CORRUPTION IN ASIA

Rethinking the Governance Paradigm

Dear Eric,

Thankyou for believing in me!

Best Wishes for the future,

Jeremy [signature]

15. NOV. 2003

CORRUPTION IN ASIA

Rethinking the Governance Paradigm

Editors

Tim Lindsey and Howard Dick

THE FEDERATION PRESS
2002

Published in Sydney by:
The Federation Press
PO Box 45, Annandale, NSW, 2038
71 John St, Leichhardt, NSW, 2040
Ph (02) 9552 2200 Fax (02) 9552 1681
E-mail: info@federationpress.com.au
Website: http://www.federationpress.com.au

National Library of Australia
Cataloguing-in-Publication entry

Corruption in Asia: rethinking the governance paradigm.

Bibliography.
Includes index.
ISBN 1 86287 421 2

1. Bureaucracy – Indonesia. 2. Political corruption – Indonesia
3. Political corruption – Vietnam. 4. Bureaucracy – Vietnam.
5. Political Corruption – East Asia. 6. Bureaucracy – East Asia.
I. Lindsey, Timothy. II Dick, Howard.

364.1323095

Typeset by The Federation Press, Leichhardt, NSW.
Printed by Ligare Pty Ltd, Riverwood NSW.

PREFACE

In the 1980s, Professor William Neilson of Canada's Centre for Asia Pacific Initiatives was laughed out of the office, with advice to return with a project involving pipes or pills, when he approached a major multilateral aid agency to seek funding for a legal institution capacity-building program in Vietnam. The wheel has now turned. Multilateral and bilateral aid agencies direct much of their East Asia activities to so-called 'governance' reform. Almost every major development project in the region must now be justified in these terms and will usually involve an element of legal institutional reform, anti-corruption initiatives or strengthening of civil society – and often a mix of all of these.

There are two main reasons why this happened and they are connected. First, the Asian financial crisis led to the sudden and unexpected collapse of banking systems and private business throughout the region and ended an era of sustained high growth. Second, the institutional weaknesses of the so-called 'Tiger Economies' were exposed, in particular, the pervasiveness of corruption, which had distorted development and so inequitably redistributed its benefits. This debacle showed up the flaws in analysis of economic and political development in East Asia. Corruption and a lack of democracy were quickly identified as the key reasons for the collapse. These two phenomena were badged together as problems of 'governance'.

The problem

The development industry, pragmatic as ever, responded to the discrediting of autocratic and corrupt regimes by embracing the discourse of 'good governance'. However, until very recently, little attention has been paid to what is meant by 'good governance' and its negative of 'corruption'. These key terms are often being used as little more than jargon. Under-theorising of the basic concepts and the haste of so many recently converted and inexperienced practitioners has led to definitional confusion, fuzzy policy, flawed projects and ineffectual reforms.

One source of confusion in relation to corruption arises from the subtle but significant conflict between the 'moralists', who see corruption as an absolute evil which must be eradicated; and, on the other hand, the 'rationalists', who see corruption as objectionable because it inhibits economic efficiency. The gulf between these two constructs is larger than it seems. The Moralists direct their efforts to education and sanctions and allow for few exceptions. The Rationalists tend to be more focused on institutions and the market and are more compromising. Not surprisingly, the prescriptions for anti-corruption reform advocated by these two groups frequently differ significantly and are sometimes incompatible.

This ideological conflict is more important than it may seem because most of the governance and anti-corruption initiatives that have marked development aid to post-crisis Asia are, in fact, major exercises in social engineering. Aid agencies and major donors are attempting not just to improve governance systems and combat corruption but, implicitly, to restructure entire national political systems and administrative structures; to democratise and build civil societies, sometimes almost from scratch. 'Conditionality' puts real weight behind these projects. If successful, they could transform the face of East Asia. Defining 'governance' and understanding 'corruption' are therefore not minor issues of terminology.

However, a great deal of optimism is required to believe that social engineering for good governance will succeed in either Indonesia or Vietnam within the foreseeable future. At the time of President Soeharto's downfall, the slogan of reform was "abolish KKN (corruption, collusion and nepotism)". For some time there was great tension between reformers who sought to bring Soeharto, his family and cronies to trial, and those who, on pragmatic or self-interested grounds, resisted this. It now appears that the status quo has for the most part prevailed.

The problems of Vietnam are somewhat different, but the outcomes are similar. Corruption is widely recognised to be a major political, social and economic issue - even by the party itself - but few cases are ever tried. The bureaucracy (including the legal system) and the party are so complicit that reform is impossible. Property rights for private and foreign enterprise are defined at law, and formal contracts are signed, but there are no mechanisms of enforcement, other than through the corrupt bureaucracy and party itself.

These systemic problems point to the basic flaw in the good governance paradigm: the imperatives of political, business and family survival militate against tackling vested interests. In the absence of rule of law, the basic institutions of these transitional societies remain largely as they were: personal connections, money politics, rentseeking and bribery. There is, as yet, no viable alternative system in either Indonesia or Vietnam. To assume that these societies are following some steady path of reform is, for the time being, just wishful thinking.

The key question is therefore not why Indonesia and Vietnam are failing to implement the good governance agenda. Why are international agencies, donors and NGOs continuing so strongly to push a new reform agenda that cannot achieve its objectives? To this, there is no simple answer. The ideals are widely shared. Jobs are being created and good consultancy rates are being paid in this new branch of the development industry. Those who are well paid to implement high ideals can sustain hope for a very long time. There is usually some evidence that progress is being achieved, at least for those who do not have a good knowledge of the local situation. And in the very long-run, some of these reforms may well come to pass, though probably modified in light of trial and error by later experts.

The argument of this book is that more might be achieved sooner by much better understanding of political, legal, commercial and social dynamics in Indonesia and Vietnam, not as they are meant to be but as they are. Multilateral agencies, donors, NGOs, scholars, local politicians, bureaucrats, business people, lawyers and journalists have much usefully to discuss. Only out of that dialogue - a dialogue between the world as it is and the world of ideals - can steady progress be made.

Structure

The aim of this book is therefore to bring more scholarly attention to bear on these problems governance and corruption in contemporary East Asia. It seeks to do so first in an abstract theoretical sense, before testing the frameworks thus established through a series of country case studies. A decision was made to restrict these studies to Indonesia and Vietnam. In part, this reflects the interests of the editors and contributors. It also allows attention to be paid to two very different Asian states: one (Indonesia) embracing a market economy and an emerging democratic system, the other (Vietnam) still socialist but in difficult transition from command economy to a limited market structure. This choice also allows interesting comparisons between civil law and socialist legal systems, and between Confucian and other Asian legal and political traditions.

In order that the case studies could be dealt with in depth by a number of writers working from different perspectives, the decision was made to exclude other Asian countries that might provide illuminating comparisons, for example, China, in relation to Vietnam; and Malaysia, for Indonesia. However, a chapter on corruption in Eastern European post-Soviet states has been included. We hope it provides a useful consideration of post-socialist issues relevant to Vietnam, as well as dealing with the consequences of a transition from 'hard' to 'soft' states paralleling Indonesia's recent experience. More significantly, it demonstrates, we hope, that the issues considered in this book are not confined to Asia.

The book is divided into three parts. The first, 'Frameworks', establishes some theoretical approaches to the problem of corruption and governance (including the East European example). The second part looks at case studies from Indonesia; and the third part looks specifically at Vietnam. A detailed glossary and list of abbreviations will assist readers unfamiliar with the countries under examination.

Tim Lindsey and Howard Dick
Melbourne
December 2001

For Imaninadira Tanya Idrus Lindsey
(and her late namesake).

T.L.

Contents

PART III – VIETNAM

Acknowledgements

This volume was inspired by an international conference at the University of Melbourne convened jointly by the Asian Law Centre and the Australian Centre for International Business. Speakers from North America, Australia and Asia were linked to three Indonesian campuses by live video hook-up through the University of Indonesia's video conference facility at Salemba in Jakarta to discuss governance, social engineering and corruption in post-crisis Asia. The administration of the conference was handled with typical calm and thoroughness by Kathryn Taylor, the Asian Law Centre Administrator, and Amanda Whiting, Research Assistant in the Centre. Thanks are also due to Peter Jones and Andrew Prasad of the Law Faculty's IT Department, who dealt with the tricky four-way live hook-up. The conference was funded by an ARC Large Grant 'Asian Laws in Transition: 1945-2001' awarded to Associate Professor Lindsey, Professor MB Hooker (Australian National University) and Professor Veronica Taylor (now University of Washington, Seattle). This book is part of a series supported by this grant.

This is not, however, a volume of conference papers. All papers were significantly rewritten and additional chapters were also invited from contributors who were not involved in the conference, Professor Leslie Holmes and Ibrahim Assegaf. Professor Holmes' paper had been previously published in a different form as "Funktionen und Dysfunktionen der Korruption und Ihrer Bekaempfung in Mittel- und Osteuropa" in Borchert J, Leitner S and Stolz K (eds) (2000) *Jahrbuch für Europa- und Nordamerika-Studien 3: Politische Korruption,* Leske und Budrich, Opladen: 117-44. Professor Brietzke's chapter is a significantly revised version of an earlier publication which appeared as "Democratization and … Administrative Law", (1999) 52 *Oklahoma Law Review* 1.

Finally, thanks go to Helen Pausacker, Research Assistant in the Asian Law Centre, who helped edit this book. Her grace under pressure is extraordinary, as is her attention to detail. The completion of this volume is largely a result of her hard work. The editors also thank Amanda Whiting and Kathryn Taylor for their support in the editing process.

Contributors

Ibrahim Assegaf is Executive Director of the Centre for Indonesian Law and Policy Studies (*Pusat Studi Hukum dan Kebijakan Indonesia*) and the Managing Director of the Indonesian law website <*www.hukumonline.com*>. He is also a member of the Steering Committee for the Establishment of the Anti-Corruption Commission and for the UNDP's Partnership for Governance Reform.

Paul Brietzke is Professor of Law at Valparaiso University Law School (USA) and from January 1999 to August 2000 was Legal Advisor at the then Ministry of Justice of Indonesia in Jakarta.

Howard Dick is Associate Professor in the Australian Centre for International Business, University of Melbourne, Australia.

John Gillespie is Associate Professor in the Law School, Deakin University, Melbourne, Australia.

Gary Goodpaster is Professor of Law Emeritus, University of California School of Law, Davis; and former Chief of Party, Partnership for Economic Growth, a joint economic policy development project of USAID and the Government of Indonesia.

Leslie Holmes is Professor of Political Science and Director of the Contemporary Europe Research Centre at the University of Melbourne, Australia. He is also the President of the International Council for Central and East European Studies.

Kanishka Jayasuriya is Senior Research Fellow, South East Asia Research Centre, City University of Hong Kong

Tim Lindsey is Director of the Asian Law Centre and Associate Professor in the Law School, both at the University of Melbourne, Australia.

Elizabeth Maitland is Associate Director of the Australian Centre for International Business, University of Melbourne.

Pip Nicholson is Associate Director (Vietnam) of the Asian Law Centre and a Senior Fellow of the Law School, both at the University of Melbourne, Australia.

Veronica Taylor is Professor of Law and Director of the Asian Law Center, University of Washington, Seattle.

Glossary

Anggaran Pendapatan dan Belanja Negara	State Budget
Azas manfaat	principle of materiality
Badan Pemeriksa Keuangan (BPK)	State Audit Agency
Badan Pemeriksa Keuangan dan Pembangunan (BPKP)	Finance and Development Audit Agency
Badan Urusan Logistik (Bulog)	National Logistics Agency
bajaj	two-passenger pedicab with motor scooter engine
ban	Commission
ban can su dang	Party Affairs section
Ban Kinh Te Trung Uong	Economic Commission
bao ke	punitive or physical intimidation
cac hoat dong hop phap	legitimate activities
can thiep	imperialist
cap trung binh	normal level
chinh nghia	exclusive righteousness
chinh sach che do	policy regime
chu truong	instructions
cong ty binh phong	companies sailing against the wind
Dewan Perwakilan Rakyat (DPR)	People's Representative Assembly or legislature
doi moi	mixed-market reforms (Vietnam)
dong	unit of currency (Vietnamese)
Dang Cong San Dan Duong	Indochinese Communist Party
duoc phap	transfer
dwifungsi	dual function (of military)
giao	unlawful allotment
giao dich thuoc nuoc	tea and cigarette money
hien dai hoa	modernisation
hoc thuyet tam quyen phan lap	separate state functions

hop phap hoa	legalising
Ikatan Hakim Indonesia (Ikahi)	Association of Indonesian Judges
kabupaten	district (administrative region)
kaki lima	mobile stall with three wheels, pushed by a vendor
Komisi Empat	Commission of Four
Komisi Pemeriksa Kekayaan Pejabat Negara (KPKPN)	Commission for Investigation of the Wealth of State Officials
korupsi, kolusi dan nepotism (KKN)	corruption, collusion and nepotism
le	ritual or code of conduct
loi ich cua nha nuoc	state benefit
luat	law
machtstaat	state based on might (Dutch)
maphia	mafia
mission civilisatrice	civilising mission
o du	umbrella
Operasi Tertib (Opstib)	Operation Law and Order
pembusukan	decomposition
penyelidikan dan penyidikan	investigation
phap luat	rule of law
phap luat va cac chinh sach, che do, the le	laws, regulations and policy regimes
preman	gangster
Program Pembangunan Nasional (Propenas)	National Development Program
quan triet	highly authoritative instructions
quan tu	(Confucian) superior men
quyen luc nha nuoc	state power
quan ly	manage
quyen su dung dat	land use rights
Rechtsstaat	state based on law
reformasi	reformation
Rencana Pembangunan Tahunan (Repeta)	Annual Development Plan
suc ep	pressure
tai hanh dong	reactionary

tap trung dan chu	democratic centralism
y tuong lanh manh	healthy markets
Thien Tu	Son of Heaven
Tim Gabungan Pemberantas Korupsi	Joint Investigating Team for the Eradication of Corruption or JIT
Tim Pemberantas Korupsi	Corruption Eradication Team
toa an dac biet	Special Courts
truong cau ~~dau~~, toa an cua nong dan	makeshift kangaroo court
uy ban	committees
uy ban khang chien hanh chinh	regional war committees
van phong	offices
Van Phong Kien Truc Su Truong	Hanoi Chief Architect's Office
vi ti nha nuoc	state positions
vi ti va quyen luc nha nuoc	position and power
vi tu co tach nhiem	responsible positions
vien chuc	public employees
xa	village

Abbreviations

ADB	Asian Development Bank
BOK	Bank of Korea
BPK	Badan Pemeriksa Keuangan, State Audit Agency
BPKP	Badan Pemeriksa Keuangan dan Pembangunan, Finance and Development Audit Agency
CPV	Communist Party of Vietnam
DPR	Dewan Perwakilan Rakyat, the People's Representative Assembly or legislature
DVR	Democratic Republic of Vietnam
GDP	gross domestic product
IBRA	Indonesian Bank Restructuring Agency
ICP	Indochinese Communist Party
IMF	International Monetary Fund
KKN	Corruption, collusion and nepotism
KPKPN	Komisi Pemeriksa Kekayaan Pejabat Negara, Commission for the Investigation of the Wealth of State Officials
MNEs	multinational enterprises
NICs	newly industrialised countries
NIE	new institutional economics
P&G	Proctor and Gamble
PAR	Public Administration Reform
PWC	post-Washington consensus
SOEs	state owned enterprises
UNDP	United Nations Development Program
US	United States of America
WB	World Bank

Chapter 1

History Always Repeats? Corruption, Culture, and 'Asian Values'[1]

Tim Lindsey

'Culture' is often simply the excuse given by proponents of law reform – particularly foreigners introducing a new law into an Asian jurisdiction – for why their new, imported anti-corruption Governance reform does not work. The instrumentalist view of law turns on an implicit equation of 'statute plus institution = change'. When the equation fails and a legal transplant does not take root, the explanations given include 'lack of local commitment', 'lack of local ownership', local legal traditions', 'local political opposition', 'lack of local support', 'sabotage' and so on. All of these fall under the rubric, sometimes explicit, of 'local legal culture' and have been part of a common experience in donor-driven law reform in Asia for many decades (Freidman 1994). Such excuses have become particularly marked as explanations for the slow progress of governance reform in East Asian states since the regional economic crises began in 1997.

Immoral Asia

In the world of legal transplantation, 'culture' has become a grab-bag of everything the foreign law reformers do not know or are unable to find out about the target jurisdiction: local ideas about law, local legal theory, the practical operation of the local legal system and political issues impinging on the operation of the local legal system. In many cases, this embraces everything encountered by foreign law reformers short of 'black letter' law (statutes, judicial decisions and formal legal institutions).

The implicit notion is that foreign legal culture is unmanageable and beyond the logic of global 'best practice' law reform. Often there is an assumption, sometimes made explicit, that Asian legal culture is opaque. It is seen as defective to the point of being immoral and corrupt, and thus just 'not worth knowing about'. The 'culture' of developing states not only obstructs reforms but also is seen as alien to the culture of developed states. It therefore comes to be seen as the basic cause of East Asian corruption.

1 This Chapter is, in part, a revised version of Lindsey (2002a).

Two examples will stand for a whole genre of analysis that views corruption as a "way of life" (Kraar 1995: 26) that is forever part of Asia.

> Running like a thread through many of the flaws of the governance systems of East Asia in an inclination towards secrecy, obedience, and incestuousness which is deeply damaging to the effort to promote a dynamic open society (Clarke 2000: 107).
>
> Respondents pondered the cultural origin of corruption in East Asia. Most agreed that the modern-day bribes and graft are descended from the traditional system practices throughout much of Asia … What was clear to most respondents is that an ancient concept of gifts exchanged or patronage to smooth relationships … has gotten out of hand in East Asian societies … (Hitchcock 1998)

As these passages show, in many accounts of corruption in Asia the difference, or 'alterity', of Asian legal cultures is emphasised and exaggerated, and thus represented as something inherently threatening and negative. This is done at the expense of attention to the often very considerable similarities between Western[2] legal systems and many aspects of Asian legal systems. These mostly arise from the longstanding colonial transfer of elements of Civil Law, Common Law or Socialist models derived ultimately from Western Europe, albeit via former colonies such America, Canada, Australia or, in the case of Marxism, via the USSR and China (Hiscock 2000). And all this, of course, ignores the fact that Western legal systems are saturated with informal 'cultural' influences as much as are Asian systems, or indeed any legal system anywhere (Freidman 1994). In other words, to assert that legal culture in Asia is the chief reason for the failure of governance transplants from developed countries is to caricature Asian legal cultures in the tradition of Western Orientalistism.

Legal Orientalism

This Orientalising of Asian legal cultures closely reflects the broader paradigm that Said (1978) identified in Western writing about Asia, with interwoven themes of opacity, seductiveness, immaturity and immorality seen as constituting the essence of the 'Orient'. In its legal form, this Orientalism can demonise local 'Asian' legal culture as immature, primitive, backward, subjective and irrational, while valorising Western laws as developed, modern and advanced, objective and rational (Taylor 1997).

Frankenberg (1997) has identified this dichotomy as hegemonic, ethnocentric and reflecting an assumed superiority of Western ideas of law. Labelling this as 'legocentrism', Frankenberg claims that most legal transplanters

> [r]emain smugly united in "belief in … the unity of legal systems constituting the 'Western' system", and in the hope for a "common order underlying the diversity of law" or a planetary system of justice" In a legal world so

2 By 'West', I mean North America, Western Europe and Australasia.

> constructed and defended one is tempted to believe that paradise is near … No wonder then that the comparativist praises the superiority – and with it the authority – of his home law … (Frankenburg 1997: 259, 260).

Thus Orientalism allows legal transplanters to assume uncritically the superiority and effectiveness of their familiar Western models. It can even blind them to the existence of alternatives. At its extreme, the consequences can be as farcical as they are destructive. Witness, for example, the Australian law firm that drafted a law based on Australia's federal model for Vietnam, a unitary state forged in a long war in which Australia fought on the other side. Or the senior American lawyer from a multilateral aid agency in his second week 'in country' who reacted with surprise to hear that Indonesia had inherited a Civil Law system from the Dutch and was not a Common Law country like the US. "But I thought it would be like Malaysia here", he said to the author.

At a less direct but perhaps more destructive level, another unfortunate consequence is that the demonising of Asian legal cultures exaggerates the importance and influence of local Asian opponents of law reform, typically members of the political elite who seek to use claims of cultural incompatibility to resist reforms that might threaten their political position. They usually suggest that real reform is inappropriate for their country and thus impossible. Accepted by reformers, this can justify the marginalising of local reformers as irrelevant or quixotic. This has been a consistent pattern in Southeast Asian law reform where, until around 2000, most foreign assistance programs ignored non-government organisations (NGOs) – consistently effective regional advocates for law reform[3] – in the false belief that political and bureaucratic elites better represented the prevailing legal culture (Lindsey 2000; 2002b).

The elusiveness of culture

Why are legal cultures orientalised in Western readings of Asian legal systems? One answer is the relative lack of detailed knowledge in the West of both the substance and the operational intricacies of Asian legal systems. Legal scholarship lags well behind other disciplines that have been active in Asian Studies since last century, for example, history, political science and anthropology (Taylor 1997: 109-10). An obvious necessity is for an increase in interdisciplinary studies in designing legal transplants for Asian jurisdictions (Lindsey 1997).

The slipperiness of the term 'culture' and its ability to evade simple definition is another reason for its unpopularity with the agencies that drive most inter-jurisdictional law reform in Asia, particularly multilateral donor and lending aid agencies such as the International Monetary Fund (IMF), the World Bank, the Asian Development Bank (ADB) and the United Nations Development Program (UNDP), as well as the bilateral aid agencies active in

3 See Neilson (2000); and Lev (2000: 84-5).

law reform such as USAID. The solution is much less clear because the problem is so conceptually confused.

The standard dictionary definition of 'culture' - for example, Oxford's - relates largely to the arts and restricts it to "the intellectual side of civilisation". This is obviously not useful in the context of law. What is usually intended by the term 'legal culture' is an anthropological reading. So, Hildred and Clifford Geertz (1975: 2-3) describe culture as 'ideas, beliefs and values' that form a 'conceptual framework' or 'pattern'. Bateson (1972), following Malinowski, has developed the theme of the pattern so far as to argue that it is fallacious even to classify the components of a society's 'patterns' or 'frameworks - traits of a 'culture' - into categories such as economic, religious, political (and, it follows, legal) sub-cultures. In 'real' everyday life, these categories overlap and partake of shared motivations and functions. Bateson argues that these categories are therefore, at best, convenient abstractions. To ascribe them independent reality as discrete aspects of a society is a 'fallacy of misplaced concreteness' (Bateson 1972: 37-8).

The significance for legal scholarship of culture as a broad panoply of complex and interacting - even competing - values and ideas, many with legal implications, has been accepted slowly. There is now acknowledgement, albeit sometimes grudging, that comparative law - whether as scholarship or as a tool for cross-jurisdictional law reform - must consider cultures as well as rules and institutions. However, the dilemma of how to deal with subject matter so unamenable to definition, and so hard to categorise, remains largely unresolved. Bateson's notion that culture cannot, ultimately, be subdivided is one resisted at most levels of analysis: scholarship, policy development and aid delivery. Some examples of the problems comparative legal theory has had in coming to terms with the intricacy of legal culture are now considered briefly. These theoretical positions have directly informed the practical implementation of law reform in Asia, particularly in the field of commercial law.

Locating legal culture in legal systems

Much comparative law thinking on legal culture traces its pedigree to Ehrlich's sociological distinction between the 'law in books' (Weber's norms sanctioned by state authorities) and the 'living law'. Originating from his study of the Austro-Hungarian empire (Ehrlich 1936; Antons 1997: 417-8), Ehrlich's notion was that social behaviour dominates rather that the "compulsive norms of the state" (Tan 1997: 4). His idea of the 'living law' has been expressed in many different ways by later theorists. For example, Katz and Katz (1975: 653) refer to 'law without law' in their analysis of the Indonesian legal system, and Hiscock (1995: 28-43) compares 'soft law' with formal 'hard law' (Hiscock. Writing on Japan, Chiba (1984, 1989) proposes an analytical model of legal culture that elaborates Erhlich's basic dichotomy of 'law in books' vs 'living law' into three competing sources of legal culture:

official vs unofficial law; indigenous law vs transplanted law; and legal rules vs legal postulates.

The problem with analysis of the sort advocated by Ehrlich and Chiba is that, although they recognise 'living law' as important, they differentiate it from 'black letter' or formal law. So the 'living law' can influence a 'neutral' formal law. It might support and supplement it, or it could oppose, modify and even undermine it, but the two are ultimately distinct (Tan 1997: 7). Yet, as Ehrlich and Chiba suggest, informal law and legal practices can play an important role in legal activity as formal laws. In some cases, including Indonesia, they may even play a more important role than formal law.[4] But this should not obscure the fact that formal and informal law are, as Bateson would argue, products of broader, overarching and diverse cultures, made of many competing and overlapping nominal sub-cultures and 'cultural traits'. Statutes are therefore as much a product of culture as is informal legal behaviour. Those who prepare and pass rules are influenced by the 'living law' and may pass 'law in books' regulations in the expectation that the 'living law' will modify them. Likewise, the application of the 'living law' is influenced by the formal legal culture.

The sharp distinction between formal and informal law is therefore hard to maintain in the reality of everyday 'doing law' and the attempt to maintain the distinction by attempting to isolate bits of actions or decisions as solely 'living law' or 'formal' law is often impossible.

The cultural web in Asian law reform

The problem for agencies trying to draft and implement concrete programs for what is, in effect, social engineering - using law as a 'kind of lever' (Lindsey & Taylor 2000: 2-14) - is that the broad meanings implicit in a Batesonian reading of 'legal culture', however accurate it may be, make 'culture' protean, evasive and unwieldy as a tool for reformers. This is especially true where the legal reform proposed involves corruption, another term that resists definition.

From the usual instrumentalist perspective of many of the international reform agencies, Bateson and Korobkin's approaches are, in a sense, meaningless. It makes 'culture' something close to 'what people do' or even 'what people think'. Are law transplanters required to grasp the whole of social frameworks and patterns of legal behaviour before they can introduce a new bankruptcy law or an anti-corruption initiative? If they are to abstract a legal 'set' from the web of culture for convenience, how is it to be selected? If this selection would be as arbitrary as Bateson suggests, will it be of any use? Cultures influencing law and governance are not inherently moral or immoral, nor do they necessarily differ radically in simple or easily predicted ways between countries or between Asia and the West. They are complex, interwoven and not easily sub-divisible. Can they be dealt with usefully at all?

4 Katz & Katz (1975); and Lindsey (1997; 1998; 2000; 2001).

The answer is that somehow they must, because they do, inevitably, affect law reform projects. This influence will always be present, whether or not it is recognised by reformers and it will never be easy to deal with. Kahn-Freund's remark (1974: 1-27) that most legal transplants fail because of political differences between donor and recipient countries suggests what makes this 'Batesonian' approach to legal culture so difficult for aid agencies. It forces recognition that law reform will inevitably involve the far more threatening realm of local political culture, amongst others, because law is inherently political. It is often difficult to win support for an aid project if its 'political' nature is obvious. The fact is, however, that almost all legal transplants, and many comparative legal projects, under the rubric of Governance are, as Frankenberg (1997: 259-261) argues, "not only academic projects but also political interventions". Law is a product of the political process and at the same time sets the rules for that process. It is therefore impossible to do much in the way of law reform – particularly, anti-corruption governance reform – if the political nature of the exercise is not accepted. To ignore this is to court failure, as in the case of the collapse of the World Bank's judicial reform project in Peru in 1998 in the face of sustained opposition from the government (LCHR 2000).

These issues explain the controversy legal culture has attracted for cross-jurisdictional governance reform, especially in relation to development assistance transplants from developed to developing countries. The history of the 'Law and Development' approach to cross-jurisdictional law reform and legal culture is illuminating in this regard.

Governance: 'Law and Development redux'?

As a specific school of thought pertaining to legal transplantation, 'Law and Development' has been discredited for some time. Ironically, although its proponents paid scant attention to legal culture, a consequence of the fall from grace of 'Law and Development' has been a tainting of 'legal culture' as a legitimate field of enquiry, both for scholars and law reformers.

The 'Law and Development' movement turned on the Weberian notion that introducing selected rules and institutions from developed 'rule of law'[5] systems (and, in particular, American interpretations of 'democracy' and 'due process') would stimulate the 'inevitable' evolution of authoritarian states in developing countries into liberal democracies (Franck 1972). Often linked to the Western anti-communist agenda of the Cold War (Trubeck and Galanter 1974: 1085-6), 'Law and Development' enjoyed brief success but was aggressively attacked in the mid 1970s by the Critical Legal Studies school and some host governments for being ethno(that is, Western)-centric, simplistic and neo-colonialist (Tamanaha 1995: 475). These criticisms were

5 On the different meanings of 'rule of law', see Lindsey (1999) on *negara hukum* in Indonesia; and Clark (1999) on the development of the concept and competing accounts.

often justified, given the failure of various, somewhat evangelic and ill-conceived Law and Development programs in the 1970s.

The problem for 'culture' was that it was implicitly central to the 'Law and Development' movement, however small a role it seemed to play on the surface. Underlying the movement was the idea that Western democratic 'legal culture' embodied in the Trojan horse of transplanted laws and institutions could (to mix metaphors) act as a benign 'germ', infecting its host with liberal democracy (Franck 1972: 762-801; Merillat 1966: 71-78). The outcome was sometimes the reverse. In many cases, the local culture swallowed colonies of foreign democratic infections whole – statutes, training courses, study tours and institutions gone with barely a trace (Watson 1996: 335-351; Burg 1977: 492-530; Merryman 1977: 457-491).

The common conclusion was that Law and Development's legal imports did not work or could not on their own deliver a liberal-democratic market-capitalist transformation. This led to a distrust of legal transplantation and thus, by extension, 'legal culture' discourse among many comparative lawyers. At the extreme, some scholars went so far as to say that "[a]t best, what can be displaced from one jurisdiction to another is, literally, a *meaningless* form of words" (Legrand 1997: 120). The consequences were strongly felt among international development agencies. Neilson (2000: 16-27; Preface, this volume) has described them as openly deriding legal development proposals in Asian countries in the 1980s. Once legal transplants had been marginalised as development assistance, there was less need to determine the role of culture.

This is not to say, however, that law reform does not have a role in the transformation of such states. Obviously it does. Any shift from authoritarianism to more open and democratic models must result in some change to the legal system, just as would a shift in the opposite direction. It is also possible – although hotly debated – that the introduction of institutions and laws that tend to support such open and democratic models may be not just consequences of a change towards openness, but may also be capable of provoking or completing it.

After a lull of 20 years or so, aspects of the Law and Development theory have been revived under the post-Washington Consensus aegis of Governance (Jayasuriya, this volume), sometimes necessarily in a opaque, even covert, fashion given the taint still born by 'Law and Development' itself. The basic motivator here is an awareness that development projects in almost every sector are usually stymied by absence of proper mechanisms for accountability and transparency in counterpart governments, that is, 'rule of law'. Governance satisfies long-standing concerns that assistance to Asian states without the 'rule of law' have often been unproductive or unsustainable, and that so much money and effort has been wasted through corruption.

This policy shift is, in part, a response to the end of the Cold War and diminishing international resistance to the American-led argument (articulated with premature fervour by Fukuyama (1992)) that there is no alternative for developing countries to "adoption of a democratic market model of state, economy and society' (Neilson 2000: 17; Rose 1998: 136). This is why Frankenberg (1997: 260) describes contemporary legal transplanters as

> [t]he juridic midwives of capitalism. It is their task to establish a rule of law that secures civil rights, facilitates investment, and complies with the demands of a globalised economy. They, incidentally, reinvent comparative law as 'Governance', ... in societies that are 'in transition'.

This 'end-of-history' triumphalism sits a little uneasily with another motivation for the rise of Governance: a sense among many aid agencies that their avoidance of 'rule of law' reform left them out of step with reform movements in recipient countries. Governance allows them to answer the criticism that the 'de-ideologised' programs that allowed these agencies to work with authoritarian governments, such as that of Soeharto in Indonesia, amounted to complicit support for oppressive regimes. To this extent, Governance is also a response to the economic crisis that hit many Asian countries from 1997 and the legal and political reforms that it provoked. Aid agencies are now embarrassed to find themselves struggling to catch up with a reform agenda that they assumed was unachievable because 'local culture' (as manipulated by the former elite) made it impossible.

The rationale of some new governance legal assistance programs therefore sometimes closely follows the logic of Law and Development and their objectives are often strikingly similar: deliver 'rule of law' and democracy through legal transplantation. In other, arguably more effective, incarnations, Governance reform breaks free from its Law and Development past and appears as less rigidly committed to American and Common Law ideas of 'rule of law'. Instead it focuses on how to locate and use compatibilities in the legal cultures of donor and recipient to build legal institutions and systems that allow diverse participation and strengthen civil societies, with an acceptance that the outcome may not necessarily precisely fit Western models. Of course these often involve liberal, 'rule of law' aspirations but need not do so exclusively - or at least not to the same uncritical and rigid level of the 1970s.

The danger for Governance is that, whatever the fate of Law and Development, the underlying problem for any program involving the transplantation of laws - any attempt to deliver cultural change in legal systems - remains the same: 'culture' is hard to locate and even harder to manipulate for actors outside it (for example, foreign law reformers). Legal cultural change is therefore a crucial part of any legal reform program, but it will always remain a crucial and unpredictable tool for those who see it as a merely ultilitarian instrument rather than, in reality, the whole of the task.

Reverse Orientalism and Asian values

These problems that culture poses for law reform are not restricted to Western governance evangelists seeking to 'save' Asia. Asian readings of Asian cultures also frequently obstruct the transplant of legal reform from

West to East. As suggested above, the 'Asian values' polemic - postulating an incompatibility between Asian cultures and Western values - is often used to argue that legal models from developed countries cannot work in Asian societies. A simplistic version of the (already simplistic) notion of 'clash of civilisations' per Huntington (1993) is usually called upon to prove that Western governance models will never take root. The argument, put most prominently by Dr Mahathir of Malaysia and Lee Kuan Yew of Singapore, and less publicly by Soeharto in Indonesia, has been summarised as follows.

> Asia has its own cultural essence, fundamentally different from that of the West; and ... this essence penetrates all Asian societies and their history so that they constitute a uniform and perennial cultural whole despite their phenomenal differences and constant changes. This dualism enables Asian advocates to charge Western concerns about human rights with cultural imperialism and to make the cultural relativist response: "Asia will go its own way". (Inoue 1998: 59)

In this sense, 'Asian Values' as applied to legal reform is really the inverse of Western legal Orientalism, except that here Asians are adopting the dualism of Western Orientalism for different purposes.

Tatsuo Inoue has disputed these claims on several grounds. First, because the Asian values argument is usually used to justify a "a system of economic freedom without political liberties" (Inoue 1998: 59), also described by Jayasuriya (1999) as 'economic constitutionalism'. This rhetoric is relied upon by elites in East Asia to insulate government and the economy from politics and opposition; to justify government by political and business elites; and to allow the development of what are, in effect, one-party systems despite their democratic shells and rhetoric (as in Singapore, Malaysia and, until recently, Indonesia). Were it otherwise, there would be no need to assert the rhetoric to justify acting against domestic opposition, because there would be none. In any Asian society there a groups who oppose the government's legal and political paradigms. Within those groups, some fiercely contest dominant 'patterns and frameworks' of values and ideas, others modify or reinterpret them. As Reid (1998: 23-8) has notably demonstrated, most Asian societies (with the obvious exception of Japan) are notable for their significant diversity of ethnicity, with each group influenced by differing historical and intellectual and philosophic traditions. Yet these are rolled into mega-categories like 'Asian', 'Chinese' or 'Indonesian' by both Western Huntingtonians and by Asian chauvinists. Orientalism in its 'Asian values' incarnation is thus a tool wielded by ruling elites for political purposes, rather than something inherent in the world-views of 'Asians'.

Secondly, Inoue (1998: 61) identifies the elevation of state sovereignty to the level of sanctification as a key component of the 'Asian values' paradigm. As embodied in the 1993 Bangkok Declaration, this is the notion that sovereignty demands that states be immune from interference in their 'internal affairs' by other states, particularly in matters of human rights. It is ironic that here East Asian states are relying on an non-Asian doctrine: "In origins and evolution, sovereignty is definitely a Western concept, and was not shared by other regions until this century".[6]

Inoue argues that, in fact, the idea of the integrity of the sovereignty of states has always been tied to, and qualified by, limits on state power. The development of the modern state since the British and French revolutions has always involved supposed liberation of subjects from the arbitrary power of rulers. Thus the modern idea of state sovereignty in fact *implies,* rather than excludes, protection of human rights, because "... such a formidable leviathan as the sovereign state should be allowed to exist only in so far as human rights are its creator and master" (Inoue 1998: 64).

Thirdly, central to the 'Asian values' argument is the 'evolutionist' view that rights and democratic systems are luxuries that cannot be delivered before economic rights: subsistence via development. Demands for rights are therefore morally 'bad' because they obstruct economic development, which must be protected from politics and criticism (Jayasuriya 1999). Against this, Inoue points out that, historically, the conferral of civil and political rights in the West preceded, or at least accompanied, social and economic rights or 'second generation rights' (Inoue 1998: 64). Few East Asian developing states have, in fact, been able to deliver lasting and social economic rights - as the economic crisis demonstrates - perhaps because of the absence of civil and political rights as checks and balances to restrain corruption and allow a more lasting and equitable distribution of the fruits of development. This argument would explain much about Indonesia's sudden collapse in 1997, after three decades of both economic growth and political repression. It also raises the question of when 'subsistence' is sufficiently secure for other rights to be permitted. Surely Singapore, for example, has reached that point?

Finally, Inoue identifies the gross distortions of history and contemporary reality necessary to maintain the extreme Hegelian dualism that underlies 'Asian values': the denial of individualism in Asia and assertion of its 'stagnancy' and unchanging communitarian nature, versus the idea of Western individualism and constant change or 'instability'. In fact, no legal culture - nor, indeed, any culture - is monolithic or static: much to the contrary. Bateson (1972: 38) reminds us that cultures complete, interact and overlap within larger national cultures and between individuals within them.

> [W]e should consider under head of 'culture contact' not only those cases in which contact occurs between two communities with different cultures and results in a profound disturbance of the culture of one or both groups; but also cases of contact within a single community ... contacts between groups of individuals with different cultural norms of behaviour in each group.

6 Richard Falk, 1993, 'Sovereignty' in Joel Kreiger (ed), *The Oxford Companion to Politics of the World*, Oxford University Press, p 851, cited in Inoue (1998: 61).

The absurdities produced by the attempt to create a dialectic of opposing monoliths, West and East, with each seeking to claim the virtues and leave the vices exclusively to other is well demonstrated by the muddle Lee Kuan Yew creates when he tries to claim anti-corruption as both an Asian value and a universal at the same time.

> TIME: It has been easy for people … blame bribery and corruption on Asian values.
>
> LEE: You owe a duty to your family and loyalty to your friends to help and support them. But you must do this from your private resources, not public resources. That's Confucianism. But this value is degraded when you use public resources through your official position to do your duty to your family and be loyal to your friends. That is wrong, and what we guard against. That is why proper systems are needed. If you want something to be built you can negotiate secretly, or you spell out the specifications and invite tenders. You open the tenders publicly and whoever meets the criteria with the best price, gets it.
>
> TIME: But this is the Western way.
>
> LEE: If it is the best way of doing business, it doesn't matter where it comes from. … The easiest way to stop corruption is to have the minimum opportunities for public officers to exercise discretion.
>
> TIME: But is there where public officials exercise discretion that gets you back into this old swamp, that "We do it because this is the Asian way."
>
> LEE: Well then you have to pay for it. … (*Time* 1998: 24).

Defining 'Indonesian' commercial culture is another difficulty in ascribing culture and race to specific modes of commercial or public sector behaviour. The ethnic Chinese minority exercises a disproportionate influence on economic activity and controls most of the heavily indebted *konglomerat* or large business groups. Nevertheless, are their business attitudes and behaviour primarily ethnic or primarily commercial?[7] The Batak of mid-Northern Sumatra and the Minangkabau of Western Sumatra are also disproportionately represented in business. Like the Chinese, both groups are noted for their supposedly 'aggressive' and 'forthright' approach to business. Yet much commercial activity, especially in the public sector and under public contracts, is leveraged off politics dominated by ethnic 'Javanese'. Under Soeharto, aspects of traditional Javanese culture were, in the words of Clifford Geertz (1990: 77), appropriated to produce a Java-centric official culture that 'muffled' and smothered the expression of other ethnic characteristics and critical expression of political and religious ideas (Pemberton 1994).[8]

Even legal cultures as ancient as Southeast Asian *adat* (traditional customary law), so often described as being an obstacle to modernity (Alisyabana 1966; Haverfield 1999), are, in fact inherently dynamic. The essence of *adat* is its procedural rules rather than substantive law. The

7 I am indebted to Jeremy Mulholland for this insight.

8 See also Lindsey (1995).

manner in which decisions are made is ultimately more important than the content of the decisions. This ensures that mechanisms for flexibility of response are retained (Hooker 1978; Haverfield 1999) as social conditions change. As the traditional Minagkabau proverb has it:

> If the river is in spate, the washing place is shifted
> With a change of rajah comes a change of *adat*.[9]

Equally, there can no doubt that cultures in Asia have changed significantly in response globalisation, by which I refer specifically to electronic communication, increased travel, rapid international capital flow and the penetration of foreign investment. The significant increase in foreign investment in Indonesia under Soeharto led to an opening of Indonesian business culture beyond the restrictions of pre-existing ethnicity to absorb international attitudes to business, predominantly from America and Japan (Taylor 1999: 279-290).

Thus, when a businessperson decides to resolve a business dispute without recourse to the Courts, it is probably impossible to determine whether this is (a) because of the influence of traditional Javanese values; (b) because of the influence of traditional Chinese family ethics; (c) a decision driven by international business culture which sees law as an inappropriate form of dispute resolution; or (d) simply a purely rational wealth-maximising decision to avoid an expensive process or a dysfunctional judiciary. The businessperson him or herself may well not understand, or be able to articulate motivations, or even care about them.

In fact this project of unravelling complex cultural constructs in Indonesian business is probably an impossible and pointless one. Rather than trying to pick a dominant culture or unpack complex moments of decision-making, it may be more productive to accept that business cultures in Indonesia today – like most urban cultures – are mestizo cultures undergoing rapid and constant change. They are made of many different 'types' all reacting and adapting to this complex environment and therefore not amenable to generalisation or stereotyping. In other words, the role 'culture' plays in any transaction – whether commercial, political or intellectual – must be understood or predicted (if that is possible) in the specific context of that transaction as well as the broader society or societies in which it takes place.

Finally, in criticising the stereotyping inherent in dualism of Asian values, Inoue (1998: 67-79)[10] also demonstrates that communitarianism of course exists in West and is indeed a basic part of liberal democratic principles and the idea of civil society itself (Inoue 1998: 73-74; Sandel 1982). He likewise identifies 'individualist' strands in Asia within major traditions such as Islam and Confucianism and points out that these two traditions themselves are part of competing value systems within individual states, Indonesia and Malaysia for example, as part of a matrix of diversity

9 JF Holleman, *Van Vollenhoven on Adat Law*, 1981, cited in Haverfield (1999: 42-73).

10 See also Friedman (2000).

common in East Asia. He also points to 'individualism' in diverse social groups within East Asian states (not least of which are political opposition groups), as well as with individuals. Inoue concludes

> Individualism is not alien to Asia ... There are perhaps no pure individualists nor pure communitarians either in the West or Asia. The two orientations are competing within us, although we may differ from each other and change ourselves in the way we strike a balance (Inoue 1998: 79)

The reasonable man versus the cultured man?

Thus, legal Orientalism, whether imposed by the West in its representations of 'Asia as travesty', for example, by Clarke and Hitchcock, or self-assertively wielded by Asian leaders like Soeharto, Mahathir and Lee Kuan Yew to represent 'Asia as righteous', inflates the authority of culture to a supreme position within states. It suggests that legal and commercial decisions are determined almost entirely by pre-existent monoliths of nationally-held values and ideas conferred at birth and confirmed by the experience of citizenship of an Asian state. This overstatement of culture is, in fact, tied to the law reformer's common problem, identified in the opening of this chapter, of ignoring culture. Local culture generalised into an immutable, overwhelming elemental force cannot be overcome or even understood by the foreigner. When trying to deliver governance reform projects, there seems no reasonable alternative to ignoring it.

The key flaw in this culture-based analysis of legal behaviour is an underlying assumption that culture-driven behaviour is not rational. On this view, culture is determined almost exclusively by ethnic, religious or traditional values, implicitly at odds with 'modern' post-industrial society and 'rational' wealth-maximising business behaviour. Legal Orientalism would therefore have it that disputants choose not to pursue a legal remedy because it offends a set of values shared by members of their ethnic or national group. Implicitly, these values are a given, definable series of attitudes and traditions that are inflexible, uniform and irrational. Hence the Indonesian failure to implement governance reforms or 'stop corruption', for example, is an irrational product of local culture, an obstacle to development, and something that is thus morally 'bad' but beyond the reach of rational, 'rule of law' reform.

Taylor and Pryles (1997) reflect on the work of Haley (1978) and others[11] on Japanese reluctance to use litigation to resolve commercial disputes. They argue that behaviour seen to demonstrate the tradition-rooted (and thus implicitly irrational) nature of Japanese legal culture – for example, dislike of Courts – can also be explained as a rational, wealth-maximising response to shortcomings in the litigation system. They follow the line of relational contract theorists such as McNeill and Linzer[12] who

11 See, for example, Ramsayer (1988).

12 See Linzer (1989).

have demonstrated that a dislike of courts as a mechanism for commercial dispute resolution is not unique to Asia and is, in fact, common in the US and other Western jurisdictions. Likewise, Asian businesses sue debtors – including other Asians – in jurisdictions where there is a functioning Court system allowing for relatively efficient, reliable and transparent debt recovery, for example, Australia, USA or (Asian!) Singapore. The point here is that 'litigation aversion' is not an irrational 'Oriental' peculiarity, fixed and incapable of change, but may also be explained as a rational response across many different cultures to similar features of Courts: their cost, the time they take, the public nature of their proceedings, the uncertainty they deliver and so on.

If this is the case, then individuals deciding how to respond to a breach of contract, illegal behaviour or corrupt demands in a state without a functioning judicial system might be influenced either by traditional legal cultures or a by rational profit maximising decision to avoid pointless and expensive litigation – or both. The two are not incompatible or easily distinguished. Indeed, 'traditional' cultural values may well adapt to suit the needs of 'rational' wealth maximisation: if the Courts do not work, avoiding them becomes part of 'culture' that is, part of common behavioural patterns, values and ideas. Otherwise, as the persistence of dynamic and responsive *adat* traditions suggests, these values would disappear.

Regardless of any judgment that may be made about the rationality or otherwise of a culture's religious, spiritual, philosophic or historical underpinnings, if it is dynamic and responds to changing circumstances, then to that extent it is not irrational. Indonesia demonstrates this very well. The failure of governance reform to 'take' and the continued Indonesian 'preference' for informal – 'corrupt' – ways of doing business can also be seen as a rational responses to first, the extreme desuetude of government systems left as a legacy of Soeharto's New Order; second, the difficulty of reforming such a system; and third, the clumsiness and lack of success of foreign-backed governance and anti-corruption reform to date.

The New Order 'franchise': Corruption as a state system

Over its three decades of power, the New Order elite – and, in particular, Soeharto and his inner circle of family and friends – consciously created a parallel 'secret' state to ensure its access to illegal or extralegal rents. It was through this system that business and administration were really carried out.[13]

By the end of Soeharto's rule, the judiciary, like the legislature, effectively functioned (or dysfunctioned) as an arm of the bureaucracy. The consequences of this were, first, the removal of any formal avenue of opposition to the executive; secondly, the absence of functioning formal mechanisms for rational transaction management or dispute resolution, whether between citizens or between state and citizens; and thirdly, the

13 This section draws on Lindsey (2002a and 2002b; and 2001).

rise of alternative, irregular and informal methods of dispute resolution and transaction management to fill the vacuum created by popular fear of Courts and politics. In other words, new 'soft' law arose – alternative, informal norms – to deal with issues that would be resolved by 'black letter law' – formal written law – in a state with a functioning legal system.

At their lowest level, these informal alternatives took the form of petty corruption and facilitation payments, as well as sophisticated traditions of informal dispute resolution. At their highest level they constituted something approaching a shadow system, a 'secret' cronyist 'black' state, in which 'real' business and policy-making took place. The New Order state thus became one predicated on bad faith: effective transacting, decision-making and politics at all levels were carried out in the shadow system, widely understood – a public secret – but not formally acknowledged.

> The officially-approved outcomes of this 'real' informal system were later legitimised in what I have called the *aspal (asli tapi palsu*: original but false) state legal system. The result is a highly developed legal formalism (hard law) and public rhetoric; seemingly impenetrable and secretive politics; state sanctioned 'corruption' and legal informality in practice (soft law norms); and apparent irrelevance and absurdity in the practice of law by reason of it being the interface between the two systems. To put it another way, there were lots of laws but, because only the politically powerful could ever win, they were reduced to nonsense (Lindsey 2001).

The creation of this system was a rational response to the state's failure to provide a functional and relevant formal system, hard law that works. As such the 'black' aspal state of soft law norms necessarily grew to monstrous, if often invisible, dimensions and permeated most aspects of Indonesian public life. It has become the only effective way to 'do' politics and commerce – and thus law.

This aspal metaphor is not, of course, confined to corruption and the judiciary. The same dynamics that drove the subversion of the bureaucracy also lay behind the institutionalisation of state violence and official criminal behaviour. The key to the creation of the 'black' state was the state's violence, which it used to force compliance. Violence became the sanction that acted as the mortar to hold the 'black' state system together. So pervasive was it that for most there was little real alternative. Complicity was the only real option for financial survival. However, for those who chose to operate outside it, either in competition as criminals, or as dissenters attempting to assert the official state systems against the 'black' state, exclusion from access to jobs or rents and, ultimately, violence were the sanctions.

Perhaps the most startling evidence of this formalised, unofficial but bureaucratic system of 'secret' corruption and state-managed violence was the extraordinary evidence given by a Ministry of Manpower official at the trial of those accused of the murder of Marsinah, a trade union activist, in 1993 (Fehring and Lindsey 1995). The official claimed that regardless of the formal industrial relations system, labour disputes in the Sidoarjo region (where Marsinah had worked) were really conducted though a secret network of government, the military and employers, known as the Sidoarjo Intelligence System, run by the local ministry office. What is more, identical networks existed all across Indonesia (Fehring & Lindsey 1995: 9).

The New Order state was thus a standover operation. The bargain it offered was the classic mafia gambit: protection (against *gali* or communists, for example) or punishment in the form of brutality. In this sense, the state was an enterprise that operated on the same basis as criminals - *preman* or, in their own slang, *jawara*, a word has long meant in common parlance bandits or gangsters or, more commonly, 'standover man'.[14] Like the *preman*, the Indonesian state still occupies an ambiguous position, surviving through a grudging acceptance underscored by fear:

> On the one hand, the *jawara* is resented for the extra economic burden he places on people, but on the other hand, there is always the attempt to keep up good relations with him … "If we are good to them, they don't hassle us." (Barker, 1999: 121, n 49)

These words could apply equally to the New Order blend of violence and corruption typified by the Sidoarjo Intelligence System: state *premanisme*. This is a model of state oppression and intervention that goes far beyond the East Asian model of authoritarian state capitalism (economic constitutionalism) proposed by Jayasuriya (1999) and others of a powerful central state committed to economic development.

This system and the ideology it produced has been memorably described by McLeod (2000) as an elaborate form of franchise. Put at its simplest, money derived from illegal rents flowed up from franchisors - office holders - to the head franchisor - Soeharto and his inner circle - in return for political favour, patronage and access to rents. McLeod's analysis can thus be seen as an economic reading of my politically-oriented 'criminal state' critique.

This formidable and now deeply-entrenched blending of state and crime, economic policy and personal power is what anti-corruption

14 *Preman* are the toughs found throughout Indonesia who extort illegal rents or *japrem* (*jatah preman*) from people living or carrying on a business in territory they have 'won' by fighting and defeating other *preman* (Barker, 1999: 119-22). Derived from the Dutch for 'free man' and used to refer first to irregular or demobilised soldiers, in everyday use the word has overlapped with *jago* (literally, 'fighting cock'), the village 'tough' of ancient tradition who in urban context became a gang boss; *rampok* bandits; and *laskyar*, militias or irregular forces, particularly during the revolutionary period (Cribb 1991a: 18-19; notes 26-77).

governance reforms seek to unravel. In other words, their target is not merely corrupt activities as such but the basic structure and mode of operation of the state and commercial sector, a mode of operation that is, in these circumstances, perfectly rational. An approach that views the decision to bribe or not bribe as simply a moral wrong, to be corrected by legislation and punishment, therefore misses the point.

'Anti anti-corruption' and hostility to foreign donors[15]

Kennedy (1999) has argued is that there are substantial problems with anti-corruption thinking and policies precisely because donor agencies and anti-corruption activists often take the moral view. Whether explicit or not, it is usually an underlying assumption driving governance policy and design. There is *no* genuinely cross-sectoral consensus in favour of the sort of programs proposed by multilateral and bilateral agencies in most developing countries. And opposition to anti-corruption "often seizes on what seems a stigmatising moral tone in the campaign that makes the effort seem unfair to the periphery [that is, the developing world]" (Kennedy 1999: 458).

The common local critique takes three forms. First is a claim is that anti-corruption is Western in origin and values, and moreover the product of double standards whereby lobbying and campaign financing in Washington is acceptable, but it is corrupt when practised in Pakistan or Indonesia. Transparency International's overt and often triumphalist embrace of the Washington Consensus politics of deregulated market economies is perhaps the most provocative example of this from local Asian perspectives (Boswell 1998).

The second is a claim that public practices in developing nations are criticised when in fact they are no different from private practices in the developed West that are not labelled as 'corrupt'. Here Kennedy compares Imelda Marcos' extravagant shoe collection with Bill Gates' wealth or lifestyle choices (Kennedy 1999: 457).

The third allegation often made is that anti-corruption is essentially about 'blaming the victim' that is, locating responsibility in local elites at national level, whereas, it is claimed, "the decisions of foreign capital and the workings of the broader world system are far more important" (Kennedy 1999: 458).

In a sense these are not true 'anti-anti-corruption' arguments but rather 'anti-Western anti-corruption' arguments. Kennedy (1999: 458) argues that they are, in any case, 'off the mark' pointing out that, after all, Marcos' fortune was obtained through blatant plunder of a state stripped of governance, whereas Gates – whatever the outcome of the Microsoft litigation – is operating within a functional system, essentially within a tight regulatory framework (hence the litigation). In other words, there *are* instances where non-Western local elites are deserving of blame for dismantling entire systems of governance.

15 This section draws on Lindsey 2002b.

Whether or not Kennedy's defence is convincing, the questions he raises are certainly live ones for the local anti-corruption movements.

The dilemma for donors

The anti-Western character of the anti-anti-corruption critique creates significant problems for foreign donors and lenders seeking to work with, for example, the Indonesian anti-corruption movement, which is predomnantly defined and led by NGOs. At best, it means that even the strongest NGO supporters of anti-corruption may be reluctant to become too close to Western donors. At its worst, it results in open hostility.[16]

The latter reaction turns, in particular, on the perceived complicity of most foreign agencies in the escalation of corruption under Soeharto, because they were active in funding Indonesian government policy in that period. Many Indonesian NGO critics argue that the foreign agencies have therefore forfeited the moral right to determine anti-corruption policy for Indonesia. It is hard to convince critics that past mistakes are not a good reason to halt further governance programs, or that cooperation between NGOs and aid agencies is essential to avoid the repetition of former difficulties.

Whatever its problems, this reply is usually more domestically palatable than the other response sometimes heard, that foreign aid agencies had no choice under Soeharto but to participate. The nature of the regime, it is argued by some donors, was such that the alternative was to withdraw completely, which would have been unacceptable. This usually generates the answer from Indonesians that they were in the same position. As argued above participation in the 'black' *preman* state as corruptor or corrupted is rarely a matter of real choice for ordinary citizens. The Indonesian NGO argument thus becomes that it is hypocritical for foreigners now to seek to reform corruption (or, more particularly, to seek to punish Indonesia by demanding action on corruption as precondition for grants and loans) when foreigners themselves participated in that corruption.

The case of Indonesia's NGOs demonstrate how the 'moral' reading of corruption, that views culture as the obstruction to governance reform programs, misunderstands the nature of the corruption problem in states like Indonesia and Thailand where corruption has been embedded cross-sectorally and for long periods. It also demonstrates how that reading actually alienates the local pre-reform constituency, further undermining the likelihood of success of any given governance reform project.

Conclusion: going behind 'culture'

Frankenberg (1997: 259) proposes a departure from the assumption that legal systems in developing countries can be remade in 'ideal' Western form.

16 See generally, Lindsey 2002b.

He rejects the idea that the solution for legal dysfunction in Asia is to inject, into a matrix of demonised and stereotyped ideas known as 'Asian culture', the set of idealised but contested ideas known as 'Western legal culture' suspended in a blend of institutions, statutes and education. Instead, he calls for recognition of Western systems not as objectives on an idealised path of a global legal evolution but as culturally specific constructs or tools, rather than as objectives of cross-jurisdictional law reform.

Perhaps we should adopt the solution of Daniel Lev, a leading scholar of Indonesian law, who bans his students from using the word 'culture' because it is usually code for something else – politics, religion or ethnicity, for example. This has the advantage of forcing precision and more careful analysis of legal transplants and local culture in comparative legal studies and cross-jurisdictional law reform. Asian cultures – business, legal and whatever – are not inherently corrupt and they are not the real obstacle to foreign governance reform initiatives. The real problem is failure to come to grips with their content and complexity in a thorough and effective way. Analysis is so often blurred by the persistent, if sometimes unacknowledged, Orientalist stereotypes still promoted by many Asian leaders and deeply embedded in the thinking of many Westerners and most governance reform assistance.

The fact is that "anti-corruption campaigns are … profoundly ideological" (Kennedy 1999: 468) and thus political. Before they design and deliver assistance, bilateral and multilateral agencies need to be aware of this and must move to better understand the specific politics and economics of corruption in the country which they seek to reform. If they do not, Governance will go the way of Law and Development before it. As yet, there is little reason to believe the lessons of the 1970s have been learnt.

References

Alisyabana, ST, (1966), *Indonesia: Social and Cultural Revolution*, Oxford University Press, Singapore.

Antons, C, (1997), *Indonesian Intellectual Property Law in Context*, in Taylor, V, (ed), *Asian Laws Through Australian Eyes*, LBC Information Services, Sydney, 401-423.

Baird, D and Thomas, J, (1984), 'Corporate Reorganisations and the Treatment of Diverse Ownership Interests: a Comment on Adequate Protection of Secured Creditors in Bankruptcy', *University of Chicago Law Review*, 51, 97.

Barker, J, (1999), 'Surveillance and Territoriality in Bandung, in Vicente L Rafael (ed), *Figures of Criminality in Indonesia, the Philippines, and Colonial Vietnam*, Southeast Asia Program Publications, Cornell University, Ithaca, 95-127.

Bateson, G, (1972), *Towards an Ecology of Mind*, Chandler Publishing, London.

Boswell, Nancy Zucker, (1998), 'New Players to Combat Transnational Bribery: The Contribution of the Civil Society/NGO Sector', 92 *American Society of International Law Proceedings* 1-4 April, 165.

Burg, EM, (1977), 'Law and Development: A review of the literature and a critique of "Scholar in Self-Estrangement"', 25 *The American Journal of Comparative Law*, 492-530.

Butt, S, (1999), 'Polygamy and Mixed Marriage in Indonesia: The Application of the Marriage Law in the Courts', in Lindsey, T (ed), *Indonesia: Law and Society*, Federation Press, Sydney, 122-144.

Carlson, D, (1987), 'Philosophy in Bankruptcy', 85 *Michigan Law Review*, 1341.

Chiba, M, (1984), 'Cultural Universality and Particularity of Jurisprudence', in Marasinghe, ML and Conklin, WE (eds) *Essays on Third World Perspectives on Jurisprudence*, Malayan Law Journal, Singapore.

Chiba, M, (1989), *Legal Pluralism: toward a general theory through Japanese legal culture*, Tokai University Press, Tokyo.

Clark, D, (1999), 'The Many Meanings of Rule of Law', in Jayasuriya, K, (ed), *Law Capitalism and Power in Asia: the Rule of Law and Legal Institutions*, Routledge, London.

Clarke, T, (2000), 'Haemorrhaging Tigers: The Power of International Financial Markets and Weakness of Asian Modes of Corporate Governance', 8(2) *Corporate Governance*, 101

Cribb, R, (ed), (1991), *The Indonesian Killings 1965-1966: Stories from Java and Bali*, Monash Papers on Southeast Asia No 21, 2nd edn, Monash University, Clayton.

Cribb, R, (1991a), *Gangsters and Revolutionaries: The Jakarta People's Militia and the Indonesian Revolution, 1945-1949*, University of Hawaii Press, Honolulu.

Delaney, KJ, (1989), 'Power, Intercorporate Networks, and "Strategic Bankruptcy"', 23 *Law and Society Review*, 643.

Ehrlich, E, (trans: WL Moll) (1936), *The Fundamental Principles of the Sociology of Law*, Harvard University Press, Cambridge.

Fehring, I and Lindsey, T, (1995), *Indonesian Labour Law Under the New Order: The Military and Prospects for Change*, Working Paper, Centre for Employment & Labour Relations, University of Melbourne

Fitzpatrick, D, (1999), 'Beyond Dualism: Land Acquisition and Law in Indonesia', in Lindsey, T (ed), *Indonesia: Law and Society*, Federation Press, Sydney, 74-95.

Franck, T, (1972), 'The New Development: Can American Law and Legal Institutions Help Developing Countries?', 3 *Wisconsin Law Review*, 762-801.

Frankenberg, G, (1997), 'Stranger than Paradise: Identity and Politics in Comparative Law', 2 *Utah Law Review*, 259-274.

Freidman, L, (1994), 'Is There a Modern Legal Culture', 7 *Ratio Juris*, 117-131.

Friedman, E, (2000), 'Since There Is No East and There Is No West, How Could Either Be the Best', in M Jacobsen and Ole Bruun (eds) *Human Rights and Asian Values: Contesting National Identities and Cultural Representations in Asia*, Nordic Institute of Asian Studies, Curzon, Richmond.

Fukuyama, F, (1992), *The End of History and the Last Man*, Free Press, New York.

Geertz, H and C (1975), *Kinship in Bali*, University of Chicago Press, Chicago and London.

Geertz, H, (1963), 'Indonesian Cultures and Communities' in McVey, R (ed), *Indonesia*, HRAF, New Haven.

Geertz, C, (1990), '"Popular Art" and the Javanese Tradition', 50 *Indonesia* 77.

Happy, S, Arif, AK and Maha Adi, IGG (2000), 'The Door isn't yet shut for Benjamin', *Tempo*, (translated by Helen Pausacker with Tim Lindsey) 5 March, 60.

Haverfield, R, (1999), '*Hak Ulayat* and the State: Land Reform in Indonesia', in Lindsey, T (ed), *Indonesia: Law and Society*, Federation Press, Sydney, 42-73.

Haley, JO, (1978), 'The Myth of the Reluctant Litigant', 4 *Journal of Japanese Studies*, 359.

Hiscock, M, (1995), 'Changing Patterns of Regional Law Making in Asia', 5 *Australian Journal of Corporate Law*, 367.

Hiscock, M, (2000), 'Remodelling Asian Laws', in Lindsey, T (ed), *Indonesia: Bankruptcy, Law Reform & the Commercial Court*, Desert Pea Press, Sydney, 28-43.

Hitchcock, DI, (1998), 'Internal Problems in East Asia', 21 *The Washington Quarterly*, 2, Spring 1998, 121-35

Hooker, MB, (1975), *Legal Pluralism: An Introduction to Colonial and Neo-Colonial Laws*, Clarendon Press, Oxford.

Hooker, MB, (1978), *Adat Law in Modern Indonesia*, Oxford University Press, Kuala Lumpur.

Huntington, S, (1993), 'The Clash of Civilizations', *Foreign Affairs*, 72 (3).

Inoue, T, (1998), 'Liberal Democracy and "Asian Values"', in Yasutomo, M (ed), *Law in a Changing World: Asian Alternatives*, Sttutgart: Frans Steiner Verlag.

Jackson, T, (1986), *The Logic and Limits of Bankruptcy Law*, Harvard University Press, Cambridge.

Jakarta Post (2000), 'Jakarta judges moved around in major govt shift', 20 April.

Jakarta Post (2000a), 'Businessman reports graft in Supreme Court', 28 April.

Jakarta Post, (2000b), 'Four new commercial Courts to be opened next week', 3 May.

Jayasuriya, K, (1999), 'The Rule of Law and Governance in the East Asian State', *The Australian Journal of Asian Law*, 1 (2).

Kahn-Freund, O, (1974), 'On the Uses and Misuses of Comparative Law', 37 *The Modern Law Review*, 1-27.

Katz, J and R, (1975), 'The New Indonesian Marriage Law: a Mirror of Indonesia's Political, Cultural & Legal Systems', 23 *American Journal of Comparative Law* 653.

Kennedy, D, (1999), 'The International Anti-Corruption Campaign', 14 *Connecticut Journal of International Law*, 455.

Korobkin, D, (1991), 'Rehabilitating Values: A Jurisprudence of Bankruptcy', 91 *Columbia Law Review*, 717.

Kraar, L, (1995), 'How Corrupt is Asia?', *Fortune*, 132, 4, 21 August, 26-7

LCHR, (2000), *Building on Quicksand: the Collapse of the World Bank's Judicial Reform Project in Peru*, http://www.Ichr.org.pubs/Peru building.htm.

Legrand, P, (1997), 'The Impossibility of Legal Transplants', 4 *MJ*, 11-124.

Lev, D, (1999), 'Between State & Society: Professional Lawyers and Reform in Indonesia', in Lindsey, T (ed), *Indonesia: Law and Society*, Federation Press, Sydney, 227-246.

Lev, D, (2000), 'Comments on the Course of Law Reform in Modern Indonesia', in Lindsey, T. (ed), *Indonesia: Bankruptcy, Law Reform & the Commercial Court*, Sydney: Desert Pea Press, 74-93.

Linnan, D, (2000a), 'Bankruptcy Policy and Reform: Reconciling Efficiency and Economic Nationalism', in Lindsey, T (ed), *Indonesia: Bankruptcy, Law Reform and the Commercial Court*, Desert Pea Press, Sydney, 94-113.

Linnan, D, (2000b), 'Indonesian Law Reform, or "Once More Unto the Breach": A Brief Institutional History', 1 *Australian Journal of Asian Law*, 1.

Lindsey, T, (1995), 'Concrete Ideology: Taste, Tradition and the Javanese Past in New Order Public Space', in Hooker, V (ed), *Culture and Society in New Order Indonesia*, Oxford, Kuala Lumpur.

Lindsey, T, (1997), 'Paradigms, Paradoxes and Possibilities: Towards Understandings of Indonesia's Legal System', in Taylor, V (ed), *Asian Laws through Australian Eyes*, LBC Information Services, Sydney.

Lindsey, T, (1998), 'The IMF and Insolvency Law Reform in Indonesia', *Bulletin of Indonesian Economic Studies*, 34 (3) 199-124.

Lindsey, T, (1999), 'Indonesia's Negara Hukum: Walking the Tightrope to the Rule of Law', in Kingsbury, D and Budiman, A, (eds) *Democracy in Indonesia: the Crisis and Beyond*, Monash Asia Institute/Centre for Southeast Asian Studies, Clayton.

Lindsey, T, (2000), 'Black Letter, Black Market and Bad Faith: Corruption and the Failure of Law Reform', in Manning, C and van Diermen, P (eds), *Indonesia in Transition*, Singapore: ISEAS, 278-292.

Lindsey, T, (2001), 'Abdurrahman, the Supreme Court and Corruption: Viruses, Transplants & the Body Politic in Indonesia', in Budiman, A and Kingsbury, D, (eds), *Indonesia: The Uncertain Transition*, Adelaide: Crawford.

Lindsey, T, (2002a), 'Culture, Insolvency and Legal Orientalism in Asia: Reaching for Goering's Revolver', in Roman Tomasic (ed), *Insolvency Laws in Asia*, forthcoming.

Lindsey, T, (2002b), 'Anti-Corruption and Non Government Organisations in Indonesia', in *Stealing the People's Money*, Partnership for Governance Reform, Jakarta (forthcoming).

Lindsey, T and Taylor, V, (2000), 'Rethinking Indonesian Insolvency Reform: Contexts and Frameworks' in Lindsey, T (ed), *Indonesia: Bankruptcy, Law Reform and the Commercial Court*, Desert Pea Press, Sydney, 2-14.

Linzer, P, (1989), 'Uncontracts: Context, Contorts and the Relational Approach', in Linzer P (ed), *A Contracts Anthology*, Andersen.

Mattei, U, (1997), 'Three Patterns of Law: Taxonomy and Change in the World's Legal Systems', 45 *American Journal of Comparative Law*, 5-44.

Merillat, HCL,(1966), 'Law and Developing Countries', 60 *The American Journal of International Law* 71-78.

Merryman, JH,(1977), 'Comparative Law and Social Change: On the Origins, Style, Decline and Revival of the Law and Development Movement', 25 *The American Journal of Comparative Law*, 457-491.

McLeod, R, (2000), 'Soeharto's Indonesia: A Better Class of Corruption', 7(2) *Agenda* 99-112.

Neilson, W, (2000), 'Reforming Commercial Laws in Asia: Strategies and Realities for Donor Agencies' in Lindsey, T (ed), *Indonesia: Bankruptcy, Law Reform and the Commercial Court*, Desert Pea Press, Sydney, 5-27.

Pemberton, J, (1994), *On the Subject of 'Java'*, Cornell University Press, Ithaca.

Ramsayer, JM, (1988), 'Reluctant Litigant Revisited: Rationality and Disputes in Japan', 14 *Journal of Japanese Studies*, 111.

Reid, A, (1998), 'Political Tradition in Indonesia: The One and the Many', 22 (1) *Asian Studies Review*, 23-28.

Rose, C, (1998), 'The "New" Law and Development Movement in the Post-Cold War Era: A Vietnam Case Study', 32 *Law and Society Review*, 93-140.

Said, E, (1978), *Orientalism*, Penguin, London.

Sandel, C, (1982), *Liberalism and the Limits of Justice*, Cambridge University Press, Cambridge.

The Straits Times (2000), 'Judges Verdict for Sale? Indonesia's Supreme Court Embarrassed by Tape' (no author), 14 April.

Tamanaha, BZ, (1995), 'The Lessons of Law-And-Development Studies', 89 *The American Journal of Comparative Law*, 475.

Tan, PL (ed), (1997), *Asian Legal Systems; Law, society and Pluralism in East Asia*, Butterworths, Adelaide.

Taylor, V (ed), (1997), *Asian Laws Through Australian Eyes*, LBC Information Services, Sydney.

Taylor, V, (1999), 'The Transformation of Indonesian Commercial Contracts and Legal Advisers', in Lindsey, T (ed), *Indonesia: Law and Society*, Federation Press, Sydney, 279-290.

Taylor, V and Pryles, M, (1997), 'The Cultures of Dispute Resolution in Asia', in Pryles, M (ed), *Dispute Resolution in Asia*, Kluwer Law International, The Netherlands.

Tempo (2000), 'The Biggest Mafia or the Highest Court?', *Tempo*, Opinion No 04/XXIX/27, (editorial - translated by Simon Butt with Tim Lindsey) April.

Time International (1998), '"Asian Values" And The Crisis: Interview Lee Kuan Yew", 150 *Time International*, 29, 16 March, 24.

Tomasic, R et al, (1996), 'Insolvency Law Administration and Culture in Six Asian Legal Systems', 6 *Australian Journal of Corporate Law*, Desert Pea Press, Sydney, 211-288.

Tomasic, R and Little, P, (1997), *Insolvency Law and Practice in Asia*, FT Law and Tax, Hong Kong.

Tomasic, R and Kamarul, B, (1999), 'The Rule of Law and Corporate Insolvency in Six Asian Legal Systems', in Kanishka J, *Law, Capitalism and Power in Asia: The Rule of Law and Legal Institutions*, Routledge, London, 151.

Tomasic, R (2000), 'Asia-Pacific Law Reforms: Directions for Indonesia', in Lindsey, T (ed), *Indonesia: Bankruptcy, Law Reform & the Commercial Court*, Desert Pea Press, Sydney, 114-124.

Trubeck, D and Galanter, M, (1974), 'Scholars in Self-Estrangement: Some Reflections on the Crisis in Law and Development Studies in the United States', 3 *Wisconsin Law Review*, 1085-1086.

Watson, A, (1996a), 'Aspects of the Reception of Law', 44 *The American Journal of Comparative Law*, 335-351.

Watson, A, (1996b), 'Legal Transplants and Law Reform', 92 *The Law Quarterly Review*, 79-84.

Zweigert, K and Kotz, H, (1985), *An Introduction to Comparative Law*, Clarendon, Oxford.

Chapter 2

Governance, Post-Washington Consensus and the New Anti-Politics

Kanishka Jayasuriya

Introduction

The recent interest in governance and issues of transparency demonstrates the emergence of a new post-Washington consensus (PWC). The lexicon of the new policy paradigm underlying this consensus includes *civil society, institution building, safety nets* and especially *governance*, all added to the conventional Washington terminology of 'open markets', 'deregulation', 'liberalisation' and 'structural adjustment'. Of course, the essential elements of this post-Washington consensus have long been evident in the thinking of organisations like the World Bank and the Asian Development Bank, which have been pushing 'governance' for some time. Even the International Monetary Fund (IMF) seems ready to be part of the new consensus.

But the shift to the PWC should not be seen as a reversal of the structural adjustment policies that characterised the Washington consensus. Rather, it is argued that the PWC should more properly be viewed as an attempt to develop a political institutional framework to embed the structural adjustment policies of the Washington consensus. From this perspective – while clearly there are different policy priorities between the policy paradigms – the PWC complements rather than replaces the policies associated with the Washington consensus. However, the politics of the PWC is a distinctive form of 'anti-politics' which seeks to cleanse economic institutions of the assumed debilitating effects of political bargaining. In essence, it attempts to constitute a form of economic constitutionalism.[1]

In this respect, governance programs are a central component of the new PWC and projects relating to corruption are an important subset. These are effectively premised on the assumption that 'politics' will necessarily diminish or muddy the clear waters of the market. Therefore, governance projects suggest a deeply antithetical attitude to politics as conflict or rational

1 See Jayasuriya (1999). I also consider "economic constitutionalism" in the context of globalisation in detail (Jayasuriya 2001).

deliberation, substituting instead a version of politics as the effective implementation of agreed technical procedures. It is a 'politics of anti-politics' which substitutes the politics of procedure for the politics of bargaining. For this reason, one of the major concerns of Governance is the development of the 'rule of law'. To this end, there has been a concerted effort to promote legal reform programs in a number of developing states. However, in the rush to promote these legal reform programs, insufficient emphasis has been given to the assumptions underlying these policies.

Foundations of the PWC[2]

While some elements of the PWC have been apparent since the beginning of this decade, it now seems clear that the Asian crisis has given great impetus to the emergence of this new policy framework. Prior to the onset of the East Asian economic crisis, there was a broad consistency between the orthodox economics literature on East Asia's economic development and the Washington consensus. "Behind the statistics of differential development performance among the countries of East, Southeast and South Asia", it was argued, was "the importance of appropriate policies" (James, Naya and Meier 1989: 21). In particular, orthodox economists sought to explain East Asia's development in terms of the outward-oriented character of the region's industrial strategies. Naya and Meier (Jayasuriya and Rosser 2001) point out that, in contrast to under-performing Latin American countries, most East Asian countries decided at an early stage in their development to pursue export-oriented industrial strategies rather than broaden and deepen their import-substitution industrial activities.

They also pointed out that most East Asian countries maintained conservative and stable macro-economic policies and, in particular, non-inflationary fiscal policies and competitively valued exchange rates. In addition, neo-classical orthodoxy placed great store on the fact that East Asian governments were remarkably successful in providing the basic public goods for competitive markets - that is, maintaining law and order, providing infrastructure and enforcing property rights (Jayasuriya and Rosser 2001).

In other words, the view of orthodox economists was that the East Asian experience provided strong evidence of how the Washington consensus could work in practice, demonstrating that the consensus was technically superior to other policy strategies. Indeed, it would not be an exaggeration to say that orthodox economic analysis of the East Asian 'miracle' was a cornerstone of the Washington consensus. If East Asia's economic success was due to free market policies, then, it was argued, free market policies must be right for other developing countries. For example,

2 This section draws on work that Andrew Rosser and I have done on the impact of the economic crisis on the 'Washington consensus'. Jayasuriya and Rosser (2001) contains a more detailed summary of the argument of this section. I thank Andrew Rosser for permitting me to use this material.

the orthodox economic reading of the East Asian miracle was vital in legitimising the Washington consensus in Sub-Saharan Africa and Latin America, as Baer, Miles and Moran (1999) have pointed out.

Here we see one of the key differences between the governance programs advocated within the framework of the Washington consensus and the PWC. In the former, 'governance' connoted the effective implementation of policies of economic liberalisation; in the latter, there is greater emphasis on governance as an instrument to promote the regulative capacities of the state. In fact, from the PWC viewpoint, one of the main causes of the Asian crisis has been a failure to reinforce the regulative capacities of the state.

Indeed, the recent emphasis on governance is reflected in the increasing attention given to the provision of regulatory frameworks in previously deregulated sectors of the economy. This is where the PWC can be clearly distinguished from the Washington consensus: it envisages a strong state - albeit restructured in a more regulatory direction - as a precondition for liberal markets. There has been a clear recognition that in the absence of frameworks like a strong competition policy, deregulation may result in a transfer of power from the state to powerful private sector oligarchies.

The recent experience of countries like Indonesia and Russia bears witness to this trend.[3] In these countries, influential networks of bureaucrats and private actors have created cartels in strategic and profitable sectors of the economy and thereby derailed the effectiveness of the reform program. Ironically, deregulation and privatisation - the cornerstones of the Washington consensus - did not lead to a flowering of liberal markets but simply served the interests of powerful capitalists whose wealth and authority had previously been based on their control of protected industries.

The PWC attempts to respond to these developments by placing an emphasis on the supply of regulatory frameworks (Stiglitz 1998a; 1998b). Therefore, the important debates within multilateral organisations in the next decade are likely to be about the future course of this re-regulation, but such a re-regulation requires that more attention be paid to issues of institution and capacity building.

Globalisation and the architecture of state

Clearly, the Asian crisis provides a proximate cause for the emergence of the PWC. However, the roots of the PWC can be traced to more deep-seated changes in the global economy. These structural changes triggered changes in the internal architecture of the state. In this respect, we need to adopt an internal, rather than an external, perspective on globalisation. Much of the literature on globalisation (see Hirst and Thompson 1996) takes what could

3 For Indonesia, see Robison and Rosser 1998; for Russia, see Holmes (this volume).

be termed an external perspective on sovereignty in that it focuses on the external constraints on state action. The standard account of how globalisation affects sovereignty maintains that the rapid integration of the global economy or the increasing intensity of trade and financial flows serves to limit the functions of the sovereign state. But the problem with this 'flow' model is that it leaves untouched the fundamental binary divide between the external and the internal. Indeed, in this binary divide, as Clark points out:

> the very unity of sovereignty thus seems to find expression in its bifurcation. In fact, it has been remarked that it was the very potency of this separation that salvaged sovereignty ... when its validity was otherwise increasingly called into question (Clark 1999: 73).

The binary divide has produced an unhelpful debate over the extent to which state power has been lost as a consequence of globalisation.

Susan Strange, in a sophisticated analysis of these changes in the global political economy, provides a twofold argument. First, that all states have had their authority and functions greatly diminished because of the integration of states into the global economy. Secondly, that

> some of the fundamental responsibilities of the state in a market economy – responsibilities first recognized, described and discussed at considerable length by Adam Smith over 200 years ago – are not being adequately discharged by anyone (Strange 1996: 14).

By identifying the significant increase in the power of non-state actors in the global system, Strange makes an important contribution to the study of state and the global political economy. In particular, she draws attention to the role and power of financial markets in constraining the ability of the state to effectively intervene in large areas of economic life. While offering a valuable and perceptive analysis of the impact of globalisation on the state, her account suffers, however, from a kind of zero-sum conception of state power and autonomy.

This zero-sum perspective is critically flawed to the extent that it neglects the degree to which sovereignty is being transformed from within the state rather than from external sources. As against this externally-driven model of globalisation, it is argued that the main sources of change are to be found in the changes to the internal structure of firms, markets and the state. Increasingly, the emergent global economy requires regulation of areas previously considered to be in the domestic domain because globalisation is a microeconomic process.

This, in turn, means examining the way state structures operate at the interstices of the domestic and international arena. For example, increasingly complex global financial markets require an almost equally complex process of harmonisation of securities regulations. But this legal harmonisation can be achieved only by institutionalised structures of cooperation between domestic and international agencies. Moreover, the regulatory cooperation implicit in efforts at legal harmonisation reflects the fact that the imperatives of a global economic order cannot be easily subsumed under the traditional notions of international law. Regulatory cooperation necessitates the removal of the very boundaries between the international and domestic that have been so central to the practice and theory of international law and international relations.

What is being suggested here is that, if globalisation is internally driven, then the very form of the state challenges the binary divide between the domestic and the international, which has been the staple of the disciplines of political science and international law. We need to pay more attention to changing patterns of political rule and order in the global economic system. From this vantage point, a key issue for any understanding of the global political economy is how economic order is produced and reproduced in the global economy. Globalisation brings with it a new ensemble of governance institutions, and it is these new structures that shape and influence the architecture of domestic states. Thus globalisation changes the internal architecture of the state.

If this argument is valid, then globalisation is serving not so much to reduce the capacity of the state to function, but rather to reshape sovereignty in the process of the transformation of the state. Clark expresses this well when he observes that:

> What is happening to sovereignty is shadow play of the transformations that the state is currently undergoing. We might then suggest that there is not only a twofold linkage - between the concept of the sovereignty and statehood - but a triangular relationship - between state, sovereignty, and globalization. All three, of necessity, are synchronized in their movements (Clark 1999: 79).

Adopting this internalist perspective on globalisation allows us to locate the emergence of the PWC as a move towards the convergence of domestic structures of governance. In short, the new global economy internationalises the previously domestic areas of governance; and this explains the priority given within the PWC to issues of regulatory capacity. In other words, the Washington consensus provided a good 'fit' for an international economy composed of national entities, but it is now clearly inadequate for a global economy where the very divide between the national and the international has become more problematic.

Governance and economic constitutionalism

One of the main features of the PWC is the 'constitutionalisation' of key economic institutions that in turn insulates these institutions from the politics of bargaining. Economic institutions themselves - central banks, for example - take on a juridical character.

These developments can clearly be observed in the emergence of governance programs in multilateral organisations. Not only is most lending tied to the effective implementation of governance programs, but multilateral agencies have followed up on these concerns with extensive aid programs for institutional strengthening or capacity building. The tenor of recent economic reforms in transitional economies and in Southeast Asian countries has been towards establishing credible and independent regulatory institutions. The NICs and Japan have not been immune from the expansion of these programmes to re-engineer the state to allow it a greater regulatory role. Michel Camdessus, the former Managing Director of the IMF, notes that the:

> IMF's role in governance issues has been evolving over the years, and good governance has taken on increasing importance in our traditional mandate of promoting economic stability and what I call high quality growth (Camdessus 1998: 1).

Moreover, he argues that the Asian crisis is ample demonstration of the disastrous effects of ineffective governance and lack of market transparency. This obviously has considerable implications for the future of the developmental state. All the recent IMF bailouts of Thailand, South Korea and Indonesia require these governments to make substantial efforts to reform their governance regimes.

Governance programs emerged out of the experience of structural adjustment programs of the 1980s. International policy makers, puzzled by the apparent failure of structural adjustment programs, began to examine more closely the capacity of economic and bureaucratic institutions to implement economic reform packages. As a World Bank discussion paper on governance noted:

> The Bank's experience has also shown that when programs and projects appear technically sound but fail to deliver results, the reasons are sometimes attributable to weak institutions, lack of an adequate legal framework, damaging discretionary interventions, uncertain and variable policy frameworks and a closed decision making process which increases risks of corruption and waste (World Bank 1991: 1).

The difference between the early governance programs of the World Bank and the PWC lies in the attention that is now being paid to enhancing the regulatory capacity of the state. Whereas early governance programs were broadly concerned with the effective implementation of structural adjustment programs, the PWC is more directly concerned with the creation of market order. Within this perspective, there is a clear shift towards a view of markets as political and legal creations that I label 'economic constitutionalism'.

The clearest example of economic constitutionalism and its politics of anti-politics is the promotion of independent central banks. Central banks have become key players because they provide the link between international regimes and the domestic state. The increasingly juridical character of central banks is a key feature in the management and regulation of this international economic order.

A major reason for the enhanced power of central banks is the growing importance of monetary policy in an era dominated by the pressure for more global financial integration. This latter trend resulted not only in a shift of policy instruments from fiscal to monetary policy, but also a shift of power *within* the state towards agencies such as central banks. While it is a truism to say that external factors will increasingly impinge on the domestic political process, the more urgent theoretical and empirical task is to examine the specific linkages that exist between external and international forces and domestic politics. Central banks are likely to play an important role in this linkage between the external and domestic political environment as they are ideally placed to provide the mechanism through which international forces are transmitted into the domestic political economies.

Nothing is more indicative of these shifts than recent changes to the South Korean central bank, the Bank of Korea (BOK). As Maxfield (1994) has noted, the BOK has not had a great deal of legislative or policy autonomy from the executive government. In fact, in South Korea real economic policy-making power lay with the Economic Planning Board and the Finance Ministry while the "central bank does little more than implement credit policies in line with overall government spending plans" (Maxfield 1994: 561). However, recent changes to the BOK have significantly altered this legislative regime in three main areas.

First, the new *Bank of Korea Act* effectively entrenches the autonomy of the BOK from the Ministry of Finance. While mechanisms of consultation between the Ministry and the BOK have been established, the executive is unable to impose on the Monetary Board a particular course of monetary policy. In fact, the draft Act was changed to reflect the IMF preference that, although the Minister for Finance and the Economy have the power to request a reconsideration of the decisions of the Monetary Board, the Minister should not be able to suspend such decisions, and any such request for reconsideration must immediately be made public (South Korea Ministry of Finance and Economy 1998).

Second, apart from those nominated by the Governor, the Minister for Finance and the Chairman of the Financial Supervisory Board, the membership of the Monetary Board will include members of the private financial community nominated by the Korean Federation of Banks and the Korean Securities Dealers' Association. The membership of these groups indicates that monetary policy will have to reflect the preferences of a financial community not likely to be sympathetic to activist industry policy (South Korea Ministry of Finance and Economy 1998).

Finally, the BOK will be expected to pursue the objective of monetary stability. The IMF stepped in to strengthen the objectives of monetary stability by adding a clause to make it clear that the prime objective of the BOK is to pursue monetary stability (South Korea Ministry of Finance and Economy, 1998).

An independent central bank strikes at the core of the developmental state in the following ways.

(i) It removes the power and capacity of central economic agencies to direct the kind of industry policies that have been a marked feature of the developmental state. In short, it shifts power from technocratic economic agencies to actors such as central banks. More importantly, it erodes the close political relationship between business and state that informed the operation of these economic agencies.

(ii) It becomes difficult to pursue the growth-oriented industry policy that often favoured the export industrial sector because the clearly defined objectives of the central bank are to establish monetary stability and, in general, to pursue an anti-inflationary strategy.

(iii) The policy of using subsidised credit as an arm of industry becomes highly problematic as a result of the BOK Act as well as the recently established Financial Supervisory Body.

All of these changes signal a significant shift towards a regulatory state underpinned by a form of economic constitutionalism. Economic constitutionalism, as noted earlier, refers to the attempt to treat the market as a constitutional order with its own rules, procedures and institutions operating to protect the market order from political interference. However, these forms of economic constitutionalism demand the construction of a specific kind of state organisation and structure: a regulatory state, the purpose of which is to safeguard market order.

Given the affinity of this term to the German ordo-liberal school of thought, it may be appropriate to call the emerging jurisprudence a kind of global ordo-liberalism. It is useful to focus on the writings of this school because it highlights the link between authoritarian politics and constitutional conceptions of economic order. Some of the prominent exponents of German ordo-liberalism were, after all, closely associated with the extremely conservative Von Papen government in the early 1930s.

Pivotal to ordo-liberalism and those of its prominent exponents such Eucken (1950) was the notion that the construction of economic order cannot be left to the spontaneous actions of the market but rather needs to be created through a consistent order-based policy (*ordnungspolitik*) of the state (Peacock and Willgerodt 1989). For the ordo-liberals the various economic, political, legal and other social processes are interrelated. Each act of government intervention must therefore be seen in connection with the total processes and overall economic order so as to ensure the "system conformity of measures" (Petersmann 1991: 63). Accordingly, the state should not attempt to conduct the economy. Instead, it should provide a system of juridical institutions that would facilitate the construction of the market. In fact, in its emphasis on the role of economic institutions in creating market order, it presages the new institutional economics. The point here is that the purpose of the state is to protect the underlying values and traits (the 'economic constitution') of the economic order.

Having chosen a certain kind of economic order, concerted political action is needed to create and sustain it. This conception of economic order places a high premium on the role of the juridical processes in safeguarding and creating market order. On this score at least it differs from those public choice accounts which emphasise the predatory nature of the state (Buchanan 1980). In contrast, the new PWC directs its attention not towards a leviathan predatory state but towards the effective capture of the state by powerfully connected vested interests.

From the PWC standpoint, what is required is not the retreat of the state, but the effective development of state institutions to protect the market order. For economic constitutionalism, a strong state was a necessary element of economic order but its role was essentially confined to providing the framework for an economic constitution that underpinned the reproduction of economic order.

The role of the state within this perspective is through indirect regulation of economic processes by providing "forms or structural conditions under which these processes could function effectively" (Gerber 1994: 47). This principle of indirect regulation is a vital element of the new regulatory state that the PWC seeks to promote.

It is possible to discern a distinctive conception of the political ramifications of notions of economic constitutionalism running through the ordo-liberal movement. In essence the ordo-liberals develop a political conception of market order where institutions are designed to protect it from the corrosive influence of politics. It is, as mentioned, essentially a politics of anti-politics.

Eucken and others were very concerned about the anti-competitive effects of society on the economy. Thus, echoing Schmitt, Eucken (1950) argued that by the end of the 19th century the state was increasingly captured by private interest groups, leading to the politicisation of the economy. In other words, the main purpose of economic constitutionalism was to protect the economy from these political pressures. This understanding of economic order implied the existence of institutions to prevent the politicisation of the economy. This could not be but anything but illiberal.

In fact, in his work in the 1930s, Schmitt (in Christi, 1998) developed a form of institutional jurisprudence which effectively recognised the fragmented nature of the state. He suggested that, rather than the twofold distinction between the state and the individual, it may be more plausible to draw a three-way distinction between the economy, the state, and the private sphere. The most interesting point here was the attempt to carve out a distinctive non-state but public sphere of economic activity. More specifically, Schmitt argued for an autonomous economic administration, that is:

> an economic sphere that belongs to the public interest and should not be seen as separate from it. Still, this is a non-state domain that can be organized and administered by these same business agents, as it happens in any genuine autonomous administration. ... Without an autonomous economic administration, in the sense of that intermediate sphere, a real new order would be hardly thinkable (Schmitt, in Christi 1998: 225–226).

This 'autonomous economic administration' dovetails with the institutionalist jurisprudence that he adopted as against 'decisionism' (his earlier preferred option) and 'normativism' (by which he meant liberal legalism).

Schmitt increasingly used the notion of 'concrete order' to emphasise how law should reflect the underlying, and of course deeply reactionary, values and norms of social and economic institutions. Schmitt's theory of concrete order finds a near perfect echo (though without any of the philosophical or political sophistication) in the work of Ellickson (1990), a leading member of the law and economics movement. Like Schmitt, Ellickson, too, places emphasis on the underlying norms - which are always seen as natural - that both order and structure economic institutions.

As Neumann (1986) pointed out, this institutional jurisprudence (and we might add here, the cognate notion of 'order' and security) became the jurisprudence of a fracturing state, characterised by polycentric centres of power. Institutional jurisprudence (be it in the form of ordo-liberalism or the law and economics movement) reflects the internal fragmentation of the sovereignty in the new global economic order. The emergence of autonomous economic administration can aptly be called a putative global ordo-liberalism. And again, the point is not the retreat of the state but the internal transformation of the state from the political structures associated with bargaining and conflict between interests to the economic constitutionalism that supports many of the governance structures of the new global economic order.

'Economic constitutionalism' attempts to place certain market regulatory institutions beyond the reach of transitory political majorities or the actions of the political executive through procedures that provide for a high degree of autonomy for a range of economic institutions. The creation of insulated institutions is designed to protect economic institutions from the influence of democratic politics. Eucken and others were very concerned about the anti-competitive effects of society on the economy (Gerber 1994). Again, this echoed Schmitt's view (Schmitt 1965) that by the end of the 19th century the state was increasingly captured by private interest groups. This led to a politicisation of the economy that in turn weakened the state.

The main purpose of economic constitutionalism was therefore to protect the economy from political pressures, and as such is anti-political jurisprudence. There is, again, a strong resemblance between the ideas the ordo-liberals in Germany in the 1930s and the recent rise of the law and economics movement. In both cases it is a jurisprudence which attempts to ground law not in a political process but in terms of the values of the institutional order, which are of course perceived as 'natural' and consequently 'disembedded' from the play of politics and power.

Economic reform and politics

Economic constitutionalism provides a sanitised version of politics that fails to acknowledge the often messy compromises and coalitions needed to implement economic reform. Markets are not just about norms: they are about power. Promoting economic reform means shifting or disrupting existing constellations of interests that benefit from economic reform. The argument here is based on the assumption that markets are embedded in politically-contested constellations of power and interests.

This stands in sharp contrast to the underlying assumptions of the orthodox, neo-classical approach which sees markets and economic strategies as somehow independent of the broader institutional context. From this perspective, all that is needed is the right economic 'fix' or strategy to correct market failure. Hence, economic strategies are seen to depend on the strategic choices of individual agents. This 'strategic' understanding of markets points to deeper ontological disagreements over the nature of markets. For example, the neo-classical perspective takes a static and abstract view of markets and views economic behaviour as independent of historical experience, institutional context, and informational or knowledge deficits. From a more political perspective, the market is seen as a structure determined by a complex historical past and one in which economic outcomes are strongly coloured by the texture of the institutional environment. Zysman (1996) neatly encapsulates this institutionalist logic when he notes that:

> Each market economy is defined by the institutions and rules that permit it to function, or to put differently, each national system can be defined by the 'institutional structure' of the economy, that which shapes how buying, selling and the very organisation of production takes place (Zysman 1996: 177).

These ontological debates over the proper constitution of markets and 'economic time' have important ramifications for the way we comprehend economic reform and policies. Adopting a dynamic conception of 'economic time' makes it untenable to think in terms of one single correct set of economic strategies. Rather, we need to understand the way different economic strategies are linked to different configurations of power and interests. Therefore, the resort to a dynamic conception of markets demands a recognition that markets cannot be disconnected from the wider ensemble of political and economic power. A comprehensive understanding of economic reform is possible only within the context of the wider set of political and institutional structures.

Indonesia provides a neat illustration of this point because, despite a deep structural crisis and the political demise of Soeharto, it has been difficult to dislodge entrenched economic oligarchies nurtured under the New Order regime. These entrenched interests have proved remarkably adept at blocking key economic reforms. The problem here is not the lack of technical fix for these problems but, more seriously, the absence of reform coalition that could underpin any significant change in the policy regime. Unless such a coalition can be identified, policy reforms – and, in particular, efforts to eradicate corruption – are likely to face severe obstacles which are fundamentally structural in nature.

This has important implications for our analysis of economic reform. To be successful, economic reform needs to have the political support of a significant group of actors. Reform strikes at the heart of deeply entrenched political and economic interests and therefore must galvanise its own political support. From this perspective, economic reform is not merely a technical exercise to implement the 'right' policies, but a political project undertaken by the putative winners of the reform process. For this reason, market transformation is likely to be a deeply contested and prolonged process. Our analysis serves to underscore the fact that markets are not neutral or abstract entities, but deeply embedded in constellations of power and interests.

Conclusion

Some of the of the key components of the emerging PWC consensus are best understood as an attempt to develop a particular understanding of politics that can ground the economic reforms advocated by multilateral agencies such as the World Bank. It is a curious kind of politics of anti-politics that attempts to quarantine economic institutions from the politics of bargaining and conflict. This economic constitutionalism drives much of the Governance programs of the World Bank and, furthermore, provides the normative rationale for the increasingly influential jurisprudence of the law and economics movement, so often in the ideological driving seat of legal and institutional reform programs.

This new politics of technical procedure may prove to be highly limited in explaining the 'how and why' of economic reform. To be successful, reform programs - such as anti-corruption initiatives - must be based on coalitions that stand to benefit from structural reform. It is much more than an exercise in technocratic management. Coalitions have to be built up and paid off and this is very different from the anti-politics promoted by governance programs. It also explains the difficulty of policy change in countries ranging from Indonesia to Japan: deeply entrenched coalitions are loath to surrender the benefits they derive from the existing configuration of markets.

References

Baer, W, Miles, WR and Moran, AB, (1999) 'The End of the Asian Myth: Why were the Experts Fooled?', 27 (10) *World Development* 1735–1747.

Buchanan, J, (1980) 'Reform in the Rent-Seeking Society', in J Buchanan, R Tollison and G Tullock (eds), *Toward a Theory of the Rent-seeking Society*, Texas A&M University Press, College Station, 359–367.

Camdessus, Michel, (1998) 'The IMF and Good Governance', address delivered at Transparency International conference, *Governments and Enterprises Facing Corruption*, Paris, 21 January.

Clark, Ian, (1999) *Globalisation and International Relations Theory*, Oxford University Press, Oxford.

Christi, Renato, (1998) *Carl Schmitt and Authoritarian Liberalism*, University of Wales Press, Cardiff.

Ellickson, Robert (1990) *Order without Law*, Harvard University Press, Cambridge, MA.

Eucken, Walter, (1950) *The Foundation of Economics: History and Theory in the Analysis of Economic Reality*, Hodge, London.

Gerber, David J, (1994), 'Constitutionalizing the Economy: German Neo-liberalism, Competition Law and the 'New' Europe', 42 *The American Journal of Comparative Law*, 25–84.

Hirst, Paul and Thompson, Geoffrey, (1996) *Globalization in Question: The International Economy and the Possibility of Governance*, Polity Press, London.

Jayasuriya, Kanishka and Rosser, Andrew, (2001), 'Economic Orthodoxy and the East Asian Crisis', 22 (3): *Third World Quarterly* 381–396.

Jayasuriya, Kanishka, (2001) 'Globalisation, Sovereignty, and the Rule of Law: From Political to Economic Constitutionalism?', *Constellations*, 8 (4) (Special Issue on 'Globalisation and Law') forthcoming.

Jayasuriya, Kanishka, (1999) 'Globalization, Law, and the Transformation of Sovereignty: The Emergence of Global Regulatory Governance', 6 (2) *Indiana Journal of Global Legal Studies* (Spring): 425–455.

Maxfield, Sylvia, (1994) 'Financial Incentives and Central Bank Authority in Industrialising Nations', 46 *World Politics* 556–588.

James, W, Naya, S and Meier, G, (1989) *Asian Development: Economic Success and Policy Lessons*, University of Wisconsin Press, Madison.

Neumann, Franz, (1986) *The Rule of Law: Political Theory and the Legal System in Modern Society*, Berg, Leamington Spa, England.

Peacock, A and Willgerodt, H, (1989) *German Neoliberals and the Social Market Economy*, Macmillan, London.

Petersmann, E, (1991) *Constitutional Functions and Constitutional Problems in International Economic Law*, Westview Press, Boulder, Colorado.

Robison, Richard and Rosser, Andrew, (1998) 'Contesting Reform: Indonesia's New Order and the IMF', 26 *World Development* 8: 1593–1609.

Schmitt, Carl, (1965) *Verfassungslehre*, Duncker and Humbolt, Berlin.

South Korea Ministry of Finance and Economy, 1998, 'Outline of New Legislation to Reform the Central Banking and Financial Supervisory Systems', Press statement, <http://kiep.go.kr/imf/hot-2-21.html>.

Stiglitz Joseph, (1998a) 'More Instruments and Broader Goals: Moving Toward the Post-Washington Consensus', 1998 Wider Annual Lecture <http://www.worldbank.org/html/extdr/extme/js-010798/wider.htm>.

Stiglitz, Joseph, (1998b) 'Lessons of the Asia Crisis', *Financial Times*, 4 December.

Strange, Susan, (1996) *The Retreat of the State: The Diffusion of Power in the World Economy*, Cambridge University Press, Cambridge.

Zysman, J, (1983) *Governments, Markets and Growth: Finance and the Politics of Industrial Change*, Cornell University Press, Ithaca, New York.

Chapter 3

Anti-Corruption and Asian Legal Professions

Veronica Taylor

Introduction

After leaving Jakarta's Catholic Cathedral one Sunday morning with an Indonesian friend I was forced to reflect on the wisdom of the anti-corruption campaign being waged by international institutions such as the International Monetary Fund (IMF) and the World Bank. It is now commonplace for anti-corruption measures to form part of the conditionality of loans made to economies in transition. Yet both the rhetoric and practice of the anti-corruption movement remain highly problematic (eg Kennedy 1999). My personal turning point was a break in the median strip in downtown Jakarta. As we u-turned, we immediately ran into a police trap and a languid indication that a fine would be levied for the 'violation'. My Indonesian friend refused to pay; instead, she put on a histrionic performance about how mortified she was in front of her foreign guest. "How can you shame our country like this?" she shouted. Abashed, the police waved us on.

In retrospect, what struck me was that she did not invoke our status as lawyers, even although she was a respected commercial lawyer at a politically well-connected local firm. In an industrialised democracy, simply saying "I'm a lawyer" would have been enough to make the police regret their attempt at petty extortion. However, as Lev (1999: 228-230) reminds us, the practising legal profession in Indonesia, like the judiciary, has long been the target of government intervention and control. The Indonesian legal 'profession' was deliberately handicapped by government, without the space or the opportunity to separate from government patronage and control. For a long time the key exception was the Legal Aid Institute (LBH: *Lembaga Bantuan Hukum*), which functioned as a political opposition to government but was by definition separate from lawyers serving government or clients connected with government (Lev 1999: 230).

Indonesian lawyers have not had the luxury of invoking professional ethics against corrupt practices. This is not solely because they have been 'captured' by government or by their clients or because they are complicit in undermining the law - although this clearly happens. Rather, they cannot invoke professional ethics because there is no Indonesian legal 'profession' in which these can be grounded.

Regulation of professions and the anti-corruption campaign

How do theories of how professions evolve relate to the broader issue of corruption in transitional economies? There are two points at which the sociology of professions connects with anti-corruption debates. Professions – particularly the legal profession – are relevant to anti-corruption regulation because they themselves are models of regulation.

The traditional hallmarks of professional organisations in the West have been those of autonomy: control over occupational training (for example, approval of the curriculum in universities); control over credentialing and entry to the profession; and self-regulation or a high degree of independence from government oversight; and control over a designated range of occupational activities (usually a monopoly granted by government). Self-regulation, of course, is never completely free of government intervention. In autocratic states, in particular, the state has a vested interest in not allowing self-regulation of professionals to evolve into the kind of political and economic autonomy that may pose a threat to state dominance. This explains, in part, the emergence of a technocratic legal 'profession' in countries such as the People's Republic of China, for example, where lawyers are unlikely to attain full independence from government (Alford 2000).

What elevates professions from other occupations, however, is their ability to sustain a 'claim to legitimacy', that is, the right to be the group – and the only group – that performs a certain kind of work in society (Abbott 1988). This protected work is the profession's 'core jurisdiction' or sphere of operation: the profession's 'claim' to government and to wider society that their members alone possess special skills and so should be given an occupational monopoly not enjoyed by potential competitors. In this way, lawyers have become more powerful than notaries; physicians are more powerful than herbalists; accountants are more powerful than bookkeepers and so on.

In economic terms, this right to protect some kinds of work from competitors is simply 'rent-seeking'. However, part of the justification for ceding professions an exclusive sphere of operation has been the implicit promise that a profession makes to government and to society that its members will act altruistically. Professionals such as lawyers claim that they will put concern for society ahead of their own pursuit of profit. We do not expect the same kind of altruism from taxi drivers or hamburger sellers.

The claim to altruism is usually expressed as 'professional ethics'. This is the point at which there seems to be a natural intersection with anti-corruption concerns. If professions can self-police their members to be 'ethical', does this not mean that professions such as lawyers will be both less inclined toward corruption and perhaps also function as a suitable social group to patrol the boundaries of corrupt behaviour? Abbott's theory of the sociology of the professions (1988) suggests that the answers are not so clear-cut.

Professional ethics are emphatically not some kind of special moral behaviour unique to people performing the same kind of work. Typically, professional 'ethics' are an undifferentiated mix of guidelines for principled behaviour and rules for controlling members of the group and excluding competitors and outsiders. Ethical rules adopted by professions are effective not because they are particularly moral, or clear or strict, but because the process of professional education and training emphasises the internalisation of professional norms. Even first-year law students in the Anglo-American legal world, for example, know that, in theory, a lawyer cannot act for both parties in a transaction, because this 'conflict of interest' would dilute the lawyer's ability to serve one or other client effectively. Some anti-corruption advocates suggest that greater 'professionalism' for government officials is the key to encouraging them to separate their public persona (government official) from their private persona (friend, relative, colleague, business partner) and thus avoid the conflicts of interest and patronage endemic in 'corrupt' regimes. (Rose-Ackerman 1999: 75) A more realistic assessment might be that 'conflict of interest' is simply a useful cognitive tool that allows people to resolve the role conflict that is a normal part of human life.

Professionals are not 'ethical' simply because they are professionals. The fact that most professions spend a great deal of time articulating and reinforcing professional norms of behaviour suggests that there is no magical moment at which a person is transformed into an ethical 'professional'. Rather, professionals comply with the ethical rules of their group because these are reinforced in a number of different ways. They are bound by professional ethics because there is a profession to bind them. Lawyers remind each other constantly about how they should behave. They gossip about who is an ethical, competent lawyer and who is not – and this gossip can have a direct consequence on the profits or business opportunities of their colleagues. Because lawyers promise the public and government that they will monitor each other, people generally trust that lawyers will behave ethically. Those client expectations also encourage lawyers to behave ethically.

The converse can also be true. Lawyers in many societies form an important social and legal institution because they can influence other people (their clients or government, for example) to comply with law and with social norms (Garth and Dezalay 1996). In this way lawyers perform an important regulatory role as an intermediate social group – an institution of civil society that mediates between government and non-government entities. Lawyers in many settings also construct themselves as non-government organisations (NGOs) although, as I argue below, this is an uneasy status that often translates into capture by government, corporate or political interests.

It should not surprise us, then, that lawyers have been early recruits to the anti-corruption movement. One example is the emergence of the non-government organisation Transparency International (TI). TI began life as a business organisation, but its membership is heavy with transnational lawyers. [1] One of the reasons that TI has become so politically powerful is that professions such as lawyers are easily able to form epistemic communities - groups of elite members who 'float' above national boundaries and share a similar outlook and objectives. Epistemic communities can formulate shared norms quickly and then argue strongly that these norms be adopted universally. Advocacy by TI is one of the reasons that other epistemic communities such as the IMF and the World Bank have adopted anti-corruption so enthusiastically (Conference 2000).

To understand how and why lawyers are being co-opted into anti-corruption regulatory roles we should focus for a moment on why corruption has emerged as such an important policy issue in development assistance.

Normative choices in the anti-corruption rhetoric

Corruption itself - particularly bribe-taking by government officials and inducements offered by clients of government - is old and well-known human behaviour. What is new is the sudden emergence of anti-corruption rhetoric within multilateral agencies such as the World Bank and the IMF. The reasons seem clear. Multilateral agencies, foreign governments and multinational corporations had become impatient with the degree to which system insiders were siphoning off money for loans, development aid and commercial transactions at its destination. The Asian financial crisis provided a recent flashpoint because of the need for speedy, large-scale bailouts of government and corporations in countries such as Indonesia. For convenience sake in this chapter I take 1997 to the present as the illustrative time frame and Indonesia as the illustrative country.

Ostensibly, the demand that countries such as Indonesia implement anti-corruption legislation and take concrete measures to curb visible forms of corruption (such as bribes to government officials) flows from an economic imperative. Theft, fraud and distortions of the market act as drags on donor funds, foreign investment and ultimately the economic development of the country concerned. Not surprisingly, multinational corporations become willing lobbyists for any kind of policy intervention that promises to make operating in their target country less costly.

The response to the economic imperative is legal formalism - fairly narrowly drafted prohibitive legislation with criminal sanctions. This too, is not surprising. The impulse to reform that is the belief that a social problem can be 'improved' with the application of more law is a conceit of lawyers across a broad political spectrum. Their new allies are economists: there are

1 See the Transparency International website: www.transparency.org

natural affinities between legal formalism and the emphasis on reducing transaction costs found in the New Institutional Economics. It is worth noting that all of these intellectual frameworks are particularly strong at the moment in the United States - they are not embraced so fervently in other parts of the common law world or in Europe.

This fusion of orthodoxies goes some way to explaining the slippage in anti-corruption arguments. What begins as an economic complaint about wastage and misallocation of economic goods in corrupt regimes quickly shifts to a critique of the political foundations of those regimes and the absence of adequate 'rule of law'. Ohnesorge (1999) deftly unmasks the apparently neutral economic objection to corruption by pointing to two of its hidden agendas: the advancement of a particular political ideology (for example, American-style political pluralism) and the advancement of multinational business interests. Jayasuriya's earlier work (1999) is significant because it flags some of the unintended consequences of this kind of political approach. He argues that 'rule of law' rhetoric has been embraced enthusiastically within East Asia (particularly in Singapore and Malaysia) as a way to bolster the legitimacy of political regimes that have rejected Anglo-American models of political democracy. Nicholson (this volume) identifies other ways in which the political intentions of the anti-corruption campaign can go awry. She shows that international anti-corruption rhetoric and show trials can serve useful political purposes for governments in places such as Vietnam, but that the results may diverge a long way from the normative agendas of multilateral agencies and multinational firms seeking a more familiar, 'transparent' system in which to do business.

The third 'orthodoxy' of much of the anti-corruption literature is its focus on the moral failings of the individual - typically the 'corrupt' government official soliciting or receiving a bribe or economic benefit. Corruption as moral failure by individuals is doubly undesirable because it leads to economic inefficiency and corrodes political legitimacy. The three orthodoxies are therefore self-reinforcing.

The moral dimension of anti-corruption rhetoric is interesting because, at its most extreme, it echoes single-issue moral campaigns against alcohol, sexual immorality and tobacco. These campaigns share a kind of satanic multiplier, where the catastrophe (in this case halting a country's economic development) is far greater than the sum of the human failings or inefficiencies being complained about. Abolitionist campaigns also share a track record of being singularly unsuccessful ways to change human behaviour. Anechiarico (1999) argues that, the problem of corruption in the United States has been constructed and policed quite differently at different points in history. He concludes that the preferred method of dealing with the problem - and in particular punitive approaches - says less about advances in understanding of the problem than about political choices and populist appeals.

A more useful approach is to acknowledge, as Rose-Ackerman does (1999: 69-88; 91-110), that corruption involves individuals and their behaviour, but that individuals are usually embedded in a bureaucratic or corporate culture. Within that, they may be caught in hierarchical relationships that determine the 'rules' for their business interactions. Scheppele (1999) reminds us that these problems are particularly acute in transition economies. Where the superstructures of an authoritarian government are being replaced with new 'marketised' institutions, the gaps between official norms and the operating norms of society are extremely wide. Accommodations that seek to bridge these gaps - including 'corrupt' practices by citizens or government officials - are rational and are unlikely to disappear just because tough legislative sanctions are introduced at the request of foreign investors or the IMF or the World Bank. Citizens and government officials are more likely to alter their behaviour when they have sufficient evidence that they will be free from scapegoating, and that local institutions will genuinely embrace procedures and resource allocation that make illegitimate acts unnecessary.

This echoes the commonsense proposition of legal sociology that individuals and legal persons sit not under some kind of seamless legislative and regulatory legal umbrella provided by the state, but in the midst of a regulatory matrix of rules (Macaulay 1991) and norms governing human behaviour generated by multiple actors. Formal laws and regulations are a part of the mix but many of the 'rules of the game' are generated by the individual or legal person itself through negotiations with other actors. Intermediate groups are particularly important: intermediaries such as bankers, insurers and lawyers and institutions such as family, church, ethnic group, the media, social groups and so on all generate normative rules. Particular industries or groupings such as professions and NGOs) also generate rules that govern their membership.[2]

One of the implications of this kind of sociological worldview is that influencing and modifying the behaviour of individuals and institutions is a more complex process than legal formalism generally acknowledges.

Normative choices guide enforcement mechanisms

How you view corruption determines your preferred policy solution. If you view 'corruption' as an aberrant behaviour by immoral individuals, then tough, top-down criminal sanctions (the legal formalist approach) would seem like a possible solution. This kind of top-down sanctioning, however, has some in-built limitations. It tends to privilege the state as the enforcer, which can lead to concentration of power in state agencies. Such formalism typically overestimates the impact of law and can lead to over-enforcement - typically the number of individuals who engage in seriously corrupt behaviour is much smaller than the amount of resources needed to detect,

2 This kind of sociological insight is now permeating economic thinking, where at least some scholars are concerned with 'institutions' that have no physical manifestation - such as the courthouse or Parliament - but which nevertheless serve as the location for formulating 'the rules of the game' (Aoki, in press).

investigate and prosecute them. The state cannot successfully prosecute every wrongdoer, and there is also a question of whether tough penalties actually discourage corrupt behaviour.

If, on the other hand, you view corruption as a failure of a political institution then 'corrupt' behaviour starts to look much more historically contingent and structurally induced. In government or bureaucratic settings we can characterise 'corrupt' practices as failures of trust - abuses of power that cause people to distrust government or business. Seen this way, you are more likely to ask: "How should we alter the structures to entrench new norms and persuade the actors to alter their behaviour?" Much of the anti-corruption writing to date is notably silent on how to redesign political and legal institutions to make them more trustworthy (Rose-Ackerman 1999; LPIB Roundtable 1999).

The difficulty with institutional design is that, to be effective, it requires intimate knowledge of the culture of the target location. These projects are also likely to be complex and almost certainly will require long time lines (much longer than the two-year 'long-term' horizon of institutions such as the World Bank: Lindsey and Taylor 2000). The advantage of what I could call the 'trust and governance' prescriptions for remaking regulatory institutions is, however, that they offer a more nuanced range of regulatory possibilities than top-down prohibition - and they are more likely to work in the long term.

Designing trustworthy intuitions

Braithwaite (1998) argues that societies work better when we maximise two kinds of trust: trust as confidence (the expectation that someone will do what we want) and trust as obligation (people accepting that they have obligations and acting to honour them). This latter definition comes close to the legal definition of trust. Obviously, many definitions of 'trust' exist, but Braithwaite argues that trust as confidence and trust as 'obligation' are mutually constituting: the more we trust people to behave in a trustworthy way, the more they are likely to do so.

The next stage of the argument is that, to maximise trust in civil society, we should design institutions based on the idea that people are more likely to be virtuous (trustworthy) than not. Braithwaite expresses this idea in a regulatory pyramid that is designed from the bottom up (1999: 353). At the bottom are virtuous actors (that is, most people or corporations or government agencies) who will comply with a norm (or a legal rule) if they are exposed to dialogue and persuasion. Dialogue and persuasion work most of the time.

If, however, the actor is a 'rational calculator' (that is, an actor who will only comply when he or she sees self-interest in doing so) then the kind of enforcement required is deterrence. So, for example, the threat of a fine or an administrative punishment may need to be made, or enforced, in order to influence the rational calculator. In the unusual case where an actor is incompetent or irrational (that is, the actor is incapable of complying or simply refuses to) then the enforcement strategy shifts to incapacitation – for example revoking a business licence, imprisonment or a heavy fine for the individual, the business or the government agency.

This kind of regulatory pyramid assumes that abuses of trust such as corruption have diverse causes. Sometimes it may be "failure to understand that the law is important, sometimes incompetence, sometimes irrational resistance to reason" (1999: 352). The pyramid assumes, however, that interpersonal trust is the most effective way to prevent abuses of trust – which people, businesses and government agencies generally respond to rational appeals to behave in a virtuous way. As it happens, mobilising interpersonal trust in this way is also efficient: dialogue and persuasion consume fewer resources than harsh intervention and imprisonment.[3]

The point of Braithwaite's argument is that the best outcome for society is one in which people comply with the norm voluntarily out of widespread trust that other people and intuitions are following the same legitimate rule. Thus the harshest form of sanction is reserved for the tiny minority of people who are incompetent or irrational. Dialogue and persuasion build a climate in which compliance is more likely. However, for the base of the pyramid to be effective, dialogue and persuasion must also signal clearly that, if trust is abused, intervention will escalate into deterrence and then incapacitation.

A second assumption of the pyramid is a state needs to supply strong institutions such as effective law enforcement and a functioning judiciary. Deterrence and incapacitation have to be credible (Braithwaite 1999: 356). Some policy makers would be inclined to respond by building very powerful state (or private) apparatuses for law enforcement, but such concentrations of power have great potential for evil (Braithwaite 1999: 357). It follows, then, that although we need strong agencies to enforce legal and social norms at the top of the regulatory pyramid, we also need institutions that will check those agencies' potential to abuse power.

In traditional political and legal theory, this problem is often addressed by talking about separation of powers between the parliament, executive and judiciary. The Braithwaite model, however, is more sophisticated and realistic than this simple separation of powers. He advocates that powerful institutions (whether state or private) need to be monitored and checked by a strong civil society, comprising a range of institutions. These intermediate institutions include the market, state agencies, the family, religious organisations, business groups, professional groups, political groups and the like. Each of these groups has the potential to become domineering and to encroach on the freedom of its members or other actors in society.

3 A Mongolian prosecutor once pointed out to me that this is a kind of Western economic fallacy – that in fact imprisonment in Mongolia is a cheap option. This may be true, but in this schema, we are not searching for just the cheapest alternative, but the one most likely to enhance civil society.

Intermediaries have their dark side as well: the Mafia, gangs, fixers of all kinds, pyramid selling groups, cults and Weight Watchers are all intermediate groups for the purposes of this argument. The dangers of intermediate groups becoming abusers of trust are lessened, Braithwaite argues, if these institutions act as guardians for each other; are guardians of the state (that is, subject state agencies to scrutiny); and are, in turn, subject to scrutiny and intervention by state agencies (1999: 366)

One of the questions we might ask about the Braithwaite model is whether it applies only to Western liberal democracies.[4] To be sure, the republican political theory that underlies it is clearly Western in its origins (Braithwaite 1999: 359-361). However, the regulatory model that Braithwaite sketches is intended to be applicable to societies that are (or aspire to be) non-totalitarian. Of course the model is an ideal type and does not operate in full in any political or legal system at present. We can thus immediately identify possible sources of resistance to this kind of model.

The first is political. The regulatory pyramid is predicated on having credible institutions at its upper end. This allows people to exert interpersonal pressure at the lower end of the pyramid in the shadow of enforcement agencies and formal laws. However, upper-end enforcement also applies to the state itself. The model requires, for example, courts and tribunals and police agencies that can and will check abuses of power by other government agencies. Yet governments in most countries tend to chafe against independent court power to veto laws or administrative practices as illegitimate or unconstitutional. More often, it is the government itself that tries to neutralise courts through under-funding, or to weaken independent regulatory agencies, or even direct legislative sabotage.

A second problem is social or cultural: how to renegotiate law and regulatory agencies when they have been distrusted for a long period? In systems such as Indonesia's, for example, where (until recently) government agencies have not had to be accountable to anyone except the President and his inner circle, there has been little incentive to build 'trust' with the citizenry or with client groups. Braithwaite's model offers no easy solution to this problem, but it does advance a useful theoretical idea. That is that we should not assume a "hydraulic relationship between the strengths of different intuitions" (1998: 366). By this he means that strengthening a regulatory institutions (for example, the courts) should not be seen as correspondingly weakening other intuitions (for example, parliament). In his view, we need a cluster of institutions that support and check each other. It is important not to rely blindly on one or a few institutions to do the regulatory work of society (1998: 366).

Many of the initial responses to widespread corruption suggest that an independent regulator (for example, an anti-corruption commission) should

4 I am grateful to my colleague Sean Cooney, of the Asian Law Centre at the University of Melbourne for asking this and other thought-provoking questions.

be established to ensure that anti-corruption legislation works and is not sabotaged by actors with a vested interest in maintaining the corrupt status quo. Alternatively, some commentators suggest that the way to proceed is to carve out corruption-free zones, in which at least one institution can be guaranteed to be corruption-free. An example of this was the establishment in Indonesia, under the auspices of the IMF, of a new Commercial Court with jurisdiction over insolvency - an experiment that seems to be failing in many respects (Lindsey and Taylor 2000). Another popular solution among anti-corruption commentators is to charge NGOs and international bodies with a 'watchdog' role and have them continually report on, and apply pressure to, the governments of transition economies (for example, LPIB Roundtable 1999). Braithwaite's argument would suggest that these approaches are destined to be short-term.

It is difficult to think of any institution in any society that remains completely virtuous over time. For this reason, Braithwaite argues, we should institutionalise some distrust in regard to all institutions, "so that their various pathologies can be checked by the strength of other institutions" (1998: 367). It is also unrealistic to believe that any social institution can exist and function free of influence from other social institutions. The key to building or re-building virtuous, trustworthy institutions is to ensure that a range of institutions - state and non-state - is strengthened together.

Lawyers as corruption-busters

We can test the Braithwaite model briefly by thinking about the problem of reinventing the judiciary in countries such as Indonesia. Anti-corruption campaigners are particularly affronted by corrupt judges. Usually this is expressed as the idea that 'rule of law' requires a judiciary that is independent of the executive and legislative branches of government and is blind to those seeking preferential treatment before the law. So, for example, it is commonplace in countries such as Indonesia for foreigners and local people alike to say "Judges are distrusted because they are corrupt" (Taylor 1999). If, however, we see corruption as the symptom of a breakdown in institutional arrangements between state and society, we are more likely to say: "Judges are corrupt because they are distrusted". That is, there are no institutional or normative measures in place that act as incentives for judges to behave in a professional, independent, consistent way that legitimises their role in the eyes of society.

Judicial independence is a concept that is frequently honoured in the breach. Most judiciaries include political appointees and are replete with episodes of political interference in the outcomes of litigation. Neither the United States nor Australia is free of political attempts to influence judges. This seems to be qualitatively different, however, from saying that a judge or judiciary is 'corrupt'.

Leaving aside the Anglo-American tradition, we can point to the long-running debate in Japanese law about the degree to which Japanese judges have served the interests of the government of the day by not ruling against it in constitutional controversies. Scholars such as Ramsayer (1993) have correlated that pattern of decision-making to judicial rankings and patterns of promotion, in order to argue that the Japanese judiciary is not fully independent of government. Yet neither those scholars nor their critics seriously entertain the idea that Japanese judges are 'corrupt' in the sense of taking bribes or bending outcomes for reasons of personal advantage. To be sure, there have been recent corruption scandals concerning public prosecutors in Japan, but the scandalousness is amplified because the instances have been rare (or rarely uncovered). Indeed, most studies of the Japanese judiciary have emphasised the ways in which compliance with professional standards is underlined during training and apprenticeship, and the way in which mentoring, scrutiny by one's peers and review by appellate courts leaves very little room for non-conformist behaviour. The net result of controlling judges' professional space so tightly in these cases seems to have been a public perception that most judges in Japan are honest most of the time.

Another problem with a court-centric anti-corruption campaign is that it does not allow for the regulatory role played by other institutions and the need for those institutions to be strong and autonomous. At the lower end of the regulatory pyramid, lawyers play an important role as 'gatekeepers' for problems. They are the ones who advise a client whether or not paying money to a government official is legal and what the consequences of breaking the law will be. In societies where lawyers are business advisors rather than simply notaries, they also sort out which claims or problems will be recognised as 'legal' and which can be solved by negotiation. Lawyers in industrialised countries frequently report that part of their role as 'trouble-shooters' in transactions is to persuade and educate their clients about what is appropriate business behaviour.

Part of the strength of lawyers as advisors in industrialised countries comes from their ability to form a strong profession and their agility in moving into new areas of work. As a professional group they also encourage us to believe that they embody legal standards. In this way, lawyers as much as judges can in a sense say, "I am the law". Lawyers are natural 'enforcers' of norms because this expands their sphere of professional activity. The other side of this role is that they also carry out much of the 'dirty work' for society in dealing with people, agencies or actions that are illegitimate, harmful or illegal.

Because lawyers perform these multifaceted roles, their relationship with the state is usually tense. Lawyers depend on the state for their grant of jurisdiction and for favourable regulation. The state relies on them (as it does on other institutions) to perform a regulatory role at the base of the regulatory pyramid. But lawyers can also be a powerful group that is likely to call the state to account at the top of the pyramid as well – something that can be uncomfortable for state actors. In Braithwaite's model, this kind of institutionalisation of distrust – or checking institutions – should be routine and uncontroversial. It follows then that lawyers too should be subject to routine checks and criticism from other actors in society.

Many legal professions in Asia are in transition from an 'advocate' model, in which lawyers operate in or near courts and in few other contexts, to a business advice model, in which their sphere of operation is much broader. Some legal 'professions' in Asia are nascent or displaced (for example, Vietnam); dysfunctional (for example, Indonesia); politically marginalised (for example, Korea); or undergoing fundamental restructuring (for example, Japan). The reality is that in many of these countries there is no single 'profession', but rather fragmented and competing clusters of more or less powerful occupational groups. The increased interest in professional ethics and professional responsibility in many Asian countries, however, suggests that there is movement underway in the legal professions that may see the emergence of better-coordinated and stronger professional groupings. If this happens, the range of regulatory options for combating corruption may broaden considerably, and the long-term institution-building contemplated by the trust and governance literature surveyed in this chapter may become viable.

References

Abbott, A, (1988), *The System of Professions: An Essay on the Division of Expert Labor*, University of Chicago Press, Chicago.

Alford, William, (2000), Book Review: *Exporting 'The Pursuit of Happiness' Aiding Democracy Abroad: The Learning Curve* by Thomas Carothers, 113 *Harvard Law Review* 1677.

Anechiarico Frank, (1999), 'Frank End-runs and Hairy Eyeballs: The Costs of Corruption Control in Market Democracies', 14 *Connecticut Journal of International Law* 379.

Aoki, Masahiko, (nd), *Toward a Comparative Institutional Analysis*, (unpublished manuscript, on file with author).

Asian Development Bank, (1998), *The Role of Law and Legal Institutions in Asian Economic Development 1960-1995*, Available online: http://adb.org at http://adb.org/Documents/Books/Role_of_Law/ default.asp (accessed 20 August 2001).

Asian Development Bank, (2000), Combating Corruption in the Asian and Pacific Economies: Conference Papers and Proceedings Available online: http://adb.org at http://adb.org/Documents/Conference /Combating_Corruption/default.asp (accessed 20 August 2001).

Braithwaite, J, (1998), 'Institutionalizing Distrust, Enculturating Trust', in V Braithwaite and M Levi (eds), *Trust and Governance*, Sage, New York.

Conference Proceedings: The Experts Roundtable: A Hemispheric Approach to Combating Corruption (2000), 15 *American University International Law Review* 759.

Gantz, David, (1997), 'The Foreign Corrupt Practices Act: Professional and Ethical Challenges for Lawyers', 14 *Arizona Journal of International and Comparative Law* 97.

Garth, Bryant and Dezalay Yves, (1996), *Dealing in Virtue: International Commercial Arbitration and the Construction of a Transactional Legal Order*, University of Chicago Press, Chicago.

Goldbarg, Andrea, (2000), 'The Foreign Corrupt Practices Act and Structural Corruption', 18 *Boston University International Law Journal* 273.

Grabowsky, Peter and Braithwaite, John (eds), (1992), *Business Regulation and Australia's Future*, Australian Institute of Criminology, Canberra.

Jayasuriya, Kanishka, (1999), 'The Rule of Law and Governance in the East Asian State', 1 *Asian Law* 107.

Kennedy, David, (1999), 'The International Anti-Corruption Campaign' 14 *Connecticut Law Journal of International Law* 455.

Lev, Daniel, (1999), 'Between State and Society: Professional Lawyers and Reform in Indonesia', in Timothy Lindsey (ed), *Indonesia: Law and Society*, Federation Press, Sydney, 227-246.

Lindsey, Timothy and Taylor, Veronica, (2000), 'Rethinking Indonesian Insolvency Reform: Contexts and Frameworks', in Timothy Lindsey (ed) *Indonesia: Bankruptcy, Law Reform & the Commercial Court*, Desert Pea Press, Sydney, 2-14.

LPIB Roundtable on Global Corruption, (1999), 31 *Law and Policy in International Business* 195-217.

Macaulay, Stewart, (1991), 'Long-Term Continuing Relations: The American Experience Regulating Dealerships and Franchises', in Christian Joerges (ed), *Franchising the Law: Theoretical and Comparative Approaches in Europe and the United States*, Nomos Verlagsgesellschaft, Baden-Baden, 179-237.

Ohnesorge, John, (1999), '"Ratch" eting up the Anti-Corruption Drive: Could a look at recent history cure a case of theory-determinism?' 14 *Connecticut Journal of International Law* 467.

Ramseyer, J Mark, (1993), 'Judicial (In)dependence in Japan' 39 *University of Chicago Law School Record* 4.

Rose, Carol V, (1998), 'The 'New' Law and Development Movement in the Post-Cold War Era: A Vietnam Case Study', 32 *Law and Society Review* 93.

Rose-Ackerman, S, (1999), *Corruption and Government*, Cambridge University Press, Cambridge.

Sachs, Jeffrey, Zinnes, Clifford and Eilat, Yair, (1999), 'Benchmarking Competitiveness in Transition Economies', *Working Paper of the Harvard Institute for International Development*, Consulting Assistance on Economic Reform II Discussion Paper No. 62 Available online: http://www.hiid.harvard.edu at http://www.hiid.harvard.edu/aer2/html/content/papers/paper62/paper62.htm (Accessed 20 August 2001).

Scheppele, Kim Lane, (1999) The Inevitable Corruption of Transition, 14 *Connecticut Journal of International Law* 509.

Silbey, Susan, (1997), '"Let them Eat Cake": Globalization, Postmodern Colonialism and the Possibilities of Justice', 31 *Law and Society Review* 20.

Taylor, Veronica, (1999), 'The Transformation of Indonesian Commercial Contracts and Legal Advisers', in Timothy Lindsey (ed), *Indonesia Law and Society*, Federation Press, Sydney, 279-291.

Taylor, Veronica, (1997), 'Rethinking Legal Orientalism', in Veronica Taylor (ed), *Asian Laws Through Australian Eyes*, LBC, Sydney.

Trubek, David and Galanter, Marc, (1974), 'Scholars in Self-Estrangement: Some Reflections on the Study of Law and Development', 82 *Yale Law Journal* 1.

World Bank, (2000), *Entering the 21st Century: World Development Report 1999/2000*, Oxford.

Chapter 4

Functions and Dysfunctions of Corruption and its Reporting in Central and Eastern Europe[1]

Leslie Holmes

Introduction

Since at least the 1960s, some analysts (for example, Leff 1964; Nye 1967; Huntington 1968) have argued that corruption can play a positive role in polities, especially during economic development and modernisation stages. Such authors typically argue that, if we are to understand corruption better, our analyses of it should distance themselves from essentially ethical interpretations and instead focus on the potential advantages – the functionality – of the phenomenon under specified circumstances.

For at least as long, other scholars and observers such as Myrdal (1968) have maintained that corruption can never be condoned and that it invariably undermines a system, including a modernising one. Perhaps the best known contemporary exponent of this position is the Berlin-based Transparency International, which seeks to eradicate corruption, particularly in international business.

In this Chapter, the advantages and disadvantages of both corruption and its reporting in the post-Communist states of Central and Eastern Europe (CEE) will be examined. It is maintained that unless it is acknowledged that corruption may under certain conditions be perceived as beneficial, attempts to reduce its levels are destined to be less effective than they could be. Expressed another way, such acknowledgement helps us better to understand the often ambiguous approaches adopted by governments in dealing with corruption.

The basic argument here is that both corruption and the reporting of corruption *can* sometimes be advantageous in the short-term, but that the former is invariably dysfunctional to systems in the longer-term and too much of the latter can be. It is further argued that the dysfunctionality can

1 Originally published in German as "Funktionen und Dysfunktionen der Korruption und Ihrer Bekaempfung in Mittel- und Osteuropa" in J Borchert et al (2000:117-44).

be particularly acute in the case of the post-Communist states. In these transitional countries both corruption and its reporting can undermine the legitimacy of the privatisation/marketisation and democratisation projects.

Definitions

Before elaborating the argument, however, a brief definitional note is required because the boundaries of the concept of corruption are still contested. There are numerous reasons for this, including the most commonly cited one of cultural difference. When does a gift of gratitude become a bribe, for instance? How useful is a definition that depends upon a rigid distinction between public and private, in an age when neo-liberalism in Western states is making the line between these two sectors increasingly fuzzy and at times even arbitrary?

There are no watertight solutions to problems such as these, so individual analysts should always specify their own preferred interpretation. Others can then decide for themselves whether or not they wish to consider the arguments and findings based on that definitional approach. Given these problems, the approach adopted here – which I have used elsewhere (see Holmes 1997a: 277-278) – is not to define corruption as such but to specify a set of criteria that must be met for an action or non-action (for example, 'turning a blind eye') to constitute a corrupt act. The four criteria are:

1. it must be carried out by either an individual or a group of individuals occupying what is widely perceived to be a public office, usually a state position – that is, it must be engaged in by *officials;*
2. the public office must be widely perceived as one of public responsibility and authority. This criterion would exclude a postal delivery worker or a train driver, for instance;
3. the official(s) must commit the act at least in part because of personal (vested) interest;
4. the officials must be aware that their actions or non-actions either are, or else might be, considered illegal or improper (this would catch cases of uncertainty where they opt not to check because the answer might not suit their interests).

An analysis of corruption in contemporary CEE that omits any reference to organised crime would be inadequate, since, all too often, there is a close nexus between the two. Yet they are conceptually distinct. Again, in attempting to define 'organised crime', the least problematical method is to identify a set of criteria to be met. Thus, in contrast to corrupt actions (or non-actions), organised crime actions involve the following five factors:

1. they are necessarily carried out by a group (typically described as a 'gang'), but not of officials;
2. they are necessarily coordinated;

3. they are probably 'bunched' or targeted (relating to drug-dealing, prostitution, loan-sharking, etc);
4. they are necessarily in part illegal, not merely improper; and
5. they usually involve physical violence, actual or threatened.

Armed with these two definitional frameworks, we can now analyse the functionality and dysfunctionality of corruption and its reporting. Where appropriate, reference to organised crime will also be made.

Functions of corruption and its reporting

At least in the short-term, there are a number of potential advantages to both corruption and its reporting. Purely for the sake of clarity, these functions can be separated into economic, social and political (although, of course, the real world is never as discrete and tidy). In each of the following sub-sections, the initial part of the analysis focuses on corruption itself, while the subsequent part is more concerned with the effects of *reporting* corruption. One final introductory point is that the analysis concentrates on the advantages and disadvantages of corruption to the state and society, not to the individuals engaged in corruption. That is a separate story, but one which is also largely self-evident.

Economic functions

The most commonly cited economic advantage of corruption is that of 'lubricating' an otherwise malfunctioning economy. The more regulated and centrally controlled an economy, *ceteris paribus* the greater potential for inefficiencies and delays. This is because the sheer complexity of modern large-scale economies means that it is unrealistic to expect to be able to coordinate in some 'planned' way the numerous factors across a whole national economy.[2] Precisely this complexity and the consequently necessarily high levels of regulation mean that the opportunities for corruption increase. But if such corruption circumvents bottlenecks, thereby facilitating an increase (and possibly also an improvement) in economic activity, this can assist economic growth.

Despite putatively similar commitments to 'marketisation' and 'privatisation' by the majority of post-Communist states, the actual level of state involvement in the economy has varied significantly during the 1990s. For instance, the Romanian economic system was not transformed nearly as substantially under Iliescu as the early pronouncements of his allegedly post-Communist government would have implied. The continuing high levels of state involvement in the economy were conducive to corruption, as subsequent President Emil Constantinescu continually emphasised during

2 The problem is further compounded by the effects of extraneous factors, over which the state has little if any control. The relevance of this in an increasingly globalised world is obvious.

his 1996 election campaign. Yet the economic problems of the Iliescu era may have been even worse had there been lower levels of corruption. Even in Czechia, whose former Prime Minister, Václav Klaus, used to claim was pursuing radical economic reform, the state still played a large role. The fact that it had a number of corruption scandals (see Kettle 1995) may partly be explained by the fact that corruption was 'necessary' for countering the inefficiency effects of excessive state involvement in the economy.

Secondly, corruption can sometimes play a positive role in encouraging private enterprise and initiative. This can be particularly beneficial in post-Communist countries in which private enterprise was, for decades, either taboo or else only reluctantly tolerated (and even then, only on a small scale). The ingenuity involved in some forms of corruption can have a highly beneficial effect on economic growth and development if redirected into more legitimate forms of economic activity.

It is sometimes claimed that one of the reasons that China's economy under Communist rule has, by many criteria, performed well in recent years, while Russia's post-Communist economy has stagnated, is that the Chinese are inherently good traders and businesspeople, whereas the Russians are not. Such cultural stereotyping is not only ethically, but also empirically, questionable. Some comparative analysts of both organised crime and corruption have, for instance, argued that the most sophisticated scams of recent years have been carried out by Russians (Sterling 1995: esp 40 and 213-283). This suggests that, under certain conditions, many Russians can, and do, display considerable ingenuity in making profits. Unfortunately, much of this ingenuity and initiative is presently directed towards criminal activity. This is largely a problem of the current post-Communist structures and processes in Russia but it also suggests that engaging in improper economic activity may teach or hone entrepreneurial skills that can subsequently be applied in more legal and constructive ways to economic development.

Thirdly, and closely linked to the previous point, corruption can introduce competition into otherwise monopolistic or quasi-monopolistic economies. If corruption 'opens up the game' to more players, this can exert a beneficial effect. Again, this is an important aspect of the transition in CEE, given the Communist legacy of near-monopolistic economies.

Fourthly, corruption may generate investment capital and assist the privatisation process. Corruption cannot be meaningfully detached here from organised crime, since they are often closely intertwined and interactive in much of contemporary CEE.[3] If, between them, they contribute to a transfer of capital from the state to the private sector, and some of these funds are then used for investment purposes, corruption has played a positive role in both the development and the restructuring of an economy.

3 For a recent scholarly analysis of the interaction of corruption and organized crime in Russia, see Frisby 1998, while a still useful earlier survey by a Russian official involved in combating organised crime and corruption is Gurov 1995. For analyses of other countries see, for example, Komlenovic 1997 and Nikolov 1997.

In assessing the potential utility of corruption to an economy, it is often necessary to specify the precise nature of the corruption. There is an important distinction between a situation in which corruption is highly regularised – in that bribe rates are 'standardised' and a potential bribe-giver knows that he or she is bribing the most appropriate official(s) – and one in which there is near anarchy even in the corruption process. An 'orderly' corruption process can increase investor confidence during otherwise highly uncertain times, as for example, during the early stages of a revolutionary transition.

Conversely, one of the most frequent criticisms from potential investors in Russia during the early-1990s was that there were often no agreed rates. One could not be reasonably certain that, having bribed one official, another would not claim that he or she was the one who really had the power to provide whatever good was being sought. Although this situation appears to have improved in recent years, it can take many years to overcome such a reputation for chaos and unreliability.

The potential economic advantages of the reporting of corruption are perhaps less obvious than the potential functionality of the phenomenon itself. However, if the reporting of corruption is perceived by potential investors as signifying that a particular government is serious about bringing corruption under control, this can encourage them to take investment risks they might otherwise avoid. Another advantage is that reporting can act as a deterrent to existing or would-be corrupt officials, as they read or see what might happen to them. If it is acknowledged that their actions (or non-actions) can have a negative impact on an economy, then another potential benefit of reporting corruption becomes clear.

Social and political functions

According to McMullan (1961: 196), corruption can make an otherwise alienating and oppressive bureaucracy appear less impenetrable and dehumanised. The argument, basically, is that if citizens can find human weaknesses in the bureaucracy, this helps the process of acceptance of the system. In addition to the fact that the officials themselves are perceived as more approachable and human – hence more acceptable – if they are corruptible, citizens can obtain goods they seek (including permits of various kinds) and which they might otherwise find very difficult to secure through the normal channels. Even if the goods would eventually have arrived via the formal routes, corruption can substantially expedite their procurement.

A limited amount of tolerance by the state of corruption among its officers can also help to retain those officers' loyalty. This is especially true during hard economic times, as typified by early post-communism. Interviews with senior Hungarian officials carried out by the author in April 1997 revealed that there was some sympathy for traffic police who accepted small bribes, on the grounds that the senior officials knew that, in the prevailing economic conditions, many lower-ranking police officers and traffic officials would have found it difficult to make ends meet if the state were to clamp down too heavily on small-scale corruption. This point is endorsed when the conditions of officials in the Communist and post-Communist eras are compared. In the former, most officials enjoyed access to various kinds of perquisites and privileges, including access to goods in limited supply, better education for their children, better healthcare facilities and so on. Although most citizens were partly aware of these privileges, the Communist authorities attempted to keep them as well hidden from the public's view as possible.

While these perquisites have not disappeared altogether in the post-Communist states, the putative commitment of most post-Communist governments to greater transparency means that officials typically receive far fewer status-related privileges than they did. Given this, the state can hope to alienate its staff less by not looking too closely at modest levels of corruption. All this demonstrates a point that will be further elaborated in the conclusion: that the potential advantageousness of state toleration of corruption depends very much on the scale of that corruption.

Developing this point, during the Communist era some tolerance of corruption could also be seen as potentially helping the state to control political unrest. If disgruntled officials could secure economic and other benefits to offset their limited rights of freedom of speech and criticism, this would take some of the steam out of their dissatisfaction and render them less inclined to act in a politically disloyal way to their employer. This could be functional to the state in two ways. First, it reduced the likelihood of political unrest among the officials themselves. Secondly it increased the probability that the officials would remain loyal to the state when called upon to suppress political unrest among the citizenry. If all this sounds fanciful, it should be noted that Milan Šimečka (1984: 133-135) has argued that the Czechoslovak leadership actually *encouraged* (as distinct from merely tolerating) corruption in the post-1968 'normalisation' period in the belief this would reduce the chances of further political unrest.

In the more open political climate of post-communism, this factor, however, does not apply to the same extent or in the same way. For three reasons this potential advantage to the state should not yet be dismissed altogether. The first is that the levels of political freedom have varied between CEE countries in the 1990s. In countries such as Belarus, or Slovakia under Mečiar (until September 1998), there has been heavy censorship and hence real limits on political freedom.

Secondly, the fact that there actually have been high levels of violent political unrest in countries such as Albania and Romania - let alone former Yugoslavia and parts of the former USSR - is clear proof that there are still possible advantages to states in attempting to secure the loyalty of their officers by 'turning a blind eye' to a certain amount of corruption. In times of mass unrest, the state needs to do all it can to ensure its officers will remain loyal to the state, rather than side with the protesters. It should not be forgotten that the collapse of Communist power in countries such as

Romania and Czechoslovakia occurred in part because the political leadership was no longer able to rely on its own coercive agencies. Memories of this are still fresh in parts of CEE.

Thirdly, and closely connected to the last point, the severe economic difficulties throughout the region during the 1990s have meant that it has almost certainly been in the state's interest not to interfere excessively in the corrupt interactions between citizens and officials. This is because such activity has probably played a positive role in reducing potentially destabilising political unrest. A certain amount of tolerance may also help to reduce the appeal of extremist political parties, although it is difficult to prove this empirically. It is only in cases of real economic crisis, as experienced by some of the countries mentioned at the beginning of the previous paragraph, that even the state's 'turning a blind eye' to illicit practices between its officers and citizens proves inadequate to maintain relative political peace.

In the aftermath of the collapse of Communist power, the Communist parties in some CEE countries were banned and expropriated. But in many cases, the Communists renamed and re-shaped themselves and were able to survive. In these cases, they typically had major advantages over other political parties. Most obviously, they had secure sources of income via their inherited wealth (in the form of buildings, etc), a developed infrastructure, and considerable political experience. Meanwhile, new laws on the funding of political parties had either not yet materialised, or else were ambiguous and insufficiently oriented towards affirmative action for *non*-Communist parties.

In such circumstances, some of these parties - be they new or revitalised ones - engaged in corruption in order to fund their activities. Given the unusual situation, it can be argued that corruption can play a useful role in the democratisation process, by helping to redress severe imbalances of various kinds between the Communists (or their successors) and other, more democratically oriented, political parties.

As part of their anti-corruption campaigns, states often encourage the public to 'whistleblow' on corrupt officials. This can have various benefits. One is that it can enhance the support for - indeed the legitimacy of - both a regime and a system, and reduce the perceived gap between 'us' (citizens) and 'them' (state authorities). But it can also play a role in developing self-initiated citizen action of a quasi-political sort. It can, in short, contribute to the development of civil society. This is more the case in countries in transition from authoritarian or totalitarian systems than in mature democracies. Thus the encouragement of whistleblowing can play its part in the overall democratisation of the post-Communist states of CEE.

Inasmuch as corruption triggers government responses, it can also play a beneficial role in institution-building in transitional states (this point has been emphasised in the Chinese context in Hao (1998). Not only are agencies either established or strengthened to fight corruption, but the existence of the problem can encourage the adoption of laws designed both to define and to combat it, including conflict of interest laws. This is yet another way in which the existence of corruption can indirectly assist the democratisation project.

One of the many reasons Communist power collapsed was that it was incapable of reforming itself sufficiently to deal with a deteriorating situation, particularly in the economic sphere. Among the numerous explanations for the inability of Communist leaderships radically to reform their systems was the fact that most attempts at decentralising and deconcentrating economic management were, to a greater or lesser extent, supposed to be implemented by the very officials such reform measures were designed to replace. It is therefore hardly surprising that these officials were often unenthusiastic about reform. By reporting corruption and mounting campaigns against it, Communist leaderships should in theory have been able to weaken the stranglehold their senior bureaucrats had on reform. Unfortunately, in practice they did not manage to do this to anything like the requisite levels.

But post-Communist leaderships often face a similar problem to that of their Communist predecessors. A prime example of the gap between a government's radical intentions on the one hand and the actuality of very limited implementation on the other, is Russia in the early-1990s. In this particular case, part of the problem was of Yeltsin's own making. As part of the strategy to build up his power base, the Russian President dramatically increased the size of his bureaucracy (see Yasmann 1993: 18). Not only can this increase the opportunities for patronage (a form of corruption) but it is also a symbolically contradictory approach, if a major objective of a government's reform policies is supposed to be a *reduction* of state involvement in the economy and society.

The reporting of corruption can, however, have some less ambiguously positive effects. One is that it can help to educate both officials and ordinary citizens about new laws and intended behavioural norms. This is particularly relevant in transitional societies, where there is often widespread confusion concerning what is and is not expected and acceptable in the rapidly changing circumstances.

The reporting in the mass media of various aspects of corruption can be beneficial to the aspirations of individual politicians and their political parties. Thus, both the print and the electronic media may be used for making allegations about opposition politicians or other political actors whom one seeks to undermine. An assumption of those making the allegations will often be that they will enhance their own standing by publicly condemning corruption. In addition to making allegations about individual political actors, politicians often make the general fight against corruption a major part of their election campaigns. Examples of politicians who have done this include Yeltsin and Constantinescu during their most recent presidential campaigns. The fact that both men made so much of the need to bring corruption (and crime more generally) under control testifies to their perception that official venality was a major concern for the electorate.

The reporting of the fight against corruption can help to increase the loyalty to the state of uncorrupted officials. If they continue to see their corrupt colleagues engage in their improprieties with impunity, there is an incentive for them to engage in corruption themselves. They may wonder if they are naïve and foolish to continue to work within the rules. It is some indication of how relatively easy it must be to get away with corruption that only four officials were found guilty of corruption and sentenced in Poland in the six years between the end of 1990 and the end of 1996. Conversely, seeing or reading reports of their co-workers being investigated and punished can encourage them to abandon any thoughts of leaving the 'straight and narrow' path.

Ironically perhaps, one of the problems of power in some CEE states prior to the 1990s was that, in their endeavours to move away from the arbitrariness and even terror of their predecessors, Communist leaderships introduced policies designed to allay bureaucrats' fears for their jobs and even lives - the result was to block channels of the upward mobility. The best-known example of this was the so-called 'stability of cadres' policy under Leonid Brezhnev (in power 1964–1982; Rigby 1970). In any system, blocked promotion paths can lead to frustration among ambitious junior staff members. Some of them will use this frustration as a self-justification for engaging in corruption. The reporting of corruption, and the anti-corruption campaigns that often accompany this, can play a useful role in overcoming frustration among junior state officials. This is because effective campaigns not only highlight corruption and its unacceptability but also make examples of officials as a way of demonstrating the serious commitment of the leadership to overcoming the phenomenon. If senior bureaucrats are removed as part of these campaigns, their posts fall vacant, typically creating promotion opportunities.

Another aspect of corruption that can enhance career opportunities is that leaderships often publicise the creation of new bodies, or else the upgrading of existing ones, as part of their endeavour to demonstrate to the public the seriousness of their intentions to reduce corruption. Unfortunately, the establishment of new bodies and the expansion of others to fight corruption increases the possibilities of patronage, including nepotism and cronyism. While this might be seen as advantageous senior political figures (as well as to the people they appoint or promote), it is also ironic that the fight against corruption can create new opportunities for corruption. Overall, the ramifications of the struggle against corruption can be part of what is best described as the anti-corruption industry. In many post-Communist countries, this is one of the fastest-growing 'sectors'.

While the reporting of corruption can help the careers of individual politicians, it can also help a government more generally by diverting attention away from economic problems. This applies in the post-Communist period just as much as it did during the Communist era. Now as then, a government can use individual officials as scapegoats for economic problems. Many citizens find it much easier to attribute economic problems to the corrupt activities of identifiable officials than to attempt to interpret such difficulties in terms of more abstract concepts such as fiscal problems, economic restructuring, or even the impact of globalisation.

A final aspect of the reporting of corruption that can be highly functional is that it reflects the growth of investigative journalism. In terms of making unsubstantiated allegations, such journalism in CEE has sometimes been irresponsible. Nevertheless, the blooming of investigative journalism is an important component of the development of civil society in the region, and hence of substantive democratisation.

Dysfunctions of corruption and its reporting

Economic dysfunctions

One of the main reasons that Russia has in recent years found it so difficult to reverse the decline of its economy is that the state has had insufficient funds to implement many of the changes that need to be introduced. Part of the explanation for this shortage of funds is the very limited success the *federal* state authorities have had in raising revenue from taxes (to some extent because of collusion between enterprises and their *local* state authorities, some of which is aptly described as corruption). So bad is the problem that one commentator (Treisman 1998: 55) has argued that, 'Russia's inability to collect taxes is rapidly becoming the greatest threat to its economic and political stability'. There is no question that a major obstacle to the more effective collection of taxes is corrupt officials, who often collaborate with organised crime.

A related problem is that often the more efficient and law-abiding firms pay taxes, while less efficient and honest companies avoid or minimise their tax payments by paying off corrupt officials. While these less honest firms still have to make payments, the bribes to officials will typically be much cheaper than paying the taxes. There are two major disadvantages to this arrangement. First, the less efficient firms are being subsidised by the more efficient. This is not conducive to a long-term improvement in a country's economic performance. At its most extreme, the inefficient firms will rent-seek from the state, expecting to be bailed out when they are in debt or even about to go bankrupt. Since the efficient and honest firms are a major source of the 'rent' being sought by the inefficient firms from the state, it becomes clear why tolerance harms economic growth.

Secondly, taxing the honest firms and directly or indirectly subsidising firms that will offer bribes in order to avoid tax payments can result in 'killing the goose that lays the golden egg'. In other words, the honest and more efficient companies may either go bankrupt because of excessive taxation, or else will simply withdraw from the market because they are disillusioned with the inequities of the corrupt system. The alternative is to join the ranks of the 'bad guys' (that is, engage in the bribery of officials themselves). A growing trend in this direction compounds the problem of an impoverished state.

There are other negative aspects to rent-seeking practices in the post-Communist world. As various analysts (for example, Glinkina 1998: *esp* 18-22; Kogan 1998: 48) have argued a major problem in CEE is that many public servants are so preoccupied with various forms of rent-seeking (including 'grass-eating' demands for bribes), that their regular duties are neglected. To the extent that the state is not fulfilling the expected tasks, its image and legitimacy suffer.

There can be little question that perceptions of excessive levels of corruption in a particular country will deter many potential investors. A recent study by the World Bank provides persuasive evidence that countries with perceived high levels of corruption are losing out on potential foreign investment, which in turn is hindering their economic growth and development. According to the unidentified author(s) of the report, a recent survey conducted on behalf of the Bank "… confirms earlier studies that corruption (as perceived by businesspeople) is negatively correlated with both investment and growth" (World Bank 1997: 2).

Even where foreign companies have opted to take a risk in a newly emerging market - and all CEE countries have such markets - they can become so irritated by the ongoing demands for bribes that they will subsequently withdraw. This was, for example, a major reason for the disengagement of the Anglo-Dutch firm Unilever from Bulgaria in 1998 (*The Economist* 1999a: 23).

Earlier, it was argued that corruption may help to generate private wealth *within* a country, which can then play a positive role in the form of domestically generated investment. But in the case of several CEE countries - Russia being the best example - just as likely is the situation where capital is exported, often either illegally or only semi-legally, from a country and deposited in banks in countries in which there are opaque banking laws (see Tikhomirov 1997).

It appears that one of the most significant differences between the role of both organised crime and corruption in the early history of the USA and contemporary Russia is that the so-called 'robber barons' (including many political figures) in the former typically invested their funds in America, whereas the latter's frequently transfer their funds out of Russia. In sum, the net economic effect of the activities of the 'robber barons' was probably positive for American development, whereas the spoils of Russian corruption and organised crime do not, in aggregate, appear to be assisting Russian economic development.[4] Indeed, if potential foreign investors see that 'rational' actors *within* a given country believe it is not in their longer-term interest to invest in their own country, this will act as a deterrent to foreign investment.

4 For a comparison of early American economic development with what is happening at present in Russia, see Lucky (1997).

In addition to private investment, developing and transitional countries can and do seek loans and aid from wealthier countries and international agencies. During the 1990s, there has been growing awareness and irritation among Western countries and international agencies that substantial portions of loans and aid have been siphoned off by corrupt officials instead of reaching their intended destinations. The World Bank - whose head, James Wolfensohn, has made the fight against corruption one of his principal objectives - introduced regulations in 1996 that require the Bank to withdraw from projects in, and discontinue dealings with, any country proven to be directing funds provided by the Bank into channels other than those for which they were intended. Some post-Communist states have also been refused loans, usually on a temporary basis, by the International Monetary Fund because they have been doing too little to combat corruption. Ukraine was 'punished' in this way in 1997 (*Business Central Europe*, 1997: 53).

Many CEE politicians and citizens have appreciated that, in the longer term, it is preferable actually to join several of the international organisations from which they have been seeking aid and low-interest loans, rather than keep hoping they will continue to be able to apply for such preferential treatment. Of the various bodies they have sought to join, the European Union (EU) is unquestionably perceived as the most important to their long-term strategies for economic growth and development.

After various delays, in early 1998 the EU began formal negotiations with five of the ten CEE countries that had applied for full membership by mid-1996. Of the political problems each applicant country needed to address, corruption was the factor to appear in all ten report-cards (European Commission 1997a: 20; European Commission 1997b: 20). In the case of the five countries whose applications are 'on hold' - the so-called 'laggards' (Bulgaria, Latvia, Lithuania, Romania, Slovakia) - the level of corruption is considered to be a serious issue. While it is perceived to be less of a problem in the five 'winner' countries (Czechia, Estonia, Hungary, Poland, Slovenia), they will also have to make concerted efforts to bring corruption under control if they are to be admitted to the EU. If the long-term economic development prospects of these countries appears to be highly dependent on their capacity to reduce corruption to acceptable levels, then corruption's potential economic disadvantages come sharply into focus.

Many analysts of economic transition in the CEE countries contrast the 'shock therapy' (or 'big bang') approach with the 'gradualist' approach. Such labels are potentially misleading, and should be used with caution. For instance, Hungary is often cited as a quintessential gradualist, yet proceeded with many aspects of privatisation and opened its economy to foreign investment more quickly than Poland, the archetypical 'shock therapist'. Nevertheless, there is some mileage in the two concepts, and their use helps to focus attention on yet another dimension of the effects of corruption.

For much of the 1990s, Poland was seen as the star economic performer among the post-Communist states of CEE. While there has unquestionably been corruption in post-Communist Poland (see Holmes 1997b), the perception is that it suffers less from this problem than do other post-Communist countries that have not adopted such radical economic policies. Equally, the radically neo-liberal Estonia, in which there is a flat-rate income tax system, emerges as the least corrupt of the fifteen post-Communist states evaluated in the 1998 Transparency International 'Corruption Perceptions Index'.[5] In 1996, Estonia was the first post-Communist state to be removed from the US Agency for International Development's list of aid recipients.

At the other end of the spectrum, Latvia is perceived by international businesspeople as second only to Russia as the most corrupt of the fifteen post-Communist states covered in the 1998 corruption perceptions index. It has not pursued such radical economic policies as its neighbour to the north. All this suggests that transitional CEE states that do not make sufficiently dramatic breaks with past economic policy may discover that the corruption that typified the late Communist era (see Holmes 1993) will continue into the transition phase and that this will hinder their economic development.

Reference was made above to Czechia's putative commitment to radical reform under Klaus. In fact, some of the analysts who took note of the comparative unemployment statistics of the CEE states in the early- and mid-1990s realised that Klaus' rhetoric was not matched by his practice. The then-Prime Minister was not permitting underperforming Czech firms to go bankrupt. In this scenario, rent-seeking and the concomitant likelihood that corruption rates would increase (or at least not decline) were a salient feature. While corruption has not, apparently, been as great a problem as might have been expected – with Czechia being one of the 'cleaner' post-Communist states in the Transparency International index – there is no question that Czech economic growth has slowed down dramatically in recent years. This is in contrast to the situation in Poland and Hungary.

Since many analysts treat these three countries as being very similar to each other, it is worth speculating on why Czechia was different. All three countries have experienced corruption in the 1990s, this did not appear to reach the very top echelons in Poland or Hungary. If potential investors and others believe that the leadership is still basically trustworthy, they are less likely to be apprehensive about investing. Conversely, Klaus' own demise in November 1997 related to corruption: it is conceivable that his failure to introduce some of the radical reforms implemented by the Poles was in part because of the excessively 'cosy' relationship he had with some of the major economic actors.

Too much reporting of corruption can lead to confusion among the state's officers, which in turn can result in their refusing to use much initiative in entering into negotiations with businesspeople for fear that this might be construed as corruption. Hence, the reporting of corruption can act

5 These indices are readily accessible on the Web at www.transparency.de.

as a disincentive to initiative and risk-taking, which is ultimately dysfunctional to economic reform and development.

One of the salient features of corruption is that it is an opaque - often largely invisible - activity. Its very cloudiness is a major reason that it usually hinders information flows within an economy. The negative implications of imperfect, or even deliberately distorted, information within an economy are self-evident.

Social and political dysfunctions

While this subsection elaborates on a large number of possible social and political disadvantages of corruption, many of these are closely connected ramifications of an overarching disadvantage, legitimation problems. The analysis will return to this larger theme following the exploration of the numerous disadvantages of corruption.

Surveys and other sources have demonstrated clearly that many citizens in CEE countries resent the growing inequality that has become a feature of post-Communist countries. Despite the fact that most citizens apparently do not seek a return to a Communist-style power system, some of the more egalitarian values of the Communist era have been deeply internalised. Closer analysis of several surveys suggests that it is not so much inequality as inequity that upsets many ordinary citizens. If those benefiting from the new economic arrangements do so less because of their honest skills and hard work, and more because of their corrupt behaviour, it is understandable why resentment levels run high. This in turn can render the legitimation of the new system more difficult.

Excessive corruption can undermine faith in and commitment to the whole democratisation and marketisation project. Survey data often hint at this problem but rarely address it directly.[6] These data show that many citizens in post-Communist states see corruption as one of the most serious problems in their country, but few data explicitly address the corruption-democratisation nexus. Nevertheless, a nuanced reading of the data does suggest that the serious reservations of many citizens have about the post-Communist order is partly - perhaps largely - explained by the association in their minds between corruption and reform.[7]

External observers sometimes note that part of the explanation for the close relationship between corruption and reform is that many of those implementing the reforms are former Communists who seek improper advantage from the new arrangements. During the 1990s, the term '*nomenklatura* privatisation' has featured prominently in analyses of problems of post-communism that relate to the legacy of the Communist era. It refers to the practice whereby former Communist officials have often benefited from

6 cf. Post-Communist Kazakhstan and Uzbekistan, see Lubin 1995.

7 There is no shortage of observers who refer to this association. Fairly typical is Fabian Schmidt (1998: 50), who maintains that corruption "presents the single largest challenge for Albania's democratic reform".

the privatisation process by having (unfair) preferential access to it. On one level, the relatively peaceful nature of the anti-Communist revolutions in CEE can be partly explained by this phenomenon. Many officials in the old system had realised by the 1980s that the Communist economic system could not compete with capitalism; and that in the future, power in the economic sphere was likely to be more important than power in the overtly political sphere. Therefore, rather than resist the pressure to replace Communist power, they yielded to it (and in some cases even led the transformative process), since they were more interested in securing a good position in the new system than defending the old.

While such attitudes might have contributed to more peaceful transitions in many CEE countries, they are typically dysfunctional in the post-Communist era. Sometimes, the former Communist officials have themselves become the part-owners of newly privatised firms, often through questionable and non-transparent processes. In other cases, they have received bribes and kickbacks from winners in tendering processes. Unfortunately, public perceptions of such corruption are widespread in CEE, which undermines the privatisation process. The effect is worse if the former Communist officials are perceived to play a continuing (as distinct from one-off) role in the privatising and privatised economies.

One reason for this is precisely the widespread perception of a close relationship between corruption and privatisation. Another is that at least *some* former Communist officials retain *some* of their former views and work methods which limit the scope of economic reforms. For instance, many will have been used to the relative security – the 'comfort-zone' – of the command economy and seek rents from the state rather than face the discomfort of real economic competition.[8] If this phenomenon is widespread, countries may take decades to move to genuinely marketised economies with an entrepreneurial, risk-taking culture.

Obtaining data on the scale and incidence of corruption in CEE states is fraught with difficulties.[9] While it is extremely probable that the amount of corruption in most of these countries really has increased in the 1990s, ultimately this cannot be proven.[10] Where statistics on corruption are either non-existent or very inadequate, public concern about the phenomenon must be based on something other than data.

Focus group research in four post-Communist states (Bulgaria, Czechia, Slovakia and Ukraine) organised by a team based at Glasgow University reveals that, while most citizens are concerned about corruption,

8 On post-Communist governments being lenient towards domestic corruption as a form of protectionism against foreign competition, see Krastev (1998: esp 57).

9 It should be noted that even general crime statistics (and not merely in CEE) are often questionable – see *The Guardian Weekly* (1998: 5).

10 For a detailed analysis of the data for Russia 1986–1995, see Luneev 1996.

far fewer have experienced it first-hand (Miller et al, 1998: 285-286)[11]. Their 'knowledge' of the corruption problem is based primarily on two sources – hearsay (gossip) and the mass media. It is, of course, extraordinarily difficult to research the former in any satisfactory manner, but coverage of corruption in the latter is relatively easy to track, albeit expensive and time-consuming. The main reason it is time-consuming is that in most post-Communist countries there have been so many reports. The frequency with which allegations about corruption are made is a major explicator of the public's perception of widespread corruption. Because this reporting can be highly dysfunctional, the reasons need to be unpacked.

First, reports are sometimes explicitly linked to government campaigns against corruption. The very limited evidence currently available suggests that the effectiveness of campaigns may be short-lived. This statement appears to be borne out by recent Bulgarian survey data. Three surveys on attitudes towards corruption were conducted between March 1997 and January 1998 by Vitosha Research, the survey research unit of the Center for the Study of Democracy based in Sofia. The number of people surveyed varied between 1032 and 1519.

The first survey preceded the coming to power in April 1997 of a new government that had made the fight against corruption one of its top priorities during the election campaign. Once in power, this new government sought to raise public awareness and disapproval of it even higher than it already was. That it succeeded in this objective is strongly suggested by the results of the second of the three surveys, conducted in September 1997. This indicated much higher levels of condemnation of corruption than the March poll had done. However, the levels of condemnation in the final survey (conducted December 1997 – January 1998) were remarkably similar to those in the March 1997 survey (all results from Vitosha Research 1998).[12] Interviews conducted by this author in Sofia during February 1998 indicated that the government's campaign had lost little impetus by then, so that the survey results suggest that the public was already becoming immune or indifferent to it.

If these findings – the typicality of which can only be surmised – are combined with inductive reasoning, it appears that anti-corruption campaigns can be functional in the short term, but ineffectual or even dysfunctional in the longer term. This is because people can become indifferent to, or even cynical about, prolonged campaigns. The cynicism arises because prolonged campaigns suggest that the government's attempted clampdown

11 For somewhat similar findings in the case of Poland see Centrum Badania Społecznej Opinii, 1994: 2. I am very grateful to Professor Lena Kolarska-Bobińska, former Director of CBOS, for having provided me with these results and to Oliver Freeman of St Antony's College, Oxford for assistance in translating them into English.

12 I wish to thank the Director of Vitosha Research, Aleksandr Stoyanov, for having kindly provided me with this report during a visit I made to Bulgaria in February 1998.

is being ineffective, and/or that the problem is so widespread that the authorities cannot bring it under control, and/or that the authorities are 'all rhetoric and no action'.

The cynicism will be greater still if it appears that the government is only paying lip-service to the corruption problem (perhaps because those conducting the putative campaign are themselves involved in questionable activities, and hence do not want investigations to probe too deeply) than where the government simply seems inefficient. In both cases public faith in 'the system' will be undermined.

Secondly, it must be borne in mind that in countries such as Russia, many of the allegations about high-ranking corruption have been made in newspapers and other media outlets that belong to, or are closely connected with, particular political parties and groupings. All too often, the allegations are ultimately not proven. This raises the public's suspicion that they might have been no more than fabrications designed for partisan point-scoring.

Parties making such allegations about their opponents *might* in the short-term undermine those opponents and enhance their own standing in the eyes of the electorate. In many cases, however, the opponents make counter-allegations. A vicious circle is established in which partisan newspapers make claims and counter-claims about corruption. Although this might be beneficial to individual parties the first or second time it occurs, it starts to become dysfunctional if it continues. While party A might only intend to undermine party B, the net effect of an iterated series of allegations and counter-allegations is to weaken public confidence in the political system generally. Certainly, surveys have revealed disturbingly low levels of trust of public figures and political institutions among the citizens of most post-Communist states (Rose et al 1998: 153-157).

Thirdly, too much, and too prolonged, reporting can make even the state's honest functionaries feel uncomfortable and insecure. This is particularly so when many of the allegations are subsequently not proven, which suggests a measure of arbitrariness. Given the experiences of arbitrariness during the Communist era, it is not surprising that this should be a potential dysfunction of the reporting of corruption. An insecure and alienated staff is not conducive to the consolidation and smooth operation of a post-Communist state.

One of the potentially most dangerous aspects of the reporting of corruption arises where the central authorities appear to be targeting a particular ethnic minority. This certainly appeared to be occurring at times during the Communist era. While there needs to be far more research into this dimension of corruption reporting under post-Communism, the high levels of ethnic sensitivity in so many parts of CEE mean that an apparent targeting of a particular group could have violent repercussions.

The observant reader will appreciate that many of the dysfunctions analysed in the last few paragraphs ultimately relate to legitimacy. While a full analysis of this issue lies beyond the scope of this Chapter, some general observations can be made.

Unlike the situation during the Communist era, there is no fundamental contradiction between the various versions of liberal 'ideology' (if this is not too grand a term!) being espoused by most post-Communist governments and the rule-of-law. This factor bodes well in the longer term for a consolidation of democracy based on abstract legal norms, as distinct from more personalised, and hence fragile, forms of power. On the other hand, at a time when the majority of post-Communist states are still fragile, system legitimation remains a major concern. Since, according to the European Bank of Reconstruction and Development, only three out of 27 had by 1999 surpassed their 1989 GDP figures (*The Economist* 1999b: 112), it becomes obvious that legitimacy based predominantly on economic performance (eudaemonism) remains a largely unrealistic goal at present. At the same time, the numerous problems surrounding the attempts to create a law-based state – which constitute both an explanation and a function of corruption – mean that the Weberian notion of a legal-rational 'modern' state is still a distant objective for many countries.

Appealing to official nationalism may therefore become a domestic mode of legitimation. The mass Serbian unrest directed against Slobodan Milosevic in mid-1999 following his defeat in Kosovo suggests that official nationalism is never a solid, long-term basis for legitimation. Yet the Yugoslav case also exemplifies just how dangerous official nationalism can be and how it can, and often does, substitute for economic performance and legal-rationality in troubled, transitional systems. To the extent that widespread and deep-rooted corruption is symptomatic of both economic problems and the weak state of law, it testifies to the legitimation problems of post-Communist transitional states.

Conclusions

While a purely ethical perspective leads to the conclusion that corruption is invariably bad (dysfunctional), cost-benefit approaches produce a more complex picture. This is particularly so if not only corruption, but also its reporting is being evaluated. A few broad conclusions can be made.

The first is that size does matter! By this is meant that citizens in most kinds of society will tolerate – even expect – a certain amount of corruption. Humans are imperfect, and most of us accept that some officials will be unable to resist temptation. But when the scale of corruption exceeds certain bounds and reaches the higher echelons of a system, corruption becomes unambiguously dysfunctional. Quite where those bounds are will vary from country to country and depend on the precise circumstances. In terms of the latter, *ceteris paribus* one would expect higher levels of corruption in transitional societies where the new 'rules of the game' are still crystallising. Nevertheless large-scale corruption is a serious problem to any government when it comes to be seen as a structural problem of the system.

The apparently high levels of corruption in many post-Communist states can be partly attributed to the transitional nature of these societies.

Whether or not it is accepted that these countries have undergone revolutions - in my own view they have - it cannot be disputed that they have all experienced profound systemic shocks in the past decade or so. Even allowing for the significant differences between, for example, the relative liberalism (in Communist terms) of Yugoslavia or Hungary on the one hand and the near paranoia and neo-Stalinism of the Albanian government (at least until Hoxha's death in 1985) on the other, all these countries were organised according to democratic centralist principles, had essentially planned and socialised economies and worked to an ideology that claimed to have answers not only to questions of economic, social and political organisation, but even to individual moral and spiritual issues such as religious belief.

There has been an enormous transformation in the 1990s, and even where politicians and others have claimed to stand for 'democracy', 'market economics' and 'the rule of law', there has rarely been consensus either on what these terms mean in the context of a particular country, or on how best to achieve them. One of the most important ramifications of such disagreement is that both governments and parliaments have often taken a very long time to agree on new laws. Moreover, the sheer scale of transformation - where governments have had to create not only new political and economic systems, but also new legal, educational, welfare, ideological and value systems, new international alignments and often even new boundaries for a given state - means that it is quite comprehensible why many of the problems, including those that relate to the growth of crime, can be interpreted partly in terms of *legislative lag*. While this problem has been more acute in some CEE states than in others, it has affected them all, without exception.

It is very difficult for a state - any state - to determine the optimal balance between condemning and condoning corruption. Although it might appear to be beneficial in the short-term for a transitional state to condone modest levels of corruption among its officials, it is all too easy for this to become entrenched, or even to get out of control - with all the delegitimising implications of this for the new and still crystallising state.

It is thus understandable why corruption has become such a problem, and why it has proven so difficult to bring it under control. Where the basic 'rules of the game' have been disputed, and economies have been in serious trouble, it is not surprising that corruption has, apparently, been so widespread. Equally, there are no inherent reasons why it should not become less of a problem as states become stronger and overcome their legislative lag, and as new legal frameworks and cultures emerge and consolidate.

Unfortunately, however, there is something of a vicious circle here. In many cases, precisely those political actors who should be devising new conflict of interest laws and other legislation that would help to reduce corruption are people who have themselves benefited economically from weak and ambiguous legislation. All too often, they still have an insufficiently developed sense of public responsibility to overcome their personal vested interests.

Despite this depressing note there are factors that leave room for some cautious optimism. First, as argued above, the *long-term* effects of corruption are overwhelmingly negative, and become increasingly obviously so. When it is appreciated that costs clearly outweigh benefits, corruption levels should decline.

Moreover, many of the reasons for high levels of corruption in CEE appear to be temporary. Most governments are slowly catching up with their legislative lags, for instance, while many countries appear, albeit falteringly, to be turning, or to have turned, the economic corner. As they do so, and appear to be making progress, not only should there be less perceived 'need' for corruption among those officials who at present engage in petty corruption primarily for reasons of basic survival, but external agencies such as the EU will be more willing to accept them as new members. This will help to bring these countries out of their vicious circles and into virtuous ones.

Finally, the significance of having genuinely contested elections should not be underestimated. In line with the argument here about the dynamism of post-communism - the situation in most CEE countries *is* clearly changing - real party *systems* are beginning to emerge and voters are becoming more sophisticated. In time, the sometimes infantile mud-slinging - much of it in the form of unsubstantiated allegations of corruption - that has typified politics in many CEE countries in the 1990s will be replaced by more constructive and consolidated politics, as electorates demand better performance from their politicians and a focus on the country's major problems rather than individual careerist aspirations. As the perception takes hold that there is somewhat less corruption than there was, the actuality of the situation might begin to follow suit.

References

Borchert, J, Leitner, S, and Stolz, K (eds), (2000), *Jahrbuch für Europa- und Nordamerika-Studien 3: Politische Korruption*, Leske und Budrich, Opladen, 117-44.

Business Central Europe: The Annual 1997/98, December 1997, 53.

Centrum Badania Opinii Społecznej, 1994, *Nieuczciwość i przekupstwo w instytucjach wymiaru sprawiedliwości*, CBOS, Warsaw.

The Economist, (1999a), 16 January, 23.

The Economist, (1999b), 24 April , 112.

European Commission, (1997a), 'Commission Opinion on Hungary's Application for Membership of the European Union', 6 *Bulletin of the European Union Supplement*, Luxembourg.

European Commission, (1997b), 'Commission Opinion on Slovenia's Application for Membership of the European Union', 15 *Bulletin of the European Union Supplement*, Luxembourg.

Frisby, Tanya, (1998), 'The Rise of Organised Crime in Russia - Its Roots and Social Significance', 50(1) *Europe-Asia Studies* 27-49.

Glinkina, Svetlana, (1998), 'The Ominous Landscape of Russian Corruption', 5(3) *Transitions* 16-23.

+*The Guardian Weekly*, (1998), 8 November, 5.

Gurov, Aleksandr, (1995), *Krasnaya Mafiya*, Yuridicheskaya Literatura, Moscow.

Hao, Yufan, (1998), 'Institution-Building: An Unintended Consequence of Corruption in China in the 1990s', paper presented at the 'International Conference on Communist and Post-Communist Societies', Melbourne, July.

Holmes, Leslie, (1993), *The End of Communist Power: Anti-Corruption Campaigns and Legitimation Crisis*, Polity Press, Cambridge.

Holmes, Leslie, (1997a), 'Corruption and the Crisis of the Post-Communist State', 27 (3-4) *Crime, Law and Social Change* 275-297.

Holmes, Leslie, (1997b), 'Corruption in Post-Communist Countries, with Particular Reference to Poland', in Leslie Holmes and Wojciech Roszkowski (eds), *Changing Rules – Polish Political and Economic Transformation in Comparative Perspective*, Institute of Political Studies, Polish Academy of Sciences, Warsaw.

Huntington, Samuel, (1968), *Political Order in Changing Societies*, Yale University Press, New Haven.

Kettle, Steve, (1995), 'Of Money and Morality', 1(3) *Transitions* 36-39.

Kogan, Natasha, (1998), 'Thinking About Corruption', 5(3) *Transitions* 46-49.

Komlenovic, Uros, (1997), 'State and Mafia in Yugoslavia', 6(4) *East European Constitutional Review* 70-73.

Krastev, Ivan, (1998), 'Dancing with Anticorruption', 7(3) *East European Constitutional Review* 56-58.

Leff, Nathaniel, (1964), 'Economic Development Through Bureaucratic Corruption', 8(3) *American Behavioral Scientist* 8-14.

Lubin, Nancy, (1995), *Central Asians Take Stock*, United States Institute of Peace, Washington.

Lucky, Christian, (1997), 'Public Theft in Early America and Contemporary Russia', 6(4) *East European Constitutional Review* 91-98.

Luneev, V, (1996), 'Korruptsiya, Uchtennaya i Fakticheskaya', 8 *Gosudarstvo i Pravo* 78-91.

McMullan, M, (1961), 'A Theory of Corruption', 9(2) *Sociological Review* 181-201.

Miller, William, Åse Grødeland and Tatyana Koshechkina, (1998), 'Are the people victims or accomplices? The use of presents and bribes to influence officials in Eastern Europe', 29(4) *Crime, Law and Social Change* 273-312.

Myrdal, Gunnar, (1968), *Asian Drama: An Enquiry into the Poverty of Nations*, Vol 2, Twentieth Century, New York.

Nikolov, Jovo, (1997), 'Organized Crime in Bulgaria', 6(4) *East European Constitutional Review* 80-84.

Nye, Joseph, (1967), 'Corruption and Political Development: A Cost-Benefit Analysis', 61(2) *American Political Science Review* 417-427.

Rigby, T Harry, (1970), 'The Soviet Leadership: Towards a Self-stabilising Oligarchy', 22(2) *Soviet Studies* 167-191.

Rose, Richard, William Mishler and Christian Haerpfer, (1998), *Democracy and its Alternatives – Understanding Post-Communist Societies*, Polity Press, Cambridge.

Schmidt, Fabian, (1998), 'Sleaze Spreads In Pauperized Albania', 5(3) *Transitions* 50-53.

Šimečka, Milan, (1984), *The Restoration of Order – The Normalisation of Czechoslovakia*, Verso, London.

Sterling, Claire, (1995), *Crime Without Frontiers – The Worldwide Expansion of Organised Crime and the Pax Mafiosa*, Warner, London.

Tikhomirov, Vladimir, 1997, 'Capital Flight from Post-Soviet Russia', 49(4) *Europe-Asia Studies* 591-615.

Treisman, Daniel, (1998), 'Russia's Taxing Problem', 112 *Foreign Policy* 55-65.

Vitosha Research, (1998), *Mnenieto na bulgarite za koruptsiyata: Mart 1997–Yanuari 1998*, Centre for the Study of Democracy, Sofia.

World Bank, (1997), 'Reducing Corruption', 8(3) *World Bank Policy and Research Bulletin*.

Yasmann, Victor, (1993), 'The Russian Civil Service – Corruption and Reform', 2(16) *RFE/RL Research Report* 18-21.

Chapter 5

Corruption and Good Governance: The New Frontier of Social Engineering

Howard Dick

Introduction

Until the Asian crisis of 1997–1998, conventional wisdom had been that economic development was sufficient both to improve material circumstances and to pave the way to a more open and democratic society. The material progress of the West, the collapse of Communism and the rise of Asia seemed amply to vindicate such confidence.

The Asian crisis sowed doubt because in several countries spectacular economic development could not be sustained by fragile institutions and political systems. The New Institutional Economics and the award of the Nobel prize to its prime exponent, Douglas North, provided the theoretical basis for rethinking development. Economic development was too narrowly based. In the new 'conventional wisdom', economic development should proceed simultaneously with institutional development. A marginal literature on corruption and 'rent-seeking' has been incorporated into a new mainstream literature referred to more broadly and discreetly as 'good governance'.

In Indonesia, as recently as May 1997 - only a year before the downfall of President Soeharto - the World Bank was still referring euphemistically to 'common local practices' (World Bank 1997). However, 'corruption, collusion and nepotism' (*korupsi, kolusi dan nepotisme* or KKN) became one of the most powerful slogans in the attack on President Soeharto and the New Order. Since his downfall in May 1998, corruption has never been out of the headlines of a newly-unfettered media. It has become a central issue in political debate; and even the World Bank now refers to it explicitly (*Jakarta Post*, 2000). Measures to promote good governance are embodied in Letters of Intent between the International Monetary Fund (IMF) and the Indonesian Government. 'Conditionality' has nevertheless proven to be an ineffective means of achieving workable reforms of law and governance (Hamilton-Hart 2001; Lindsey and Taylor 2000).

As a basis for policy, the newly fashionable discourse of good governance is still under-theorised and flawed. First, 'corruption' and 'good governance' are not scientific concepts but ideological slogans, one negative, the other positive. Secondly, they assume a convergence model of a known linear direction and time path to sustainable development. Thirdly, practitioners often continue to apply the old conventional wisdom that politics is disruptive to stability, being at best a luxury and at worst harmful to development (Jayasuriya, this volume). This chapter argues that the challenge of sustainable development should be reconceptualised as a problem of 'search strategy' in which politics are an essential part of the process and institutions are formed to embody learning-by-doing. Corruption and rent-seeking are not trivial problems but intrinsic to the political process. Gains can easily be redistributed through political reform but the overall incidence is unlikely to fall except by long-term political evolution. Institutional reform is not a politically disembodied 'quick fix'. The chapter begins with a brief discussion of definitional issues and suggests that 'good governance' should be deconstructed in terms of power relationships and discourse. It explores the problem of the time path of development and argues for a reconceptualisation of it in the terms just mentioned. It then applies such thinking to 20th Century Indonesia with brief comparative references. The conclusion suggests how ideology and power may be invoked to deconstruct the new conventional wisdom.

Corruption, rents, good governance and discourse

'Corruption' is defined in various ways but 'abuse of public power for private benefit' (Tanzi 1998) or 'violation of formal rules' (Khan 1998) are fairly standard definitions that have scarcely evolved since Nye (1967) and Scott (1972). These simple definitions beg a set of questions. There is a predicate. What power is being abused and who wields that power? A subject is implied. 'Corruption' is reflexive. Power is abused by the person(s) who holds that power. If the abuse is solely for personal gain, the circle is completed. Second parties may enter the picture as beneficiaries of the action or, rather, transaction. The third party – the unseen and unstated eye – is the critic, who determines the nature and extent of the abuse, or indeed whether there is abuse at all.

Corruption is therefore a normative concept. Defining corruption as a violation of formal or legal norms assumes that the *ideal* society is one governed by rule of law. Perhaps few would challenge this ideal, but by a slide in logic it then comes to be accepted that any departure from law in an *actual* society may also be regarded as corrupt, irrespective of the fairness and administration of those laws and the nature of the political system, economy and society. Again, many would see this as reasonable. For example, "in the age of globalism the world is reduced to only one marketplace, which means there is just one set of rules" (Backman 1999: 5). This rigid ideological stance ignores, however, the important questions of which agencies set these rules and what leeway, if any, is allowed in their enforcement.

A similar normative problem arises with the concepts of rent and rent-seeking. 'Rent' is a classical term reintroduced to the literature by Krueger (1974) to refer to excess returns or incomes above the competitive norm (Khan and Jomo 2000: 5-6). However, a purely competitive market is an *ideal* state. It is not so easy to quantify rents under conditions of imperfect competition that apply to actual economies. The target is plain enough: the same corrupt beneficiaries whom Adam Smith targeted in his famous polemic against mercantilism, monopolies and economic privilege (Smith, 1950). Rent-seeking is found everywhere but the term has been applied pejoratively and with particular force to developing countries.

Since subjectivity is unavoidable, the best approach is to make it explicit. Corruption and rent-seeking is in the eye of the beholder. Like crime, corruption and rent-seeking are agreed to be a Bad Thing, but their scope and content are less well defined. They are not precise terms of social science but codewords denoting practices engaged in by someone else and regarded as illegal or unethical by the commentator, whose set of values are projected onto the behaviour of others. Perceptions correlate with the shared values, experiences and practical purposes of the group or society (Heidenheimer et al 1991). When foreign observers or agencies pass judgement upon other countries, they project their own values onto behaviour in different political, legal and social systems. Such an approach is implicit in the much cited corruption rankings compiled by Transparency International (TI) and Political and Economic Risk Consultancy PERC, which involve questionnaire surveys of *expatriates*. 'Corruption' implies that 'you' are different from 'us'; the corollary being that 'you' should become more like 'us'; and not that 'we' should become more like 'you'. Thus every reference to 'corruption' is part of a discourse with cultural and ideological dimensions.

The term 'good governance' is therefore not much help. Governance itself is just a broad concept like motherhood. Good Governance, in fact, means more or less the same as Good Motherhood. As a norm it enjoys universal acceptance. No-one is in favour of Bad Governance or Bad Motherhood. The content, however, is unspecified. It is a powerful ideological battering ram for whichever groups set the intellectual and policy agenda. The most interesting aspect of the good governance literature so far is that the content is so little contested.

Even simple deconstruction is therefore sufficient to demonstrate that the terms 'corruption', 'rent-seeking' and 'good governance' are the new cutting edge of a very long-running ideological campaign. Two hundred years ago, the polity against which Adam Smith fired his salvoes was one of the first nation-states; the newly industrialising economies of Asia with their neo-mercantilist policies are among the newest. The campaign by a new discipline of economists for a set of secular, universalist and internationalist principles of free trade was part of the ideological shaping of the modern world. Its counterpart was the political campaign that gained unstoppable momentum from the American and French revolutions for democracy, rule of law and political (now human) rights: Liberty! Equality! Fraternity! Born of the same source, these two revolutionary forces have both complemented and opposed each other. They have complemented each other in their attack on old privilege, but conflicted over the vehicle of nationalism, which has become the basis for new privilege.

The outcome has been indeterminate because of a third and reactionary force, namely the rational bureaucratic state, in both civil and military guise. If nationalism has been the ideological propulsion, the rational bureaucratic state has been the organisational basis for modern society, forming the well-known amalgam of nation-state. Such concentrations of bureaucratic and military power have been able to resist international and domestic pressures for economic liberalisation and/or political reform – in the case of some South American countries for almost two hundred years. After the shock of the 1930s depression and in the environment of the Cold War, authoritarian regimes in these and other newly independent nation-states, including Indonesia, were encouraged to apply state-directed policies to promote industrialisation and development through planning and protection. Now that the global ideological agenda has shifted towards free trade and democratisation, it has become necessary to hack away at these bastions of new privilege or, at the very least, give them some respectability.

The dominant international discourse is the neo-liberal reform agenda, promoted by the IMF and World Bank, supported by international business and informed by the new institutional economics. Neo-liberal orthodoxy maintains that good government is small government; that an efficient legal system is needed to provide a stable, low-risk investment climate for private capital; that government/private sector relations should be transparent according to law; and that corruption and rent-seeking should be minimised. Until the recent economic crisis, many Asian governments had argued for a counter-orthodoxy of the *dirigiste* or developmental state (Wade 1990; Johnson 1982): strong government was good government, even at the cost of economic and political freedoms. Their case was underpinned by the achievement of sustained high rates of economic growth. State intervention apparently could improve on market outcomes. The currency crisis has all but destroyed the credibility of this counter-orthodoxy. The perceived role of 'corruption' as a source of vulnerability is seen as confirming the perils of over-government and the virtues of what used to be called the 'free enterprise' system: "We told you so!"

Within Indonesia the international discourse reinforced an anti-Soeharto, anti-New Order and pro-reform, pro-democracy discourse. The accumulating evidence of 'collusion, corruption and nepotism' by the Presidential family, business cronies, ministers and senior officials was all grist to the mill. Perceived greed and abuse of power undermined the legitimacy of President Soeharto and New Order power holders, while justifying change in the system and structure of government. Above all, it strengthened the argument for stronger legal process (rule of law) and more democracy. The fact that 'corruption' was such a dirty word internationally gave tremendous force to the slogan of KKN (*korupsi, kolusi dan nepotisme*);

generated sympathetic media coverage; and won international support. Technocrats, especially displaced ones, also supported calls for greater accountability and transparency.

The anti-corruption campaign therefore unites under one banner and in one virtuous cause a disparate moral alliance of domestic radical critics, technocrats, multinational business, foreign governments and international agencies. The common element in international and domestic discourses is that they are both critiques of power. It is not necessarily in the interests of the protagonists that the term 'corruption' be deconstructed, because that would tend to expose their differing goals and motivations. Social science analysis, however, requires these separate discourses to be identified and understood in their own terms. Otherwise academics abandon their trade to become mercenaries in a moral crusade with poorly specified political and economic objectives.

Time path, search strategy and politics

Because 'corruption', 'rent-seeking' and 'governance' are normative concepts judged against an ideal state of society, Improvement/Progress/ Development become exercises in comparative statics. Society is to be moved from an old, corrupt equilibrium to a new, ideal one. It is the proper task of government to achieve this transition. The driving force is the pressure of domestic and international expectations. The question is how this is to be achieved and how long it will take.

First, a corrupt regime may not share this objective. It may indulge the rhetoric, but not seek to give it substance if it threatens power and privilege. Secondly, even if the goal is embraced and translated into policy, what is the policy mix and time path? In the Cold War era an expedient compromise was reached between authoritarian regimes, Western powers and international aid agencies to promote economic development with only token political reforms. In the case of some Asian and South American countries this produced spectacular results, but the shock of the Asian crisis of 1997–1998 gave rise to a crisis of confidence. Economic development might not be sustainable without institutional development. But could institutional development be achieved without destabilising political reform? Would not popular politics retard economic development before economic prosperity had been secured?

What drives economic and political development is expectations. Economic expectations for greater material prosperity are powerfully reinforced by envy, demonstration effects, mass advertising and formal education. Universal primary education, the diffusion of television, urbanisation and rural/urban migration reinforce these expectations. In the case of politics, expectations for rule of law, democracy and basic human rights are reinforced by the demonstration effect of foreign countries, media and the diffusion of populist ideology. Rule of law, democracy and human rights have been powerful aspirations since the American and French revolutions in the late eighteenth centuries. Each country that overthrows authoritarian rule, most recently in former Communist countries, South Korea, Taiwan, Indonesia and now Yugoslavia, sends a strong signal to the rest of the world. If they can achieve this, why not us? In what respect are we inferior?

Countries seeking to move beyond the status of an underdeveloped country (UDC) face the challenge of a double transition: an economic one from poor to rich; and a political one from autocratic to democratic. This can be illustrated by a simple matrix.

	POOR	RICH
AUTOCRATIC	**UDC**	Developmental state
DEMOCRATIC	Poor Democracy	**DC**

Countries which complete the double transition from the upper left to lower right of the matrix become a modern Western country, typically a member of the OECD, like the nations of Europe, North America, Japan, Korea and Australasia. Ideally they would progress smoothly along a linear diagonal time path with simultaneous economic and political development. Sub-optimally, they might move through the matrix either clockwise or anti-clockwise. A nation could achieve a transition to democracy while remaining economically backward, like India or the Philippines, but this is uncommon. More typically countries achieve an economic transition but retain authoritarian regimes. These are sometimes known as developmental states, of which Singapore and, until very recently, South Korea may be taken as prime examples. The expectation is that such states, like South Korea, will eventually democratise but the time path is unknown.

Another possibility, however, is that countries may get stuck in an intermediate zone where lack of economic progress frustrates political reform and lack of political reform frustrates economic progress. The matrix can be hollowed out to show this.

	POOR	(transition)	RICH
AUTOCRATIC	**UDC**		Developmental state
(transition)			
DEMOCRATIC	Poor democracy		**DC**

A state which looked to have achieved a successful economic transition may regress with downfall of a corrupt, authoritarian regime. Such a process of circular frustration could last for quite a long time without any clear outcome. Various African, Asian and Latin American countries would appear to fall into this amorphous intermediate zone, albeit at different stages of development. This perspective is hardly reassuring. Many countries get lost in no man's land. There is no good theory that explains why some escape to achieve a double transition, or is able to predict how or when others may do so. In short, there is no time path. We can only rationalise history after the event.

It may therefore be useful to dissolve the matrix into a simple square along the same two dimensions of economic and political development. Nations begin in the top left-hand corner as Third World countries and seek to achieve the double transition to the bottom right-hand corner as a prosperous and democratic nation. The inside of the square, however, is empty. It is unmapped terrain across which a society seeks to be led or to conduct itself in the shortest time without extreme hardship. What makes the task so difficult and so slow is that progress is mostly in groups and in small steps, whether by coercion or voluntarily. The transition is not achieved until the large majority of the population has made the transition, not just a ruling clique or the urban middle class.

The problem of the double transition can be reconceptualised as one of complex 'search strategy'. Search involves learning, by rejecting unviable paths and trying to identify those offering the best prospects. Since the essence of such social learning is conflict and its resolution, each stage of learning is represented by an institution or set of rules which embody that knowledge like a built social feature in formerly unknown terrain. In this way social capital is accumulated, translated into behaviour and eventually embodied in culture. Analogy with the built environment is rather apt as sets of institutions become the basis for complex communities, from villages to towns and cities.

One approach to finding the time path is the engineering/authoritarian one of directing society by the shortest possible distance along a known or predetermined path. A post-Asian crisis example is the relationship between the government of Indonesia and the IMF as formalised in successive letters of intent and annual reviews by the consortium of aid donors. As it happens, this is also the model of educating children under a state-directed curriculum. Children graduate from year to year through prescribed curricula, assessed by examination, until they are judged to know enough to earn the status of adults and citizens with rights to drive and vote.

This rational meritocratic model is so pervasive in the West and among the middle class in developing countries that it is accepted implicitly. Indeed, many members of the urban middle class are themselves part of the civil and military state apparatus. But what if the state does not know best? What if the time path is not known and an alliance of strong-willed governments, donors and international aid agencies are leading or coercing a society along an unsustainable time path? The decision-makers themselves are likely to be well remunerated and may not suffer material loss if the strategy fails. However, coercion may eventually produce a hostile political reaction that overthrows the state and its development strategy.

An alternative path of searching and learning can be likened to pre-modern child learning. Until the last hundred or so years, children grew up by following adults around and learning by doing, progressing at their own rate according to the opportunities. This is a model not of rational, graded progression but of exploring life and finding a way through its maze by an iterative process of learning. The question is whether it can also be applied to society as a whole. In the double transition a society may be influenced by foreign models and ideologies but still needs to experience the learning by doing, which is a process of resolving conflict and consolidating a social consensus.

A better metaphor is the search pattern of ants. Disturbance or relocation initially gives rise to random search patterns. As each ant returning to the nest passes back information to outgoing ants; movements stream and tends towards a single main flow. Random search with feedback and iterative learning is an efficient search strategy for a society of ants. It accumulates knowledge of the entire terrain, which would be missing from focused linear explorations, thereby minimises long-term risk, and allows energies to be focused most productively.

A more sophisticated model for human society would allow for outside intervention. Such intervention might be benign, in allowing for the possibility of accelerating learning from drawing on the experience of other societies, or may be malevolent, in forcing society into unproductive or fatal search strategies. It is probably not an unfair criticism of multilateral institutions like the IMF, World Bank and ADB to say that they have used Third World ants' nests as a means to their own corporate learning. Strategies have been imposed, studied, and revised in the light of their success of failure. It is not always clear, however, that the ants being experimented upon are gaining equal benefit, especially when programs are carried out with borrowed funds that must be repaid.

Such a perspective allows a rethinking of politics. Politics are conventionally seen as ways of contesting and wielding power, which is indeed what is acted out upon the stage. However, from the viewpoint of long-term institutional development, politics may better be seen as the search and learning strategy that gives rise to institutions. Until around two hundred years ago, kings and aristocracy governed by birthright. The institutions of popular sovereignty and republicanism made politics immensely more complex, just as nations and nationalism were emerging to respecify the units of government. It has been easier to 'imagine' nations and endow them with high constitutional ideals than to develop structure and institutions that enjoy popular legitimacy and allow public choice.

To deprive a nation of politics, as has been done to Indonesia for most of the 20th Century, is not only to disempower society but also to prevent it from developing to maturity by making choices, committing mistakes, learning from the experience and embodying that knowledge in appropriate institutions. Rules are specified and observed because they are seen by learning to be functional and better than the alternative. 'Muddling through', as it used to be known in Britain, can make a lot of sense as a search and learning strategy.

The conventional dichotomy between economics and politics, as illustrated by the above two-dimensional square, is therefore dangerously misleading. Such a dichotomy may be imposed as an authoritarian act, but it is certainly not intrinsic to the process of development. Development theorists and policymakers have been right to read the Asian crisis as a crisis of the old conventional wisdom, namely that economic development will deliver both material and social goods. They have correctly identified the need for simultaneous institutional development. However, they have maintained the old fallacy in a new guise, namely that economic and *institutional* development will proceed best in the absence of (messy and disruptive) politics. Hence the emphasis is on passing better laws and trying to enforce them without much regard to the political process needed for 'rule of law' to take root. The significance of institutional development is that both economics and politics are needed for social integration and a sustainable development trajectory.

The requirement is therefore not *less* politics but more efficient politics. Can broad coalitions be formed and sustained as policy-making governments, which is the challenge of leadership? Can conflicts be resolved and, through feedback, can better formal and informal rules-of-the-game be incorporated in organisations? Can corruption and rent-seeking be kept within reasonable limits to resolve conflict and hold coalitions together without too high an opportunity cost to society? (Khan and Jomo 2000) A sudden transition from authoritarian rule, as in contemporary Indonesia, creates high expectations that the new political elite struggles to meet. Competition between unstable vertical organisations in the form of political parties has to be reconciled with the need for cooperation across alliances and coalitions. Public interest collides with vested interest. Ideals and ideologies have to be aligned with realities. All this is the very stuff of politics but at the outset the game is being played by unskilled participants. It is bad enough to see the 'sausages' being made, but to see them being made badly is even worse.

In Southeast Asia, the objection to politics is sometimes made by citing the case of the Philippines, a country which pre- and post-Marcos has had a surfeit of elite politics but ineffective government and a poor record of economic growth. However, the weaknesses of governance in the Philippines may have more to do with the nature of politics: local political and business dynasties override national parties and programs (Sidel 1999). By contrast, Indonesia has a tradition of national parties and ideologies. For all their faults, parties and their local machines tie ordinary people into networks of loyalties and give them a stake in the political system and its institutions at the central, provincial and local levels. In Thailand political parties have become enmeshed with national and local political and business interests, giving rise to a system of 'money politics' (Phongpaichit et al, 1998). The new Indonesian democracy would appear rapidly to be taking on some of these characteristics. If there is no low-corruption democracy on offer, a corrupt democracy may still be preferable to and more sustainable than corrupt authoritarianism.

The seductive appeal of 'anti-politics' is that it leaves power in the hands of the experts: authoritarian presidents and ministers, senior bureaucrats and military officers, their cronies and their international advisers and funding agencies. The experts decide what is best. Order is good; disorder is bad. This is the old reactionary police state in modern guise; and it is no more ready now to surrender power than in its authoritarian and colonial past. As at the time of the French Revolution, popular, participatory politics threatens the power and privileges of the ruling elite. There is a lot to lose. Does the elite stand and fight or does it embrace and seek to control the new democratic politics?

Twentieth-century Indonesia

In the case of Indonesia, the interaction between political development and economic development can be seen from a joint periodisation for the course of the Twentieth Century. Allowing for some rounding of years to get a reasonable fit, the result is set out below with periods of marked political reform or economic progress indicated in bold.[1]

Period	*Politics*	*Economy*
1901-20	**Ethical Era**	**Expansion and boom**
1920-30	Reaction	**Expansion** (after 1923)
1930-42	Repression	Depression and recovery
1942-45	Occupation	Catastrophic decline
1945-49	**Revolution**	Uneven recovery
1950-57	**Parliamentary Democracy**	**Rehabilitation**
1957-66	Guided Democracy (1959)	Stagnation and decline
1966-73	**Modest reform**	**Economic recovery**
1974-98	Repression	**Rapid development**
1998-	**Democratisation**	Crisis and stagnation

1 This periodisation is taken from Dick (2001) and DHLT (2002), where the underlying political and economic periodisations are examined in more detail.

This joint periodisation shows that in only three periods has political reform coincided with economic development:

1901-20	The early enlightened years of the colonial Ethical Policy
1950-57	The first years after the recognition of Independence in December 1949
1966-73	The early 'coalition' years of the New Order

Altogether these three periods total 32 years, just one-third of the 20th century. Even the longest was only 20 years, the other two a mere seven years. No single period was long enough to build and embed solid institutions and inculcate new patterns of behaviour. Nor did later periods build on earlier foundations. After the disruption of the Japanese occupation and the Revolution, the 1950s were a new start; as were the early years of the New Order after the downfall of Soekarno and the elimination of the Communist Party. In each case a new political system and new institutions have had to be devised. The same applies to the most recent period of Democracy and Reform. The transition to democracy appears not to have solved, but to have compounded problems. There are high ideals and clear goals, detailed letters of intent, and policy, but, so far, no feasible time path. Without the rewards and sanctions of authoritarian rule, top-down government no longer works, but neither can the new political parties formulate a new consensus and translate it into policy.

The other two-thirds of Indonesia's twentieth century divide into periods of economic development without political development and vice-versa. Since there is no inherent reason why political and economic development should coincide, neither can it be assumed that their disjunction is necessarily harmful. As mentioned above, during the New Order conventional wisdom was that political reform could wait while economic development was pushed with all speed to provide society with material resources. Rapid, and apparently sustained, economic growth seemed to justify this approach. The analogy can be drawn with a relay race. The reality was not necessarily so benign. Tightening political repression in the last two decades of colonial rule, as also under the New Order after 1974, eroded the legitimacy of capitalist economic expansion. Conversely, the 1940s and the period of Guided Democracy, as again since 1998, were periods when society was preoccupied with politics and when the consequent instability put paid to economic expansion. The outcome has been not a relay race but a 'flip-flop' cycle of frustration. In terms of the matrix of development and democracy discussed above, Indonesia remains stuck in no man's land, lurching from one side to the other but without progressing along any definite time path.

Three aspects of this pattern can be drawn out. First, it is not altogether true that Indonesia experienced no institutional development under the New Order. Former World Bank country director de Tray remarked at the end of his term that the only strong institution had been President Soeharto (de Tray 1999: 1). This understates the tremendous consolidation and extension of the power of the centralised state, the culmination of a process which had begun under Governor-General Daendels almost two hundred years earlier (DHLT 2002). Under the New Order not only was the bureaucracy greatly strengthened as an instrument of centralised, authoritarian rule (Rohdewohld 1995). Control of the civil bureaucracy was taken over by the Armed Forces exercising its claim of dual function (*dwifungsi*), a combination of military and civic mission to achieve the goals of Stability and Development. This whole system was in turn manipulated and controlled by an extensive intelligence and surveillance apparatus (Tanter 1991). Despite the absence of rule of law, there were implicit and explicit 'rules of the game' which were enforced by patronage and reward; and also at times by harsh and violent penalties (McLeod 2000). Institutional development therefore did occur, but it was narrowly based to support an authoritarian structure. Institutions that were inconsistent with this structure, such as political parties, trade unions or the legal system, were suppressed, corrupted, or co-opted. The state and middle class prospered, but at the expense of civil society. In terms of social capital, the opportunity cost was terribly high, the consequences of which have been seen since May 1998. Reforming authoritarian institutions amidst a weak civil society can seem a Sisyphean undertaking.

Secondly, in the midst of such acute political, economic and institutional crisis, it is myopic to see corruption and rent-seeking as the fundamental problems. They are not trivial problems, especially for foreign investors. Nevertheless, they are symptoms or distortions caused by authoritarian rule. They are not the cause of authoritarian rule. If an infection causes fever which in turn causes a rash, a good doctor may treat the rash to alleviate discomfort but she should not diagnose and prescribe only according to that which is most visible. In the case of Indonesia, there is no short-term social engineering that will suddenly dissipate corruption. In the absence of rule of law, there is no means of enforcing property rights and contracts other than through patronage and payment.

Thirdly, the incidence of corruption is not obviously lower under the new democratic regime than under the old one. In year 2000, much old corruption was exposed but a series of new cases also came to attention, while society waited to see whether the government had the means or the will to act (ICW 2001). A few members of the former regime have been imprisoned or are under trial, but new corruption seems to escape sanction as long as it does not become too gross, or the perpetrators lose political favour. Such a strategy may be better than none, but it redistributes, rather than reduces, corruption and reinforces an already-high level of social cynicism. The situation may therefore be akin to that in 1970, when the Soeharto allowed the Committee of Four to investigate several great scandals but refused to act on their findings (Mackie 1970; Assegaf, this volume). The state oil company Pertamina escaped sanction then; and thirty years later was still notorious for corruption, of which the Soeharto family had been the principal beneficiaries. The apparent unsustainability of economic development, combined with chronic institutional weakness and signs of national disintegration, are breeding frustration and pessimism.

Conclusion

North (1990) and other new institutional economists are on strong ground in arguing that some states and associated property rights regimes are more conducive to economic development than others. On the whole Western Europe and North America (excluding Mexico) look much better than far Eastern Europe, South America, Asia and Africa. Nevertheless, it would be simplistic to try and explain the history of Europe or North America in terms of 'good governance', like an updated version of Weber's 'protestant work ethic'. In the late 1930s and 1940s the future of Europe, like that of Southeast Asia today, was still opaque. Could one imagine in 1945 the IMF drawing up a post-war recovery plan for continental Europe in terms of programs of anti-corruption, rule of law and good governance? It would not have been entirely silly to do so. Nazi Germany was one of the century's most corrupt and violent regimes. Elsewhere, authoritarianism was the norm. Except in Sweden and Switzerland, democracy had been snuffed out. In the event, the Marshall Plan combined massive capital transfers with restoration of political rights. Sovereignty and agency was restored to the people of each nation to find their own way. Spain and Portugal, however, remained under authoritarian rule until the 1970s; Greece reverted to military rule in the mid-1960s; Eastern Europe was held under Communist dictatorships until the fall of the Berlin Wall in 1989; and the rump of Yugoslavia achieved proper democracy only in 2001. The political record is therefore patchy. Europe may be a story of the triumph of democracy and good governance, but only in the past fifty years, which is not so very long ago.

Myrdal (1968) argued that a 'strong state' was the necessary handmaiden of economic development. Until the Asian crisis, the success of the 'high performing Asian economies' and the lagging development of India and the Philippines seemed to justify this insight. The authoritarian 'developmental state' seemed to work. Post-Asian crisis the situation is not so clear-cut. A benevolent authoritarian state with sound institutions - of which Singapore stands out as the prime and perhaps the only example - still fits the model. But in other countries, repressive and corrupt authoritarian states - of which Indonesia was the prime example - may have become an obstacle to development by undermining the institutions and eroding the social capital of civil society. The authoritarian response is to reconstitute the strong or developmental state and to impose a better set of institutions so that economic development can proceed. Such social engineering, which is widely advocated by multilateral agencies and western interests, takes little account of the local dynamics of transformation.

The other and bolder response, as in Europe after World War II, is to try and restore vitality, skill and credibility to the domestic politics, to allow society to make political choices and hope that it will 'muddle through'. In the very long-run, as mentioned, 'muddling through' may be the better strategy for searching and learning, the shortest and least painful way to achieve the dual transition.

Indonesia is not the only country, even in Asia, still struggling to achieve the double transition from underdeveloped to developed country. The Philippines faces similar problems of a soft economy, weak democratic government, and regional insurgency. Communist Vietnam suffers political and economic stagnation. Burma and Cambodia are categorised as 'narco-states'. This already accounts for five of the ten ASEAN countries. Before the Asian crisis, Thailand and Malaysia were hailed along with Indonesia as 'high performing Asian economies' (World Bank 1993). Thailand has advanced farthest along a virtuous time path of political and economic development but has since come under IMF tutelage and found it difficult to accelerate institutional reform. Malaysia has had more success in economic recovery without as yet confronting the crisis of authoritarian rule. Singapore has achieved the rare feat of an economic transition under authoritarian rule but with solid institutional underpinnings. Even without tiny Laos and Brunei, this is a very mixed bag.

A very long-term perspective may be gained from the history of the technology transfer of the modern rational bureaucratic state. The basic institutions were introduced to Java, the core of modern Indonesia, at the same time that they were being introduced to Europe and as part of the same political process of the French Empire. The linking agent was Governor-General Daendels, a republican marshal sent out to Java in 1808 by the Dutch king, the brother of Napoleon (DHLT 2002).

Daendels applied the Napoleonic model: a rational bureaucratic hierarchy with specified tasks and salary scales; organised into prefectures; and linked by post road for fast official communication. The model was elaborated by his successors but never altered in these fundamentals. Indonesia is thus a new democracy but by colonial descent a very old modern state. Outside Europe, its contemporaries are the former Spanish states of South America. Similar reforms were not introduced to Japan, Thailand or Vietnam until the 1870s. Hence, the political problem is not that Indonesia failed to acquire and adapt modern political institutions, but that it acquired modern authoritarian institutions very early and democratic institutions very late. The authoritarian tendency was reinforced by the subsequent transfer of modern rational bureaucratic military systems. Here in outline is a historical argument that has much more bite than the vague discourse of good governance and property rights as disembodied institutions. Moreover, it portrays the problem of political transition not as specifically Indonesian, or even Asian, but as part of world history of the past two hundred years. Indonesia may be lagging, but its problems are by no means unique – even leaving aside the troubles of Africa.

This historical approach also challenges simplistic arguments that corruption is the product of traditional cultural traits. Of course, corruption is culturally embedded and all countries have a patrimonial heritage - even the United States. However, the notion of traditional culture as a given set of traits is virtually meaningless. All the Asian countries mentioned - and especially Indonesia and Vietnam - are polities which have synthesised elements of the modern bureaucratic state: democracy, global business institutions, traditional kingship and patrimonialism. The amalgam is not traditional but a transitional modern form. Current efforts to impose good governance will have some effect - most notably in the appearance of greater conformity to international norms - but underlying realities will continue to be very different. This will reflect politics and political choices as much as culture.

References

Backman, M, (1999), *Asian Eclipse: Exposing the Dark Side of Asian Business*, Wiley, Singapore.

Dick, HW, (2000), 'Corruption and Good Governance: The Beginning or the End of Development?', in D Kingsbury & A Budiman (eds), *Indonesia: The Uncertain Transition*, Crawford, Adelaide.

Dick, HW, (2001), 'The Challenge of Sustainable Development: Economic, Institutional and Political Interactions, 1900-2000', in G Lloyd & S Smith (eds), *Indonesia Today: Challenges of History*, Institute of Southeast Asian Studies, Singapore.

Dick, H, Houben, V, Lindblad, T and Thee KW (DHLT), (2003), *The Emergence of a National Economy: An Economic History of Indonesia, 1800-2000*, Allen & Unwin, Sydney.

Eggertsson, Thrainn, (1990), *Economic Behavior and Institutions*, Cambridge University Press, Cambridge.

Hamilton-Hart, N, (2001), 'Anti-Corruption Strategies in Indonesia', 37(1) *Bulletin of Indonesian Economic Studies*, April, 55-72.

Heidenheimer, AJ, Johnston, M and LeVine, VT, (1991), *Political Corruption - A Handbook*, Transaction Publishers, New Brunswick and Oxford, 3-14.

Indonesia Corruption Watch (ICW), (2001), *Laporan Tahun 2000*, Jakarta.

Jakarta Post, (2000), 'World Bank Wants Good Governance, Anticorruption', 12 May.

Johnson, C, (1982), *MITI and the Japanese Miracle: The Growth of Industrial Policy*, 1925-1975, Stanford, Stanford University Press.

Khan, MH, (1998), 'Patron-Client Networks and the Economic Effects of Corruption in Asia', 10(1) *The European Journal of Development Research* 15-39.

Khan, MH and Jomo, KS (eds), (2000), *Rents, Rent-Seeking and Economic Development: Theory and Evidence In Asia*, Cambridge University Press, Cambridge.

Krueger, AO, (1974), 'The Political Economy of the Rent-seeking Society', 64(3) *American Economic Review* 291-303.

Lindsey, Timothy and Taylor, Veronica, 2000, 'Rethinking Indonesian Insolvency Reform: Contexts and Frameworks', in T Lindsey (ed), *Indonesia: Bankruptcy, Law Reform and the Commercial Court*, Desert Pea Press, Sydney, 2-14.

Loveman, B and Davies, TM, (1978), *The Politics of Antipolitics: The Military in Latin America*, University of Nebraska Press, Lincoln.

Mackie, JAC, (1970), 'The Commission of Four Report on Corruption', 6(3) *Bulletin of Indonesian Economic Studies*, November, 87-101.

Marshall, K, (1998), 'Combating Corruption in Indonesia', Aide Memoire of the World Bank Team, Jakarta, 20 September.

McLeod, R, (2000), 'Soeharto's Indonesia: A Better Class of Corruption', 7(2) *Agenda* 99-112.

Myrdal, Gunnar, (1968), *Asian Drama: An Inquiry into the Poverty of Nations*, Pantheon, New York.

North, DC, (1990), *Institutions, Institutional Change and Economic Performance*, Cambridge University Press, Cambridge.

Nye, Joseph, (1967), 'Corruption and Political Development: A Cost-Benefit Analysis', 61(2) *The American Political Science Review* 417-427.

Phongpaichit, P et al, (1998), *Guns, Girls, Gambling and Ganja: Thailand's Illegal Economy and Public Policy*, Silkworm Books, Chiang Mai.

Rohdewohld, Rainer, (1995), *Public Administration in Indonesia*, Montech, Melbourne.

Scott, J, (1972), *Comparative Political Corruption*, Prentice-Hall, Englewood Cliffs (NJ).

Sidel, J, (1999), *Capital, Coercion and Crime: Bossism in the Philippines*, Stanford University Press, Stanford.

Smith, A, (1950), *An Inquiry into the Nature and Causes of the Wealth of Nations*, edited by E Cannon, Methuen, London.

Tanter, RC, (1991), *Intelligence Agencies and Third World Militarization: A Case Study of Indonesia, 1966–1989*, PhD thesis, Monash University, Clayton.

Tanzi, V, (1998), 'Corruption Around the World: Causes, Consequences, Scope and Cures', 45(4) *IMF Staff Papers*, December: 559-594.

Tray, D de, (1999), 'The World Bank's Lessons from the Indonesian Economic Crisis', Speech given at the Farewell Luncheon hosted by the Indonesian Forum Foundation, Jakarta

Wade, R, (1990), *Governing the Market: Economic Theory and the Role of Government in East Asian Industrialization*, Princeton University Press, Princeton.

World Bank, (1993), *The East Asian Miracle: Economic Growth and Public Policy*, Oxford University Press, Oxford.

World Bank, (1999), 'Indonesia: From Crisis to Opportunity', Country Report, World Bank, Washington DC.

Chapter Six

Reflections on Corruption in Indonesia[1]

Gary Goodpaster

> Just as it is impossible not to taste honey or poison that one may find at the tip of one's tongue, so it is impossible for one dealing with government funds not to taste, at least a little bit, of the King's wealth.[2]

Indonesian pundits often say that Indonesia has a 'culture of corruption',[3] or that Indonesian society is permissive and tolerates corruption. Proposals to establish a social norm that condemns corruption usually follow (*Jakarta Post* 2001a). These claims are efforts to explain why there is widespread, endemic corruption in Indonesia and why it persists over generations, notwithstanding general notice and constant condemnation. Sadly, cultural explanations are often 'that's just the way it is' explanations. Even if in some sense correct, there is not much explanation. Cultural explanations also call for cultural remedies, such as education of children (efficacy of which one may doubt for the world of adults).

We need a 'real' analysis, something that generalised cultural explanations do not provide, to understand how corrupt activities enter people's lives; what it does for them; and why they would tolerate it, given public condemnation. We must also begin by recognising that what we call 'corruption' serves legitimate human needs; it solves problems of making a living and getting ahead; and, depending on the circumstances, there may be impelling incentives for people to act corruptly. We need to understand how that occurs and why it is so difficult to do anything about it.

1 I would like to thank Jeff Povolny and Thomas Timberg, my colleagues at the Partnership for Economic Growth, Jakarta, for reviewing earlier drafts of this paper and providing helpful comments.

2 Kautilya, "The Arthashastra", quoted in World Bank (2000: 135)

3 Indonesia's first vice president, Mohammad Hatta, said this a long time ago, but it is often repeated, most recently by T Mulya Lubis, a prominent Indonesian lawyer and reformer, in a speech in Washington, DC, to the United States-Indonesia Society (Lubis 2001).

Corruption, collusion, and nepotism (corruption for short)[4] are natural, not aberrational, behaviours. Consider the countries and governments of the world and their histories and you will conclude that, at some stage of national development, what we call corruption constitutes a norm of behaviour. Much history comprises tales of corruption and nepotism, from the courts of Rome and Byzantium, through the palaces of popes, kings and renaissance princes; down to the robber barons and tammany halls of yesteryear; to the political patronage, backroom deals, mafias, triads and *yakuza* of today. By our standards, Elizabethan England[5] and the late 19th Century United States were quite corrupt. Corruption is also widespread in developing states and transition economies - particularly those, like Indonesia, where the state controls much of the economy (World Bank 2000: 151, n 1). It appears in post-colonial states - there are 'states' in Africa that could give lessons to the Devil - and in many of the states formed from the dissolved Soviet empire (Holmes, this volume).

Throughout history it is actually the countries and governments that are deemed not corrupt, or that control corruption successfully, that are abnormal. Corruption is the normal, or ordinary, state. On this proposition, what needs explaining is not corruption, but moves away from corruption. History suggests that countries overcome or 'graduate' from corruption, learning that it is an evil to fight and conquer. In democracies, the development of democratic voting; effective opposition parties and interest groups; and regulated yet 'free' market economies are catalysts in this process. Even graduates, however, do not always completely succeed in eradicating corruption, but rather in confining or limiting it. The recent French and German political corruption scandals and the unseemly story of 'money politics' in the United States and most Western developed countries attest the difficulty in wholly exterminating corruption.

What we call corruption is a form of seeking personal gain. It is natural for individuals to seek their own advantage and that of their family

4 Collusion is just cooperation for gain given a negative cast. It is very common, as noted by Adam Smith two centuries ago: "People of the same trade seldom meet together, even for merriment and diversion, but the conversation ends in a conspiracy against the public." As for nepotism, evolutionary theories of the selfish gene and kin selection provide a biological and evolutionary basis for favouring one's own. In fact, nepotism is natural: if required to make a choice between relatives and strangers, most would choose relatives. An example will make the point. In 1997, in the United States, out of 4,000 kidney donors, only one gave a kidney to a non-relative (Burnham and Phelan 2000: 204).

5 The Crown practice of granting monopolies or special privileges in order to obtain revenue or to reward services "reached its climax while Elizabeth was in power. A list of her grants includes patents giving the sole rights to sell or manufacture currants, salt, iron, powder, cards, calf-skins, feels, ouldavies, ox-shin bones, train-oil, lists of cloth, potashes, aniseed, vinegar, sea-coals, bottles, lead, accidences, oil, calamine-stone, oil-of-blubber, glasses, paper, starch, tin, sulphur, new drapery, dried pilchards, beer, horn, leather, Irish yarn, importation of Spanish wool, and transportation of iron-ordinance" (Miller, 1907: 1, 2).

members or relatives. If the government controls access to economic opportunities or has large, exploitable resources, I would, of course, approach the government to gain access to them. As long as what I got justified the expenditure I had to make to get it, it would be rational for me to pay, in some way, for that access. From the individual's point of view, corruption is just securing some gain or advantage - and not unfairly, for others can do what I do. In fact, I am not likely to see how my gain hurts anyone else, except perhaps competitors for the deal. If I don't receive the gain, then someone else will. As between us, I am at least as deserving; and I would, of course, prefer that I or mine receive it. Once I and people like me secure a productive position, or more grandly, capture the state policy and decision-making apparatus, we will use it to benefit ourselves and ours as much as we can. In the latter case, we will push programs in directions that provide the greatest opportunities for rent-seeking.

To say that humans are naturally inclined to corruption is not to say that it is good; nor to claim that nothing can be done about it; nor to preclude judgements about corrupt activities. Claiming that corruption is natural no more endorses it than saying that wars are natural endorses war. Just like other natural human inclinations we would perhaps like to disown - say, the tendency to overeat or inclinations to vice - corrupt behaviours can be brought under conscious control. It takes some learning and discipline, however. The case must be made why corruption is bad for you, or - if you personally profit from it - why it is bad for others and society; and why, in the long run, it may be bad for you and yours. To those who make livings corruptly, where many people do so, this is not an easy case to make. Worse, even when made, collective action problems may ensure that while all agree in moral concert that corruption is an evil, no substantive remedy entails.

Assuming that humans naturally tend to engage in what we righteously condemn as corrupt behaviours, however, also suggests that moral condemnation alone no more serves to stem corruption than it does the classic human vices or the expression of genuine human needs. It may comprise a gesture of solidarity with the good and the right, but as Bertold Brecht once famously said, "*Erst kommt das Essen, denn die Morale* (Eat first; moralise later)". Put otherwise, corruption is bound up with making a living for oneself and one's own, either through corruptly generated income or self-protectively through payments of bribes and corruption taxes to get on with one's business. People with full bellies and shelter are much more likely to listen to moral arguments than people without; and we cannot disassociate issues of corruption from issues of self-provision. Corruption is primarily an economic and social issue and only down the line a matter for sermons.

All this said, there are scales and degrees of corruption. Corruption can be narrow or widespread; petty or grand; restricted or free; disorganised or organised. On deeply infiltrating state instruments, corruption works a qualitative change in the way a society is organised and operates. Call this condition 'structural' corruption, that is, corruption woven into the fabric of governance, so that governmental powers are co-opted to enable corrupt activities and into the weave of a society's social and economic affairs. Corruption can become so insinuated that, like a brain worm,[6] it takes over its host, or at least some of its functions, for its own purposes. Eradicating structural corruption is immensely difficult because it operates as a governing economic and social system in itself and because so many livelihoods depend on it.

Widespread corruption, such as now exists in Indonesia and some other developing countries, forms a parasitic economic and social system. That is, it comprises adaptive and interconnected ways of making a living; certain kinds of incentives; characteristic ways of relating to others; and persistence across generations. It is not a self-sufficient or stand-alone system but depends on co-existing economic and social systems, for example, on the agricultural economy; on markets or state enterprises; on the self-employed; on small and medium enterprises; on the informal or black economy operating outside, or on the contestable margins of, the law. In Indonesia, corruption interpenetrates these and other systems and lives off them.

Corruption is, in considerable part, exploitative. That is, many corrupt activities are non-productive and the corrupt make their livings rentier-fashion by extracting wealth from others. Corruption may involve productive activities, for example, an overpriced power supply contract, but these are generally priced at greater than market prices - and are exploitative to that degree; or depend on theft, such as illegal logging; or other illegal activity, such as smuggling. Even legitimate business activities - such as some of those the Indonesian military undertakes - while themselves productive, are sometimes intertwined with corrupt activities that are exploitative.[7]

Corruption feeds on poverty and widespread unemployment. Many find those desperate for employment particularly easy to exploit. For example, systematised illegal gold mining in Kalimantan primarily uses poor migrants from Java and Madura for its workforce (Kleden 2000). The migrants get start-up funds from local businessmen, who then receive half. To insure there are no governmental raids on the illegal mines, the businessmen then must pay off local police, the military and government officials (Kleden 2000).

6 A brain worm is a parasite that infects ants. Ants, in scavenging, eat a larval form which then makes it way to an ant's basal ganglia. From there it somehow impels ants to climb stalks of grass. Ruminants crop the grass, ingesting the ant and the brain worm, which then goes through another stage of its life cycle in the intestines of the ruminants.

7 For example, in Medan, trucks that have a sticker from a military foundation routinely pass through checkpoints at which money is demanded from truck drivers whose trucks do not carry the sticker. Recently, truck drivers plying the Banda-Aceh road staged a strike to protest illegal levies demanded at ten to fifteen different checkpoints. One of the drivers spoke out: "We are tired of the levies demanded by officers and hoodlums along the road. Every day we have to spend millions of rupiah to pay these levies" (*Jakarta Post* 2001b).

To the degree that corruption joins or creates organised criminality, as occurs in Indonesia, it threatens ominous social system consequences. The example reveals that systematic corruption may require large-scale cooperation. It also shows corruption as a 'black', or inverse, kind of governance through which government officials protect illegal activities for a price, with their own 'take' functioning much like a tax for government services. Finally, note that while productive, illegal mining is extremely costly in adverse environmental consequences, resulting in despoliation, deforestation and in mercury and cyanide poisoning of streams and rivers. It is also costly in terms of public goods such as governmental authority, rule of law and accountability. There is a looting lawlessness in all this that is astonishing. There is, however, also an order in the lawlessness: a system of expectations, incentives and arrangements that creates profit and grants impunity from law.

As detailed below, Indonesians economically support large, and largely unproductive, rentier and pariah classes. The rentier class forms a kind of aristocracy, basing its position partly on capitalist profits derived from governmentally conferred privileges; and on rents extracted from businesses and from lower classes. The pariah class is composed of hoodlums and lower level officials and police officers who can use their official positions to coerce small payments from many people. There are also shadowy ties between these classes, with the former often employing the latter for various illicit purposes.

As an economic system, what is good about corruption is that it provides livelihoods. To a certain degree, because corrupt payments for protection operate like a tax, corruption may also, in theory at least, serve to dampen certain undesirable activities, but that is an unintentional consequence. Indeed, because corrupt payments often protect what should not be protected (for example, prostitution or drug trafficking) they may actually encourage them.

What is bad about corruption is that it comprises essentially non-productive behaviours or behaviours excessively costly to the host. It does not, in economists' terms, use resources efficiently nor give people the incentive to engage in productive activities. Studies of the economics of corruption suggest that officials' proclivity to rent seek increases and public investment distorts, because investment provides rent-seeking opportunities (World Bank 2000: 145, n 1) and causes all sorts of public losses (Mauro 1997: 6-7). In governance terms, it does nothing to provide for the common good and, in fact, actively detracts from it.

As a social system, corruption also appears feudal or colonial in character, with lower ranks supporting the upper. And it seems particularly adapted to strongly stratified societies in which the state asserts a commanding role in economic life. Interestingly, it also seems to thrive in situations in which, as in Russia, the central state becomes enfeebled and loses the authority it once had. Indonesia falls into *all* of these categories.

An overview of rent-seeking in Indonesia

Ordinary rent-seeking

As Indonesian basic salaries are quite low, workers welcome any additional increment of income. Many Indonesians hold several jobs and most are on a constant lookout for additional sources of income. This is true even of government employees, a fact that often surprises foreigners who assume that government employees are already paid to provide government services. Indonesia's bureaucracies, however, have been employment sinks for the country; and they are notoriously overstaffed. Low salaries accommodate these large numbers and explain some of their work habits. There is a common saying that Indonesian government employees are paid a salary to show up, not to work. These employees expect that if they are assigned special tasks, then there will be additional remuneration to carry out those tasks. This creates a certain kind of entrepreneurialism in government offices. Projects, and assignments to projects, are prized because there will be a payment associated with the work, beyond the basic salary.

More broadly, there is an expectation that if anyone provides a service, there will be some payment for it. This is something like the custom of tipping, but has an even more mandatory character. The deliveryman who wrestles the new refrigerator up to your flat, although a paid employee, nonetheless expects some additional money for the service. Speakers, presenters, moderators, organisers and news reporters at conferences expect, and routinely receive, payments. Indeed, when, as sometimes happens, a foreign speaker rejects the 'fee', there is befuddlement and consternation on the part of the organisers. They have no procedures for dealing with a refusal to take a payment. In fact, as the organisers usually get a percentage of what is paid out, it is in their own interest to insure that the participants receive their fees. It is also customary to offer attendees at conferences a 'transportation fee' and even an 'attendance fee', in addition to free meals. These fees are usually small, but they evidence the basic attitude. If someone does something at your request, you are expected to pay something for it. And if you are a government official, you are expected to have access to, and provide, information and services that a citizen wants, if he or she is willing to pay.

In this transactional economy, these service payments to government officials may or may not count as corruption, depending on the degree of organised 'farming' involved, as I will clarify below. If corruption is defined as the abuse of public power for private gain, then the 'transaction fees and payments' charged and offered primarily reflect a dysfunctionally incentivised administrative structure. In this structure, the economic incentives of public employees are to guard access to public information and services and to deliver them only in exchange for payment of a fee. In a sense, the ordinary functions of government have been quietly 'privatised' in what we would think of as perverse ways. This comprises a certain kind of economy and a widely accepted way of making a living. Nonetheless these practices are quite close to what we think of as corruption. Indeed, close enough that it is easy to cross the admittedly indistinct line.

What, really, is the difference between a government employee who expects an extra payment for participating in an assigned project and a police officer who expects payment for providing 'protection' to a business? The difference lies in what is 'privatised' and in what we define as an abuse of public power. The abuse lies not in providing information and service or work for a fee, but in the deliberate distortion, or avoidance, of laws, rules and lawful procedures in order to secure a private gain. It also lies in appropriating the state's monopoly of coercive power for private purposes. For example, to get a passport or driver's licence renewal, a citizen may have to make a payment, beyond posted fees, to expedite the renewal. But when a policeman 'shakes down' a private citizen, threatening to use his power of arrest or citation unless a bribe is paid, the policemen enlists the coercive authority of the state to extract a gain. Law 'enforcement' becomes an unauthorised tollgate. The policeman provides no lawful service of any kind, but rather victimises citizens at will and as arbitrarily as he or she wishes.

Corrupt rent-seeking

We cannot, however, classify all low and mid-level bureaucratic rent-seeking as petty and as signifying only administrative dysfunctionality. For example, many positions in the bureaucracy are bought and sold. They are marketed because they are income generating, and the purchase of a position creates incentives to extract more rents and extract them systematically: what I call 'farming'.

The positions include the more desirable positions for traffic police, customs and immigration officials and court clerks. Junior officials must pay their superiors a quota from their earnings to secure these spots. Any money raised by taking bribes from members of the public over and above their agreed quotas they keep. Those who fail to meet their quota are moved on in favour of those who can (Backman 1999).

This practice is also an example of a payment hierarchy or pyramid, something that seems common and that offers a glimpse of the organised character of predation. It is also clear, as noted below, that there is a substantial amount of leakage in departmental and state enterprise budgets, particularly development budgets, and that many rivulets of cash divert to eagerly grasping hands, then to be used for private purposes.

Even outside the gloomy halls and offices of many state bureaucracies where the underemployed wait, government officials interacting with citizens on the street abuse their authority to engage in petty illegalities that impose additional regressive bribery taxes on the producing populace. Poor villagers in West Java, for example, were baffled when their government rice supply suddenly dried up. Suppliers complained that their payment was 60 million rupiah ($6,300) in arrears. But villagers were adamant that they had paid the bills, the *Jakarta Post* reported. It was discovered that one local official had collected money from 4,000 poor families and used it to build himself a house. Another village chief spent the money he was handling on a car. A third financed a wedding party. A fourth financed a second wife for himself. Investigators found that there was one village chief who had used the money to buy rice, as he should have done. But instead of distributing it to the needy villagers, he handed it out free to electors to win power for himself. "Oddly, none of these officials has been prosecuted", the newspaper reported. An article on the same page of the same newspaper reports that a survey revealed 12,000 malnourished children in the central area of Java alone (Vittachi 2000).

Consider also the case of weigh stations or bridges. A major reason for the establishment of weigh stations throughout the provinces is to prevent road damage from overloaded trucks. Ironically, weigh stations ensure the opposite. This is because Department of Transport officers openly misuse the weighbridges, forcing drivers to stop for the extraction of illegal payments. To compensate for these and other illegal payments the police require, driver and traders must overload to ensure adequate margins.[8] There are many other examples of similar rackets involving illegal taxes and charges on the movement of agricultural goods. Interviews with farmers, truck drivers, traders and shippers in South Sulawesi reveal that officers including air/sea police; customs; port authorities; the forestry department; and local police officers collect these levies. For example, from the rice producing area of Sidrap to the port town of Pare-Pare (approximately one hour by road) there are usually two police posts where payments must be made. Further payment to the police is required for entry into the port of Pare-Pare. Each post requires payment of between Rp 3,000-5,000[9] (although some drivers complain that demands are often for larger amounts). From Sidrap to the provincial capital, Makassar (approximately four hours to the south) there are seven police posts, as well as three

8 When there are no weighbridges on the planned route, drivers tend to reduce their load. However, this is rare, because there are so many weight stations. For a province with a relatively small population, South Sulawesi has a large number of weigh stations. For example, on the road from the northern part of the province, Kabupaten Luwu Utara, to Makassar (the capital in the south) there are six weigh stations, including two that are less than 25 km apart (in the town of Datae in the Kabupaten Sidrap and in Lumpue near the port of Pare-Pare). The amount each truck must pay is between Rp 5,000–20,000 (A$1.00–$4.00, as at December 2001), depending on the amount of excess weight. Provincial Department of Transport offices establish maximum truck weight capacities in ways insuring that all product transport vehicles are overweight. For example, six wheeled vehicles with a six to seven ton capacity have a four ton limit, 12-13 ton capacity vehicles have an eight ton limit. Drivers insist that transporting at, or under, the maximum tonnage allowed is extremely uneconomic. Of course, drivers do not abide by the limits even though, under regulations, any transport vehicle found at a weigh station to be overweight supposedly must be unloaded. This never happens. Drivers know that while in violation of the load limits, they can pay to avoid a citation and be on their way.

9 A$0.75 – $1.00, as at December 2001.

weighbridges. Drivers and traders transporting cattle from Bone (on the East coast of the peninsula) to Makassar reported that the five-hour trip might involve the payment of around 20 illegal charges. Traders typically estimate the largest expected loss from these charges and pass these losses on to farmers in the form of lower prices (Ray and Darma 2000).

Grand rent-seeking

Many people, within and without Indonesia, when reflecting on Indonesian corruption, immediately think of the grand scale corruption that Soeharto and his chosen ones represented. Such corruption involved the conferral of special economic privileges on Soeharto family members and favoured associates. These granted monopolies, inflated government contracts and leases; and allowed access to departmental 'off budget' slush funds. They also permitted misdirection and misuse of state enterprise and reforestation and social insurance funds; mandated bank lending to the favoured and well-connected in violation of prudent lending rules; and authorised diversion of development funds to personal uses. Soeharto also seemed to encourage ministers to enjoy the largesse or, *noblesse oblige,* looking smilingly aside when they did.

A World Bank report stated that approximately 20-30 per cent of development aid was stolen or

> diverted through informal payments to GOI (Government of Indonesia) staff and politicians ... Most GOI agencies have sophisticated informal systems for diversion of 10-20 percent of the development budget under their management and for utilising the proceeds diverted to supplement both their inadequate operations funds and their compensation.[10]

Recent audits of Pertamina, the state oil and gas company, and Bulog, the state logistics agency that deals with grain, disclosed massive 'inefficiencies' and corruption, much of that due to corrupt contracting practices. A Price Waterhouse Coopers audit of Pertamina, completed in mid-1999, reported losses of US $6.1 billion over the two-year period between April 1996 and May 1998.[11] Similarly, an Arthur Andersen audit of Bulog found corruption losses of US $2 billion over the four-year period between April 1993 and the end of March 1998 (*Suara Pembaruan* 1999).

Note, however, that while certain individuals - the aristocracy of the corrupt - profited handsomely from grand corruption, there is more to it than that. The rule 'follow the money' is a tool we can use to give us some insight into the real economy of corruption in Indonesia. Consider the Bank Bali scandal.[12] This involved the transfer of approximately US$80 million out of $123 million owed to Bank Bali - under a government guarantee scheme

10 Quoted in Schwarz (1999: 316).

11 *Gatra* (1999). The Indonesian government later revised this figure downward.

12 An excellent description and chronology of the Bank Bali scandal can be found at *Tempo* (2000).

on inter-bank debt – to a private company as a fee for 'assistance' in collecting on the guarantee. The scandal was first disclosed in the midst of a national election campaign. It was alleged that the money was to be used as a slush fund for Golkar party election campaign activities and that then-President Habibie and his lieutenants were deeply involved.

One enlightening result of the audit, however, was the disclosure that the $80 million was distributed to an extraordinary number of businesses and private parties.[13] While it is difficult to discern exactly what the distributions were for, not all, perhaps not even most, appear to have been intended for political purposes. What the Bank Bali funds flow chart shows is an immense network of corrupt payments and associations beneath the surface of a single grand corruption scheme. There are evidently large pay-off pyramids associated with grand corruptions, pyramids apparently the inverse of those noted concerning rent-farming in bureaucracies. There money flows up; here down. In either direction, however, the flows implicate many people. We can now sense an unseen Indonesian economy organised as a web of corruption networks, networks that are perhaps more than just distribution systems. The payments, particularly those downward, must buy *something*. Networks useful for one purpose may be useful for another.

While I have used examples from the New Order era, there are many allegations that not only has grand and mid-level corruption continued, but that it is worse than ever.[14] Habit, opportunities for those new to the feeding chain and 'money politics' are reasons; the breakdown of authoritarian rule, which in some sense controlled and directed these corruptions, is another. I consider these matters below.

Judicial and legal system corruption

It is widely accepted in Indonesia that the judiciary is largely corrupt (ICJ 1999; Lubis 1999); that there are many corrupt lawyers willing to pay for decisions; and that there is serious corruption among Indonesia's prosecutors and police as well.

Indonesians have a very low level of confidence in the integrity and competence of their judicial system. Corruption is rampant; decisions can be

13 A chart of the funds flows can be found at *Jakarta Post.com* (nd).

14 "Di sisi lain, praktek korupsi yang menjadi penyebab ambruknya perekonomian hingga saat ini tidak ada yang diusut secara tuntas. Bahkan, praktek korupsi itu kembali terulang dalam pemerintahan Gus Dur dalam skala dan kualitas yang makin tersistem … Kroniisme kini merebak di seluruh jajaran kabinet. Dan kantor kepresidenan agaknya mulai berubah menjadi bursa KKN …" (*Suara Pembaruan Daily* 2000 and *hukumonline* 2001). [On the other hand, there has still not yet been a thorough investigation of corruption, which is the cause of economic collapse. The practice of corruption has even returned again under the Gus Dur (Abdurrahman Wahid) administration on an increasingly systemised scale and quality. Cronyism has now cut deeply into the entire cabinet. And the presidential office is beginning to become rather like a KKN (corruption, cronyism, nepotism) stock exchange.]

purchased; the courts are subject to political interference; and legal transparency is inadequate. In many legal cases, plaintiffs are not seeking justice, but rather are using the judicial system as a mechanism through which to extort third parties. Such problems are by no means limited to the judicial system: they also extend to the legal profession, the attorney general's office, administrative agencies, and, especially, the police force (*Van Zorge Report on Indonesia* 2000).

The corruption of so many actors in the legal system means that it cannot serve as a proper tool of governance nor as a just means of dispute resolution. Those who would bribe their way out of a legal problem have many gatekeepers to approach. Police, prosecutors, lawyers, and several layers of judges can each dispose of or divert cases. If one does not, another may. Corruption in the legal system eviscerates Indonesia's reform efforts because the system by and large cannot be trusted to render honest decisions, but may be trusted to protect corrupt activities.

The cost to Indonesia of this corrupt legal system is incalculable. Aside from loss of governance capacity and social disaffection because people cannot use it to remedy real problems, there are clear economic losses. Donors, creditors, and potential foreign investors look upon the system with immense frustration, particularly at blatant fraud practised in the courts. Indonesia's new foreign investment is negligible, something that limits its ability to grow economically. While political instability is asserted to be a principal reason, investors also point in horror at the legal system because they know that, under current conditions, they have no security of investment whatsoever. Worse yet, they have come to realise that if they do invest, they may be subject to arrest on the complaint of a fraudulent debtor who is likely to have paid off the police (*Wall Street Journal* 2000).[15]

Police, military, and related corruption

The police, trustworthy confidential sources say, engage in three levels of organised corruption. There is a large-scale protection racket where police provide protection to paying businesses. The protection may be from police predation or security from payment demands from other groups and may also include services in labour disputes. There is also street-level corruption, the extortion of money from ordinary citizens through threats of arrest or citation. The police also require payments when someone seeks to file a police report, such as for the theft of a car. Police know that insurers demand police reports before paying any theft claims and so they charge substantial 'filing' fees in such cases.

Then there is the purchase of positions within the police force itself. To become a policeman requires the payment of two years' salary up-front. The rookie expects to recoup this payment within six months of employment.

15 In at least two cases, fraudulent creditors have appeared in Indonesian bankruptcy composition proceedings to defeat claims of legitimate creditors (Goodpaster 2001).

Higher-level offices are sold, and offer extraordinary opportunities for gain. The 4.5 million rupiah[16] monthly salary that police generals earn does not match the mansions and fleets of luxury cars that some own. Finally, as noted, this is all well-organised. There is a pay-off pyramid in police departments which is enforced through designation of some officer, a 'hard plant' or quartermaster, to collect and distribute payments.

Where the *raison d'etre* for the police force is moneymaking and the collection of rents, there is no public order and safety mission. Ordinary Indonesians understand this quite well and openly state that they hate the police, viewing them primarily as criminal forces preying on members of the public. Store owners and traders; bus and *bajaj* (motorised rickshaw) drivers; and owners of nightclubs and discotheques must all pay protection money to the police. If anyone needs convincing, the police can send thugs to demonstrate what it is like not to pay protection. Jakarta newspapers often report such 'visits' by mysterious and unnamed groups that sometimes resulting in substantial property damage.

The Indonesian military, although alleged to engage in similar practices, is also a more difficult case. It operates many businesses, legal and illegal. The justification for its business empire has been the state's notorious under-funding of the military. The income the military derives from its businesses and foundations, however, is 'off budget'. No outside observer has a good idea of how much money the military takes in, nor exactly how it is distributed. A large part of it appears to go to military personnel, with commanders commanding a large portion of that (*Van Zorge Report on Indonesia* 2001). The military also has close but shadowy connections with many Indonesian conglomerates. There is apparently some cross-shareholding in enterprises and conglomerates have, in the past at least, allegedly provided funds for some of the military's blacker operations (Aditjondro 2000).

Without denying the military's need for resources beyond those provided by the state, the secret control of immense resources derived from sources legal and illegal without accountability for their use is a structure for mafia-like corruption. There are, for example, allegations that the military has used its resources to fund the violence in the Maluku islands (*Van Zorge Report on Indonesia* 2001). There are also allegations that the military has extensive arrangements with wealthy businessmen, under which the military provides "low-cost military manpower and equipment, threats and intimidation of business competitors, eviction of smallholders from land, and beatings and murder of those who might threaten the system" (*Van Zorge Report on Indonesia* 2001).

Premanism – local gangster, mafia-like activities – are an associated phenomenon. *Preman* gangs charge businesses monthly fees to ensure there will not be any 'disturbances' that interrupt business operations. Of course, since the *preman* gangs themselves are the source of these disturbances,

16 A$1,200.00 as at December 2001.

these guarantees are effective. Such gangs also appear prevalent at certain markets and transportation terminals, charging store owners; *kaki lima* (portable, hand-pushed vending carts); *bajaj* (motorised rickshaws) and taxi drivers fees for operating from the area.

One example from Medan shows the extent and seriousness of the *preman* problem. On 21 August 2000, 17,000 local transportation drivers called a strike to protest against *preman* activities. Drivers stated that they had to pay *preman* 5,000 rupiah each day or suffer vehicle damage. They demanded police action (*Kompas* 2000c). Protest actions like this are not uncommon (*Kompas* 2000b). *Preman* gangs, of course, can operate where police forces are either not effective or choose not to be effective. There is also evidence that in some places, *preman* gangs are in league with members of police forces (*Kompas* 2000d); and that *preman* are hired to undertake demonstrations and violent mass actions (Randall 1998). There may be military involvement as well and certainly there are pay-off pyramids.

Aside from the monetary losses this rent-seeking imposes on the populace - and note that the 'bribery tax' is highly regressive as far as the poor are concerned - there are additional and immeasurable social and monetary losses. These arise from the failure of the police to do what police and armed forces are supposed to do, namely provide security, safety, order, and defence; as well as the active doing of what they are *not* supposed to do. For we must add to this already scandalous story the illegal activities that these forces either protect or undertake themselves: drugs, prostitution, gambling, illegal logging and mining, smuggling and the like. Leaving aside the vice crimes and social costs attributable to them and focusing just on material losses, the illegal logging and mining cause direct theft losses to the state and its people through the destruction of natural capital and also greatly increase the rate of natural resource depletion. The smuggling of goods such as subsidised kerosene and gasoline to places like Singapore diverts and appropriates the subsidies intended to help ordinary people. Police and military involvement in illegal logging, mining, and smuggling also results in a larger web of corruption. It entails either 'hush' or 'facilitation' payments to bureaucrats, inspectors and local officials or threats of violence or, indeed, actual violence, against interference or disclosure.

Money politics

'Money politics' is a term used to describe the purchase of political favours or influence (Dick, this volume). It is a problem in all countries, even the most robust democracies, and reform efforts directed at money politics only narrow its scope. rather than eliminate, it. There is a question of what part of 'money politics' we should classify as a form of corruption. Of course there are degrees. Paying money for a legislative vote or to buy a governmental office is one thing.

Donating to a political campaign is another. Although it is a complicated issue, 'ordinary money' politics, I think, should not count as corruption. By 'ordinary', I mean the use of money to *support* particular candidates or particular parties. Politics is about power, gaining it and using it. We can no more separate money from politics than we can separate stargazing from stars. Abnormal money politics would, however, include using money to *buy* votes or offices, under-the-table transactions to procure governmental decisions, and the like.

While Indonesia has a mostly 'democratically' elected national legislature, it is not yet a democracy where ordinary citizens' opinions matter much, nor where office-holders are meaningfully accountable to citizens. Those who hold political power now did not gain it by offering platforms that citizens endorsed by voting. At the national level, elections to high office are indirect, as people vote for parties rather than individuals. This essentially means that the parties control seats. If the electorate votes for a party rather than for an individual, anyone wanting a seat can simply pay the party to designate him or her as the elected official, something which appears to have happened frequently. In addition, no party in the national legislature holds an absolute majority and every decisive action requires the building of coalitions. Coalitions are as readily built (perhaps more readily) with money than with ideology or shared interests.

In this way, the nature of 'money politics' in Indonesia is closely tied to its electoral system - and there is a lot of 'money politics' going on. In fact, if one draws inferences from various clues that surface from time to time, and credits allegations and rumours, Indonesian politics is fundamentally 'money politics' of the worst kind. People, offices, and votes are bought and sold.

For those in power, and those who seek power, access to sources of money to play deadly serious political power games is an absolute necessity. Those who have money use it skilfully to defend their interests. It is also clear that Indonesian political parties use every avenue they can to obtain funds. Everyone suspects the intense political jockeying around 'cash cow' portfolios, such as IBRA (Indonesian Bank Restructuring Agency) or state enterprises, discloses that parties are looking for fountains of money for present and future political activities and power.

The immense foot-dragging of Indonesian officials in debt restructuring and privatisation – where vast interests are involved – is perhaps best explained by 'money politics'. There are widespread suspicions that the government's favouritism toward three of its largest debtors,[17] expressed through the IBRA bailouts and decisions not to prosecute, is also the result of money politics. In fact, an assumption of payment goes far in explaining a lot of otherwise mysterious, erratic and puzzling official behaviour.

The redistribution of corruption: Decentralisation and kinds of bandits

Mancur Olson, in discussing 'governmental' incentives to tax or take assets from subjects, makes a useful distinction between 'roving' and 'stationary' bandits. Suppose a situation of anarchy in a given territory. Warlords moving through it will appropriate whatever they can, wherever they can. Because they steal, and steal all they can, they have no interest in ongoing productive activities. When an area is exhausted of wealth, they will simply move on to other territories and other plundering opportunities.

By contrast, where a warlord takes over a territory and stays there, he has an interest in ongoing productive activities and output. He can steal from, or 'tax', the same people on an ongoing basis. Since he has secured his source of revenue, he may even wish to protect the people from other predators. Eventually, his own predation may evolve into something like governmentally-provided security - and even into the provision of public goods. After all, as he takes some percentage of the revenue generated in the territory, if the people generate more revenue, he will get more too. In other words, his interest in increasing his wealth is allied with the interests of the populace in increasing their wealth. He has what Olson (2000) refers to as an 'encompassing' interest.

Soeharto was a 'stationary bandit' running a stationary bandit regime. Under Soeharto, businesses that bribed or shared wealth to obtain economic opportunities, advantages, or protection did get services in return. They obtained licences, land and environmental concessions, security of investment, contract enforcement and assistance in managing labour disputes. The Soeharto system of highly-centralised rule did not eliminate

17 "On October 2, the Financial Sector Policy Committee (FSPC) approved major debt restructuring deals between IBRA and five of its top obligors: Texmaco Group (US $2.1 billion); Tirtamas Majutama (US $596 million); PT Kimia Kertas (US $275 million); Sinar Mas Group (Rp 1.2 trillion swap); and Banten Java Persada (Rp 1.4 trillion compensation for return of assets). While some analysts supported the terms of the deals as the best the government could hope for, others criticised them as expensive bail-outs that exposed the government to high levels of contingent risk. The Texmaco and Tirtamas deals are particularly controversial because of the complex holding companies created as vehicles for the government's equity stakes as well as the deals' generous financial terms. According to press reports, the local IMF and World Bank representatives wrote to the Indonesian government shortly after the deals were announced urging that they be reviewed. However, Coordinating Minister Ramli has vigorously defended the terms of the deals" (United States Embassy, Jakarta 2000).

the uncertainties and indignities suffered by business people trying to invest in the regions. A variety of local officials reporting to different ministries based in the capital oversaw various aspects of the business climate, from the environment to labour affairs to land use and taxation – with regulation often dependent on bribery. Police and military officers were frequently active in the selective prevention, and at times, active instigation, of labour disputes, with labour control bought at a price determined by local commanders and the superiors to whom they owed fealty.

Companies operating without the benefit of good connections in Jakarta would tend to suffer from these forms of irregular and illegal exactions. However, these pay-offs went to local bureaucrats (representatives of the central government), rather than local politicians. Jakarta's insistence on the encouragement of private investment inculcated a measure of restraint and predictability based around central government interests in increasing the flows of private capital into the provinces (Oxford Analytica 2000).

With Soeharto gone, Indonesia's stationary bandit government is gone, and the territory is open to roving bandits. With fiscal and governmental decentralisation, power has flowed to the regions and *kabupatens* and has created greater opportunities for local corruption through regulatory activity. Their greater independence and a possible 'it's our turn now' mentality also encourages predation.

Quasi-democratic politics, the emergence of political parties from rigorous government control and decentralisation have created local contests for influence and power.

> [These processes] have politicised all aspects of business operations. Companies must now make under-the-table payments to a considerably broader range of politicians than before .... (Oxford Analytica 2000).

With decentralisation, businesses dependent on local government licences, contracts and regulation now have shifted:

> ... to spreading their money around different parties or else affiliating themselves with one or another party in the local assembly. In this regard, businesspeople operating in real estate, construction, and various criminal activities have become especially prominent ... (Oxford Analytica 2000).

Why corruption is hard to end: Collective choice problems

Widespread corruption, in the aggregate, creates collective choice problems. The first is overuse of resources; the second is the free rider problem.

When everyone may use a resource freely, the resource will be overused. The individual user, whose percentage of the use of the whole may be small, does not see that cumulatively, if all use as he does, the commons will be overrun – overgrazed if it is cattle land; over-fished if it is a fishery; stripped if it is a forest. The threat of overuse, of course, is commons collapse. Indonesia's 1998 financial crisis and sharp economic decline evidence just that kind of event. Many, perhaps most, of Indonesia's banks siphoned off bank liquidity credits, freely granted by Bank Indonesia to try to weather the crisis, in corrupt ways. This, along with other factors, resulted in a collapse of the Indonesian banking system, a catastrophe from which Indonesia has yet to recover.

As mentioned, corruption also presents a free-rider problem. Aside from whatever changes hands, there are passed-on costs of corruption that someone pays, but those who gain are not among them. In a normal case of high-level corruption - over-inflated construction contracts or money siphoned from state enterprises - the population at large pays through loss or diversion of revenues or resources or through higher taxes. No one suffers a loss in any clear, direct way and the small losses allocable to everyone are not sufficient to cause large numbers of people to organise and unite to fight them. In the case of street-level corruption, those victimised pay directly and suffer a lower standard of living through what amounts to a highly regressive tax (World Bank 2000: 146, n 1). But street-level corruption victimises classes of people whose response is typically silent rage and suffering, not organised resistance.

There are also large, but intangible or unquantifiable costs - such as loss of governmental authority and legitimacy; absence of rule of law; misallocation of talent; and abuse of citizens. Those involved in corruption, of course, gain far more than their allocable share of any loss. For practical purposes, they can view any loss as entirely passed off to others. In this respect, corruption resembles environmental pollution; another case where individual actors do not internalise costs and do not consider the externalities of their actions.

Anti-corruption programs are a common good, but these collective choice problems make the task of remedying or preventing corruption very difficult. Few who profit see the harm in their own behaviour. The harms - aside from direct immediate financial losses - are diffuse, sometimes intangible, often difficult to measure. The remedy requires strong governmental commitment; and that may require broad societal consensus. This will not arise naturally.

> In a really large group, the typical individual receives only a minuscule share of the benefit of an action he or she takes in the group interest. This minuscule share does not typically motivate individuals in a large group to voluntarily act in a way that is consistent with the common interest of the group. (Olsen 2000: 77).

By contrast, it is much easier for small groups to organise and coordinate activities among members. Not only are communication problems much less severe but member shares in any pay-off of group success are also much greater. The corrupt, as members of various webs and networks, are much more effective in achieving policy and practical goals than the general public or the many unrelated victims of corruption.

Because the individual share of benefits from collective action is so small, voluntary collective action almost always fails in large groups. Small groups, however, are successful and have powerful incentives to undertake collective action – here, with respect to anti-corruption efforts, to prevent corruption. To these insights, we can add another important reason for the failure of the victims of Indonesian corruption to act. The Indonesian military, the police, government officials, the judiciary and *preman* enforce structural corruption in Indonesia. Directly or indirectly, through threats, violence, buy-offs and cover-ups, they protect the system through which they make their livelihoods.

Remedying corruption in Indonesia

Corruption on Indonesia's scale is immensely costly to the state and society. There are enormous economic efficiency losses and huge costs arising from misallocation of resources. There are competitiveness costs, as corruption is a principal reason for Indonesia's notoriously high transactions costs economy. There are large lost opportunity costs from all the investors, both domestic and foreign, that withdraw or forego investing in Indonesia because of corruption and its associations. I have already noted the other immense, but unquantifiable costs in individual and societal well-being and losses in the provision of public goods.

At present, only some NGOs and a few sectors of the public have made ending corruption in Indonesia a priority issue. Government officials, with the short-lived exception of now-deceased Attorney General Lopa, have done little – and the little that has been done has not been effective. Aside from serious collective choice problems, the lack of clarity in what an anti-corruption campaign would do and how far back it might reach may have something to do with this. Even reformed sinners would not relish time in jail or loss of wealth and reputation.

Powerful vested interests and networks of corruption beneficiaries that profit from the status quo continue to foil anti-corruption efforts. While anti-corruption advocates have made the moral case against corruption, no one in Indonesia has deeply investigated and explained the economics of corruption, nor exposed in any thorough and convincing way its social and political costs. Nor have corruption studies focused sufficiently on the future consequences of continued corruption, the intergenerational losses and costs: the destruction of Indonesia's commons; the plundering of resources; and the environmental losses and illnesses. For today's currently costly economy of corruption is also a spendthrift economy, destroying many livelihoods and lives of tomorrow.

Careful studies exposing in detail the systems, networks and social and economic costs of corruption are essential tools in the anti-corruption campaign. Will, as Buddha noted, attends knowledge.

Study and persuasion is not all there is to be done, however. Recent influential stances on corruption view it as a governance problem (World Bank 2000: 135-168, n 1; Asian Development Bank 1999). Indeed, the good governance program is part of the donor prescription for Indonesia. The program calls for key reforms (World Bank 2000: 152-159, n 1). Including enhancing competition in the economy through demonopolisation and deregulation and promoting the accountability of political leadership through public disclosure and transparency rules. It also includes creating merit-based and service-oriented public administration; transparency and accountability in public expenditure management; and promoting the rule of law.

While most would agree that these are excellent and essential reforms, they have proven controversial, primarily because they supposedly ignore the realities of politics. Some critics believe that those who champion the good governance program, primarily the World Bank and the Asian Development Bank, import worldviews that do not fit the needs and realities of developing countries. For example, Jayasuriya (this volume) asserts that the new paradigm for development donors is toward enhancing the regulatory capacity of the state. This entails that the state should not itself seek to conduct the economy, but instead create a set of regulatory institutions that facilitate the creation and proper operation of the market.

> Economic constitutionalism ... refers to the attempt to treat the market as a constitutional order with its own rules, procedures, and institutions operating to protect market order from political interference. However, these forms of economic constitutionalism demand the construction of a specific kind of state organisation and structure: a *regulatory state*, the purpose of which is to safeguard market order.(Jayasuriya, this volume)

Jayasuriya critiques the new paradigm for seeking to insulate the market from politics. Dick (this volume) agrees, stating:

> Development theorists and policymakers] have maintained ...that economic and *institutional* development will proceed best in the absence of (messy and disruptive) politics.

Both believe that it is not possible to separate markets or economic reform from existing constellations of powers and interests that shape politics.

To be successful, economic reform needs to have the political support of a significant group of actors. Reform strikes at the heart of deeply entrenched political and economic interests. Therefore, to be successful a program of economic reform must galvanise its own political support. From this perspective, economic reform is not merely a technical exercise to implement the 'right' policies, but a political project undertaken by the putative winners of the reform process. For this reason, market transformation is likely to be a deeply contested and prolonged process.

As I have argued, corruption in Indonesia *is* a governance problem because Indonesian corruption is intimately bound up with Indonesian governance. It is also true, as the critics of the governance paradigm have it, that you cannot insulate the politics of markets and the economy from politics. However, sometimes *something* causes reform politics to grapple seriously with corruption: we have evidence that countries can grow or evolve away from thoroughgoing and systematic corruption. The United

States, for example, did it over a period of about fifty years, roughly between 1870 and 1920.

All things that evolve, do so because of variation and what the evolutionary theorists call 'selection pressure'. The environment in which the creature lives, and that includes other creatures that prey on it and on which it preys, favours some particular variation over another. The moth that happens to have better camouflage and looks like tree bark when it lands on a tree will more likely escape bird predators and reproduce. These moths will generate successfully, compared to others - even of the same species - and, as long as the trees on which they hide remain the same and as long as their predators do not evolve better detectors, they will survive and prosper. At present, money politics and all it entails in the worst sense, and corrupt ways of making livelihoods, dominate the Indonesian environment. Survival in this environment appears to require playing the political game as a deadly serious power game or gladiatorial contest, where money is the primary weapon to wield. Outside the political game, survival requires doing whatever is necessary to make, or protect, a living, and corrupt activities are an accepted way to do that.

If these observations are correct, it is a mistake to view the 'good governance' paradigm as an effort to evade politics. Indonesian corruption *is* a matter of governance, and there is no way to address grand and petty corruption, and all intermediate forms, without engaging politics and political actors. If donors, in promoting the good governance paradigm, think that they can elude politics and insulate the economic realm from it, they are clearly wrong. But I do not believe they hold these views. They have other failings. The donor failures are impatience, short-term time frames and inability to stay the course. The donor demand for good governance, the negotiated letters of intent, the reviews and the granting or withholding of tranches dependent on the fulfilment of promises, create a substantial *selection pressure* in the Indonesian environment: it changes it. Donors say: 'do this'. Indonesia agrees to comply in order to get donor money. Indonesia does not fulfil its promises, and the donors deny the money. Indonesia returns to its reform promises and tasks and eventually complies, rarely completely, but sufficiently to get the tranche.

The point of the story is that there *is* movement in the right direction. There may be no stunning conversion, no mass baptisms in the anti-corruption faith, but there is change that would not have occurred otherwise. Through continued selection pressure and through changes stimulated in players in the system, donor involvement is part of the political mix. Indonesia may do its politics any way it wants to, but if it wants to take into account the money it needs and the donors are willing to give, *on conditions,* it will change and evolve in the direction of donor desires. One must also remember that there are reformist forces in Indonesia, both outside the government and within, and they are part of Indonesia's developing politics. Donor conditionalities, advice, and good governance ideas support them and help them make gains they would not otherwise make.

Remedying corruption in Indonesia - which ultimately only Indonesians can do - will likely take a long time, perhaps at least a generation. Although it is true that some polities - Hong Kong and Singapore, for example - overcame their corruption in relatively short periods of time, they are very different cases involving small, non-democratic jurisdictions and strong, centralised governmental authority. These conditions do not exist in Indonesia. The worry for Indonesia is, in fact, not the good governance paradigm or program, however flawed they may be, but *donor fatigue:* donors giving up after a few years of stalled or stymied efforts. The game is selection pressure, consistent and constant selection pressure over a *long* period of time - not mandates to insulate the economy from politics. Indonesian politics must now take into account what donors are willing to do. It must take into account whatever selection pressures globalisation brings - and these will be considerable indeed. In the long-term, Indonesia will learn and evolve and confront the corruption that seriously damages its economy and polity, holds back its development and victimises its people.

References

Aditjondro, George, (2000), 'Financing Human Rights Abuses in Indonesia', International Action for West Papua (IAWP) website, <http://www.koteka.net.part2.htm>.

Asian Development Bank, (1999), *Good Governance and Anticorruption: the Road Forward for Indonesia*, paper presented at the Eight Meeting of the Consultative Group on Indonesia (Paris, July 27-28 1999).

Backman, Michael, (1999), *Asian Eclipse: Exposing the Dark Side of Business in Asia*, John Wiley & Sons, Singapore, New York.

Burnham, Terry and Phelan, Jay, (2000), *Mean Genes*, Perseus Publishing, Cambridge, Massachusetts.

Delhaise, Phillipe F, (1998), *Asia in Crisis: The Implosion of the Banking and Finance Systems,* John Wiley & Sons (Asia), Singapore and New York.

Gatra, (1999), 'Pertamina Stabbed by Audit Documents', 36/V, 24 July.

hukumonline, (2001), 'ICW: Politik Uang di DPR Makin Marak,' 23 January, <http://www.hukumonline.com/cetak_artikel.asp?code =1733&artikel=berita>.

ICJ, (1999), *Ruler's Law* (The Report of the International Commission of Jurists Mission to Indonesia) 24 (unpublished, on file with author).

Jakarta Post, (2001a), 'New Interpretation of Laws Sought to Fight Corruption', 30 January.

Jakarta Post, (2001b), 'Truck Drivers Strike against Extortion', 2 February.

Jakarta Post.com, (nd) Bank Bali Scandal - Long Form - Funds Flows, <http://www.thejakartapost.com/bbscandal_lf_fundsflows.asp>.

Kleden, Anzis, (2000), 'Illegal Miners, Transient Merchants Thrive amid Extortion Culture' *Indonesian Observer*, 25 November.

Kompas, (2000a), 'Pungutan Preman Palembang Mengganas', 8 February.

Kompas, (2000b), 'Tanahabang, "Emang Abang Yang Punye"?', 29 June.

Kompas, (2000c), '17.000 Armada Angkot di Medan Mogok Total', 22 August.

Kompas, (2000d), 'Pemicu Bentrokan Preman di Blok M diduga Oknum Polisi dan TNI', 15 November.

Lubis, T Mulya, (2001), speech in Washington, DC, to the United States-Indonesia Society, *USINDO Brief*, <USINDO@aol.com>, 18 January.

Lubis, T Mulya, (1999), 'The *Rechtsstaat* and Human Rights' in Timothy Lindsey (ed), *Indonesia: Law and Society*, Federation Press, Sydney, 171-185.

Mauro, Paolo, (1997), *Why Worry about Corruption*, International Monetary Fund, Economic Issues Series, No 6, 24 February.

Miller, Sidney P, (1907), 'The Case of the Monopolies', 6(1) *Michigan Law Review* 2.

Olson, Mancur, (2000), *Power and Prosperity*, Basic Books, New York.

Oxford Analytica, (2000), *Asia Pacific Brief*, December (on file with the author).

Pope, Jeremy (ed), (1999), *The TI Source Book* (3d ed) (on file with author)

Randall, Jesse, (1998), 'Political Gangsters', *Inside Indonesia* 53, January-March, <http://www.insideindonesia.org/edit53/preman.htm>

Ray, David and Darma, Rahim, (2000), Field trip to South Sulawesi, April. Report on file at the Partnership for Economic Growth Central Office, Jakarta, Indonesia.

Schwarz, Adam, (1999), *A Nation in Waiting: Indonesia's Search for Stability*, Allen & Unwin, St Leonards, NSW.

Suara Pembaruan Daily, (1999), 'Inefisiensi Pertamina US$2,005 Miliar', 11 October, <www.suarapembaruan.com/News/1999/10/111099/Headline/h103/h103.html>.

Suara Pembaruan Daily, (2000), 'Sjahrir: Gus Dur Sebaiknya Mundur', 23 October, <http://www.suarapembaruan.com/News/2000/10/23/Utama/ut01/ut01.html>.

Tempo, (2000), Kronologi Kasus Bank Bali (Jejak Penelusuran PwC) (Description and chronology of the Bank Bali scandal), 11 May, <http://www.tempo.co.id/harian/fokus/16/2,1,4,id.html>.

United States Embassy, Jakarta, (2000), 'Recent Economic Reports: Economic and Financial Highlights', October-November.

Van Zorge Report on Indonesia, (2000), 'Transforming The Legal System: From Rulers' Law to Rule-of-Law', Volume I, 28, 4.

Van Zorge Report on Indonesia, (2001). 'Indonesia's Army: Friend or Foe?', Volume II, 16, 7.

Vittachi, Nury, (2000), 'Travellers' Tales', *Far Eastern Economic Review* 96, 7 December.

Wall Street Journal, (2000), 'Indonesian Stake Leads to Legal Mess for Canadian Insurer', 6 December.

World Bank, (2000), *The Quality of Growth*, Oxford University Press, New York.

World Bank, (2001), *World Development Report 2000/2001*, Oxford University Press, New York.

Chapter 7

Administrative Reforms in Indonesia?[1]

Paul H Brietzke

As this chapter goes to press, an Indonesian transition looks precarious - even compared to the shaky transitions seen in many other countries. Although no one publicly urges a restoration of a Soeharto-style New Order regime, Indonesians may, tragically, have to wait for another turn of the 'history wheel' before it becomes possible to unscramble the eggs of the economically, politically, ideologically, legally, and morally bankrupt New Order regime.

In this light, fresh and creative analyses are urgently needed of what, precisely, development (doing well) and democratisation (doing good) mean in an Indonesian context. The same is true of 'good governance' - the thesis of these qualities - and of their antithesis: corruption, organised violence and other abuses of power. These analyses are needed because there are no convincing historical models or theories of causation about Indonesia's type of 'transition'. Historical perspectives on Indonesian *reformasi* do, however, suggest that a Hegelian 'dialectical' approach to good governance is appropriate and this is what I attempt in this chapter. 'Where you stand depends on where you sit' and, for eighteen months, I sat as a USAID contractor in the Indonesian Ministry of Justice. My observation of everyday corruption during that time informs this chapter.

Bureaucratic discretion and rationality

John Gillespie (1999: 122-123 argues that East Asia 'authoritarian states' relied on fluid relations; on a neo-liberal legalism restricted to introducing marketplace predictabilities; and 'on bureaucratic power implemented formally through politically insulated state and quasi-state institutions'. This tactic was successful for a long time in a far-from-democratic Japan, but the cumulative lack of flexibility in such a system grew too complex for

1 This article is loosely based on Brietzke (1999). While I thank Howard Dick, Tim Lindsey and Amanda Whiting for their helpful comments, errors of fact and judgment are my responsibility.

direct management, until the cumulative effects of excessive rent-seeking proved fatal. As International Monetary Fund (IMF) and World Bank (WB) 'Protestants' should be aware, Asian consumer cultures are also very different from the Protestant cultures that gave rise to a neo-liberal, rational choice theory (Gillespie, 1999: 132).[2] I doubt, however, that, in making this distinction between cultures Gillespie means to throw the rationality baby out with the neo-liberal bath water. Insights into a culturally-distinctive rationality can be gleaned through a 'progressive' law and economics approach that is informed by institutional insights. If we cannot postulate a prevalence of rationality, what are we left with? Savigny's *volksgeist* or the philosopher-kings of Plato, Marx or Confucius, explanations which may strike responsive chords in Javanese culture? 'Rule-versus-discretion' is a misleading dichotomy. Assessments should be based on the capacity to implement policy, even through discretionary licensing, at least until new norms become better embedded (Gillespie, 1999: 139).

This is a convincing argument providing new norms can indeed be embedded while discretion continues to be tolerated. It also assumes a particular answer to an empirical question: to what extent are discretion-based decisions better than, or (almost) as good as, rule-based decisions? My reading of the sad history of Indonesia and many other countries[3] is that broad bureaucratic discretion almost always breeds a lethargy that must be overcome by bribes or credible threats. Platonic, Confucian or Marxist philosopher-kings seem very thin on the bureaucratic ground.

Enculturating reformasi dialectically

Bates (1995: 27) comments on the need to find a mid-point between championing the market and defending the state - the latter to capture sources of economic growth neglected by a market focus (Bastone and Brietzke 2000). The World Bank seems to be coming around to this view. In the latest World Development Report (Pearlstein 2000), it stresses the need for better institutions; permitting a gradual phasing-in of free trade and unrestricted capital flows; the need for intervention where markets create under-investment; and the moral unacceptability of a mass poverty amid global prosperity. Clark (1999: 28) finds that 'good governance', like 'rule of law', is a doctrine or ideology about how government should act. Even critics of the IMF and WB admit that these multilaterals' litany of transparency, accountability, predictability and public participation is a worthy addition to a good governance/rule of law doctrine.

2 In the same vein Borosage (2000 - quoting Joseph Stiglitz) describes these organisations as sending 'second-rate economists from first-rate universities' to evaluate the performance of IMF donees against a reactionary economics dogma, while peddling misery and leaving devastation in their wake.

3 See, for example, Robert Klitgaard's *Tropical Gangsters* (1991).

The essence of this doctrine is that policy must be formulated and implemented through law to attain coherence and consistency, to promote policy-favouring behaviours, and to suppress behaviours that circumvent or negate democratising and developmental policies. The 'design' question is how to create the best incentives and organisations for the 'social field' of Indonesia. Khan (1995: 75) and Bates (1995: 31) comment that the solution is to realise more collective gains and reduce rent-seeking by changing incentives or enabling coordination and monitoring. A common Indonesian assertion thus amounts to a contradiction in terms: 'We now have many good laws, but they are badly implemented' (Lindsey 1999: 176-79; Seidman 1998).

From our positions within Indonesian bureaucracy, Timberg and I (1999) proposed a laundry list of Indonesian reforms that might go some way to responding to this complaint. Some of the details and techniques in this list proved popular enough to find their way into the lists of some Indonesian reformers but one of our central recommendations has been all but ignored. We argued that three time-consuming, thoroughgoing, good governance reforms - the bureaucracy, the judiciary and anti-corruption measures - are inescapable preconditions to the success of easier, more minor reforms. Limited legal reforms of the Indonesian Supreme Court have, admittedly, been drafted and more detailed anti-corruption law reforms have been passed, but the bureaucracy has curiously been left untouched.

Skilful bureaucratic and judicial reforms would reduce opportunities for corruption and thus take some pressure off anti-corruption efforts. However, no political will to promulgate *and* implement any of these three reforms is yet evident. Locked in struggles with predatory elites, a weak government seems unable to do much more than survive in office. 'Reforms' thus amount to 'quick fixes' that will have little effect other than soothing the multilaterals.

Reformers face the paradox of needing massive governmental intervention to end massive governmental intervention. They are expected to use state power to promote the very institutions of civil society that will eventually constrain and check state power. Meanwhile, fearful of their potential loss wealth and power, incumbent Indonesian elites - cronies, tycoons, and senior bureaucrats - are delaying, circumventing, or negating reforms, just like the *apparatchiks* and *nomenklatura* of East and Central Europe (Holmes, this volume). These elites are trying to perpetuate the 'internal colonialism' of Soeharto's New Order by a 'defensive modernisation': the minimum of adaptation that permits them to survive *reformasi* more or less intact, perhaps by admitting some new members and sacrificing an egregious few. In confronting such resistance, Indonesian reformers are tempted to become the kind of authoritarians they were empowered to replace.

Administrative law reform

Does administrative law offer a solution? Ideally, it transmits new developmental and democratic aims to the state, economy, and society, while implementing the IMF/WB virtues of transparency, accountability, predictability and public participation (Jacobini 1991:1; Pierce et al 1985: 521; Smith 1988: 89). Immediate success is not possible in Indonesia but there are grounds for hope that a start can be made. However, a Dutch-style Indonesian *Machtstaat* – a state based on might, as opposed to a *Rechtsstaat*, a state based on law – still remains very much in place. The positivist legalism of the late Soeharto reign carries much of the rhetoric but little of the substance of the rule of law, despite recent formalistic declarations of *reformasi*. Collaboration among judges, police, prosecutors, the military and other bureaucrats continues to create an authoritarian concentration of power, as opposed to a British-style concentration within Parliament or a Franco-American separation of powers. There is a longstanding bureaucratic power to override Indonesian statutes 'in the national interest', and an overriding interest in protecting state institutions.

Bourchier (1999: 234-235) states that East Asians take a communitarian view of the public interest, implemented through the state-centric, top-down law that Indonesia inherited from the Dutch. He comments that the New Order's 'legal engineering' amounts to a Court/Ministry of Justice/Attorney General "wired to the will of the executive" (1999: 238). Citizens who complain about bureaucratic actions may therefore be treated like traitors: enemies of the integralist state, who place themselves outside the *volk* and are thus liable to punishment. The net effect is that public law institutions have become mere shells; ideology no longer keeps corruption in check; expertise and integrity count for little; and bureaucracies thus merit little public trust or support.[4]

In Indonesia's broad and vague Civil Law tradition, even 'organic,' statutory language gets 'implemented' through administrative regulations. These regulations are sometimes *ultra vires* and almost always grant broad state discretion, lacking in transparency and accountability. They seldom descend to the level of specificity needed to define particular tasks and require that they be performed. There is almost no administrative law in Indonesia today, in the sense of rules that apply (even vaguely) beyond a particular task in a particular ministry or agency. The consequences of this are apparent wherever you look in Indonesia: little coherence or consistency in state actions – especially with regard to the implementation of policy initiatives by the Wahid or Megawati governments. This confusion – which has served to perpetuate Soeharto's New Order – still plays into the hands of incumbent elites and others who would direct state (in)action through bribery or credible threats.

4 Bourchier (1999: 234-236); Jayasuriya (1999: 1, 11-12); Lev (1999: 92, 100); Lindsey (1999: 182-184; 2000a and 2000b).

Law is one form of political, economic, social and moral thought and the failure to do anything about this manifest chaos arguably reflects a lack of thought, consensus and political will within the government. Opportunities for democracy and development will dissipate sooner or later if there is no coherent process for formulating and implementing the 'public interest' and for then peaceably resolving the disputes that inevitably arise. Yet, perhaps dreaming the Indonesian dream of good men rather than good laws, many legal reformers are tinkering with existing, demonstrably unworkable, solutions. They seem unwilling to risk the uncertainty of something new, especially if it means substantial revisions of the Indo-Dutch top-down system. This matter has less than full IMF/WB attention because of a very different but equally unrealistic dream: a new 'withering away of the state' involving the deregulation of almost everything (Bourchier 1999: 235; Lindsey 2000a).[5]

Max Weber's ideal reforms

Democratising and developmental trends neither create nor strengthen a state, which remains an elite-favouring, colonial hangover. Without broad reforms in Indonesian administration and administrative law, nothing will work the way democratising reformers might hope.

Ideally, Max Weber's 'legal-rational legitimacy' offers the best means for rebuilding an incompetent and often-malignant Indonesian state. Many Indonesian reformers now identify themselves as Weberian modernists because they recognise that past efforts to create a law-less predictability usually proved futile. Predictability - that is, no sudden, non-evolutionary changes in the 'rules of the game' or in their application - is essential to promoting public confidence and such (other) investments as can only be recouped over a number of years.

Weber does not lack for academic critics but it seems that most Indonesians would prefer to enjoy the economic and political benefits of

5 Bourchier (1999, 239) quotes *Tempo* magazine editor Goenawan Mohamed as follows, "The worst aspect of the past thirty to forty years of modern Indonesian history has been the breakdown of law". Jayasuriya (1999: 7) mentions that both modernisation and rational choice theories stress the rise of a liberal outlook through representative democracy; an independent associational life; an independent and neutral bureaucracy; and growth of a civic language. Khan (1995: 72) states that institutional reforms require analyses of the inherited balance of power and of the political settlement (but I would add that the terms of the latter are still under negotiation). Sims (2000: A10), quoting Arbi Sanit, states that the dream of some Indonesians, described in the text, echoes the sometimes statist, neo-Confucian or Marxist reliance on 'superior men' that Gillespie (2001) attributes to Vietnam.

Weber's modernism before pondering the angst analysed by his post-modern critics (Jayasuriya 1999: 3-4, 9, 17; Lindsey 2000a and 1999: 186).[6]

Following Hans Kelsen as well as Max Weber, a thorough Indonesian remodelling would begin with an appropriate Constitution and then broaden downward, in an increasingly specific and concrete application of norms through administrative laws and regulations. The policy and authority for each application draws its justification from a higher source in a public law hierarchy. Of course, gaps and weak points in such a process can be identified in all countries, but what makes Indonesia 'special' is the frequent lack of a coherent, concrete and stable *content* in a formally-elegant hierarchy. The Indonesian administrative 'system' is thus, ironically, largely defined by its gaps and weak points. This creates an *uneven* state, where most actions lack justification and thus legitimacy, and a parasitical bureaucracy that cannot be termed a 'civil service'. This unevenness can be dealt with thorough a planned hardening of Myrdal's Asian 'soft' state, which is far from soft on the poor and powerless, along with a softening of Lindsey's Indonesian 'hard' (if criminal) state (Myrdal 1968: 1126, 1132, passim; Lindsey 2000a and 1999: 182).[7]

Many Indonesian administrative law rules are both too soft (they create so much discretion that the bureaucratic power to do nothing is frequently exercised) and too hard, especially on private parties who want to plan their conduct according to calculations of what bureaucrats will, in fact, do. Hard law, but not always the hard state, is exemplified by the criminalisation and heavy punishment of even trivial misbehaviours. This is largely a futile exercise, since would-be violators heavily discount the prohibition by the low likelihood of getting caught, prosecuted and convicted.

Ideally, administrative law is like a good newspaper article: it describes who does what, when, where, and why, describing the control options available to 'governance system designers' for application before or after the fact (Thompson 2000). Revising legal content should enable government to get the state under control by punishing *and* rewarding bureaucratic

6 Lindsey (2000b), glosses Richard Tanter's comments on an Indonesian 'insecurity state' which relies on constant and official precariousness to justify its own lawless ways. Many of the recommendations in Thompson's excellent article on the state of public administration (2000) cannot now be adopted in Indonesia, given corruption, incapabilities, high information costs, and other artifacts of bureaucratic underdevelopment.

7 Lindsey (2000a and 1999: 182) contrasts Indonesian 'soft' and 'hard' laws, especially the hard law formalism of the black state. But this is not a 'hard law that works,' at least in desired ways. Lindsey (2000b) goes on to describe an Indonesian *preman* (what I would call hard) State, which uses mafioso gambits like violence, brutality and protection rackets. Booth (1995: 303) asks whether Indonesia will evolve 'from a predatory to developmental state?' Clark (1999: 37) discusses an Indonesian 'soft authoritarianism'. According to Harriss (1995: 10), "the state is invariably a reflection of the holdover power within a society, representative of the dominant economic groups" and perhaps of weak and corrupted market signals.

behaviour in nuanced ways: on the basis of what administrative law and policy encourages; permits but does not encourage (tolerates); discourages without prohibiting; and prohibits. Such a planned redirection of incentives and organisations would help create a culture of bureaucratic professionalism and creativity, that of a civil service.

The evolution of such a culture also requires time and the growth of a media-informed public opinion; improved public education, especially in 'civics' and a street-knowledge of bureaucratic rules; improved Parliamentary[8] and agency monitoring and evaluation of bureaucratic performance; and an explicit linking of pay, promotions, and agency jurisdictions and budgets to bureaucratic performance evaluations (Burgess 2000). Even James Wolfensohn advises his 11,000 World Bank staff to break up the old bureaucratic culture, speak your mind and do more to help the poor (Burgess 2000). Such justice (rather than charity) properly begins at the Bank's opulent homes.

Most bureaucratic activity can be defined as specific tasks, which permit ongoing and relatively neutral evaluations of performance by the bureaucrat's superiors. That is, most Indonesian bureaucratic jobs are like those of grass cutters in the park, rather than like those of Cabinet Ministers. Ministers obviously need more discretion, but they are also more likely to be called to account, politically or by the media. The main reason for specifying bureaucratic performance under an administrative law is to reduce the major bureaucratic discretionary power: the power to do nothing, unless bribes or threats overcome the bureaucrat's lethargy.

My time spent in the bowels of the Indonesian Ministry of Justice is instructive here. Brown bags of cash change hands in the men's room.[9] Some bureaucrats have mastered the fine art of appearing busy: shuffling papers and drinking endless glasses of coffee or tea. Other bureaucrats seem content to sit idle in between chats, reading newspapers or taking turns playing Free Cell (a form of Solitaire) on the only computer located on their floor (which, incidentally, lacks an Internet connection).

Devising and enforcing bureaucratic tasks would markedly reduce this vast idleness throughout Indonesia, but how should these tasks be defined? Discretion should be reduced by reducing the number of issues to be decided and by requiring written, reasoned decisions wherever possible. Resources and decision-making inputs should also be described clearly: those the bureaucrat must have; those she may use; and those she is prohibited from using (for example, prejudicial matters). Outputs should also be clearly defined, leaving the bureaucrat free creatively to maximise outputs from given inputs, subject to obeying procedures that promote public participation and accountability. Audits and information management systems should be improved and 'rat-proofed'. Jurisdictional conflicts

8 *Dewan Perwakilan Rakyat* or DPR, People's Representative Council.

9 Of course, if the payer is a women and the payee/bureaucrat is a man, his female colleague will be seen going into the women's toilet with the payer.

among ministries and agencies should be resolved. Joint responsibilities and hierarchies of evaluation should be clarified (National Economic Research Associates, 1997). Many Indonesians are close to being behind John Rawls' 'veil of ignorance', rationally uncertain of their position in the new society that emerges fitfully. Bureaucratic reforms should reduce this uncertainty wherever possible, since it slows down democratisation and development.

Improved administrative law would encourage everybody to define their ends and means carefully; prompt the 'political' resolution of jurisdictional and value conflicts that otherwise remain hidden from view; and improve the coordination and 'fit' among agencies old and new. There is a great deal of overlap and infighting among Indonesia's religious, business, economics and law reform agencies. The many Indonesian agencies and individual bureaucrats with no real purpose or task would then stand out like sore thumbs, and could be cashiered, reorganised or reassigned accordingly. Organisations and individuals forced out of their longstanding sinecures can be expected to fight back, and the Indonesian bureaucracy's hitherto powerful 'lobby' may reduce huge efficiency gains to merely significant ones - and redundant bureaucracies may go to work for local governments, under the decentralisation initiative.

Adequately publicised ('socialised'), bureaucratic performance criteria enable citizens to know when to demand action and/or complain to the bureaucrat's superior. This superior would also be evaluated, in part on how effectively she deals with such complaints. A cluster of these criteria, adjusted into a reasonable workload, constitute the bureaucrat's job description that is amendable to a relatively objective evaluation by a superior.

By contrast, most Indonesian evaluations are currently based on services performed for elites and patron-client networks, whether these fit rudimentary job descriptions or not. Promotion/demotion and salary increases/decreases should be based on such evaluations, subject to internal procedures safeguarding the fairness of the process. A premium should be offered for the bureaucratic ability to distinguish essential tasks - improved rural healthcare, for example - from merely desirable ones, such as creating more elite leisure facilities.

Real-world opportunities

External accountabilities

There is nothing particularly democratic about a bureaucracy being made to get its own house in order. Such a step would serve an authoritarian regime almost as well. Democratising and developmental potential emerges from meaningful public participation and accountability to citizens and institutions outside the politicians' and bureaucrats' sphere of influence.

Soeharto's New Order embodied the antithesis of such participation and accountability. Laws were rammed through with little opportunity for consultation or debate. Law was excluded from the process of resolving disputes between the Indonesian state and its citizens, who were sometimes treated like traitors (Lindsey 2000b and Lindsey 1999: 180). The Indonesian military punished the poor and powerless in an arbitrary fashion (hard state) but never punishes elites who have not fallen from grace (soft state). The military's lawless near-monopoly over the means of violence is now eroding quickly, but things otherwise remain much the same under Wahid and Megawati as under their predecessors, Habibie and Soeharto. This hamstrings the regime's democratising and developmental potential. If citizens, NGOs, and even multilateral and foreign donors do not know and understand a law, they cannot evaluate its implementation and its other social effects. And if members of parliament do not have the facts to understand the logic of a proposed law, they cannot communicate between government and the governed or monitor bureaucratic performance (Seidman 1998).

Publishing enforceable codes of conduct - guides to a civil service culture, to the reconciling of private interests and public duties in non-corrupt ways - and publishing regulations in a draft form are useful beginnings. The drafters of these regulations should be required to consider oral and written comments by citizens, not just from elite lawyers and special interest groups. They should also be required *either* to re-draft the regulations *or* to justify their refusal to do so in a written opinion.

Paul (1989: 67) describes the many rights related to an effective public participation, rights which should be strengthened under Indonesian law: rights to meet; to form self-managed organisations; to federate with domestic and international NGOs; to possess a corporate status; to sue (and be sued); to raise money; to have a private communications system; to gain access to the media; to receive information from government; and to demonstrate and electioneer non-violently.

These rather elaborate (and admittedly costly) procedures would encourage everyone to take the regulatory process seriously, but the consensus is that formal appeals mechanisms are also required to redress any demonstrably adverse effects of laws, regulations and their application. This is accountability, but by, to and for whom? Worldwide, the permutations and combinations are almost endless, but processes in countries like Indonesia tend to be driven by the demands of foreign investors or (what largely amounts to the same thing) of multilateral donors (National Economic Research Associates 1997). Like the rule of law of which they are an important part, accountability devices assume the official fallibility that few politicians and bureaucrats are willing to concede in practice (see Clark 1999: 34-35).

A few courageous Indonesian judges revived public hopes for state accountability through the courts (Millie 1999) as the Supreme Court sought public support through 'populist' decisions beginning in 1992. Soeharto, however, overturned these for 'thin' reasons, to the dismay of lawyers and the public (Bourchier 1999: 245-46). The judiciary is now currently and widely seen as part of the good governance problem rather than the solution. Lindsey (1999: 185) even views Indonesian judges simply as facilitators, standing at the other end of the food chain that runs from commerce. There is thus little chance in the medium term that most Indonesian judges will consistently spot and apply the relevant facts and rules. When excessive delays and corruption are factored in, it seems clear that an American or French-style, judge-centred, administrative accountability would frequently fail Indonesians. In any event, such accountability is extremely expensive and is thus dominated by elites or special interest groups keen to veto worthy, as well as abusive, policies.

A rudimentary Indonesian separation of powers is embodied in a broad judicial power to declare statutes and regulations ultra vires, as is a vague power of judicial review (of the constitutionality of laws, regulations, and bureaucratic actions) under the Supreme Court Draft Law (2000). This law has yet to pass the Parliament, let alone be implemented. Thoroughgoing constitutional reforms should be preconditions to implementing so much jurisdictional power (Bourchier 1999: 233).

A fair amount of ink has been spilt over the superiority of Indonesian Administrative Courts (within a bifurcated, civilian-style judiciary) created under a 1986 Law and discussed in Bourchier (1999: 239-42), Jayasuriya (1999: 17) and the sources they cite. But there is little current evidence of salutary Administrative Court effects, either in the media or on the ground. Hopes now rest on the Ombudsman Commission, created by a 2000 Law. It remains to be seen whether it will follow the Tanzanian model, tidying up "procedural irregularities, delays, inconsistencies, and other assorted problems," as a "poor man's lawyer" (Jacobini 1991: 208). This would be a noteworthy advance for Indonesian law as a whole, if effective access were no longer merely a function of the applicant's wealth and power. Still, judges and ombudsmen are always at the mercy of a prevailing political and legal culture which has been softened, but not fundamentally changed, by Indonesian *reformasi.* Denied legal ammunition by the broad discretion conferred under existing administrative laws and regulations (if they even chose to consult the latter) Indonesian judges and ombudsmen will have to guard their flanks against undemocratic veto groups.

In sum, the prospects for external accountability of the Indonesian state are not encouraging. The legislature could reorganise its Committee structure and practices and especially overhaul the ways its politics are conducted. Among other benefits this could result in a more informed scrutiny of draft laws and regulations and a regular oversight of bureaucratic performance. But such scrutiny and monitoring is hard work. It also makes enemies in the bureaucracy and among special interest groups, while delivering few benefits on election day.

If Indonesian civil society continues to develop, we can expect NGOs and an investigative media to play ever-more significant accountability roles. The unravelling of several instances of bureaucratic misbehaviour after Indonesia Corruption Watch publicised the Bank Bali Scandal is instructive (Tjiaw, et al 1999). Such self-empowered groups tend to humanise bureaucracy and reduce social distances in a democracy. But their sponsorship by well-intentioned foreign donors can have the paradoxical consequences of subverting NGO independence and zeal and of contributing to a 'corporatism' of special interest groups - so well organised that they can create a 'gridlock' by vetoing one policy after another. For example, trade associations of ostensibly small businesses may succeed in 'hijacking' the Indonesian Competition Law (No 5 of 1999) and the Commission it creates.

Especially sensitive is the Indonesian advocate's role in promoting administrative accountability. If lawyers do not look after accountability and citizens' rights from their informed, and sometimes technocratic, perspective, then who will? Certainly not the many politicians and bureaucrats who are preoccupied with pursuits they hope will remain unaccountable. Rather than an NGO, Indonesian lawyers may soon form a semi-governmental organisation under the Advocates Law (2000). Since the percentage of lawyers committed to accountability and citizen rights is small in most countries, we hope that a new Advocates' Association will give Indonesian administrative reformers support and 'cover'.

The 'prize' to be gained through an effective accountability and public participation is worth striving for from as many directions as possible: bureaucratic legitimacy. This is a scarce and valuable resource, since bureaucratic orders regarded as legitimate need fewer other 'political' resources to secure compliance: coercion, administrative capacity and so forth. Like legitimacy, these resources are scarce in all countries relative to need - and especially in Indonesia.

Five entry points for Indonesian reforms

The creativity, sustained political commitment and other 'resources' needed to implement Weberian-style administrative reforms are unlikely to materialise soon in Indonesia. The advantages of such an integrated approach to reform are clear, but progress can nonetheless be made through the partial, piecemeal and opportunistic reforms characteristic of recent Indonesian politics. However, Weber's precepts should be kept in mind whenever possible. Otherwise, and as in the many recent reforms 'sponsored' by multilateral donors, a political, economic and legal jumble will have the effect (if not always the purpose) of favouring domestic and foreign elites. A thoughtful plan is thus required so that the existing administrative jumble is not made worse and so that bits of reform are kept moving in predictable, politically-agreed directions. Limited political commitment and administrative capacities mean that only a few of the most serious problems can be tackled initially. But this 'patching' should be done in systematic ways that create leverage for additional reforms in the future.

For the *first* entry point, a moribund Ministry of Administrative Reform could be revived and progressively empowered to plan and implement the many tough decisions that are required and an Administrative Law Reform Commission could be established. However, Soegih Arto (1999) reminds us that Indonesia is over-organised in police-state fashion - and especially with regard to economic, business, legal, and religious councils. Rationalisation and an improved coordination and 'fit' are thus in order, perhaps as preconditions to other 'structural' reforms.

For a *second* entry point, Indonesia created many ostensibly-independent regulatory commissions from 1999 onwards, for competition, consumer protection, human rights, anti-corruption, the judiciary, advocates and so forth. This seems an almost desperate gamble on a device with a proven democratic potential in other countries: one that circumvents more intractably authoritarian bureaucracies. There are economies of scale and scope in devising general procedures for all Indonesian commissions at the same time. These procedures emphasise neutral evaluations of bureaucratic performances and public participation and accountability, consistent with the commissions' independence. If this is not done, some commissions will be regulated well, others poorly - and all differently - thereby creating a jumble of law and policy that would be unique even in Indonesia. Commissions that perform well under such generic procedures should be favoured by expanding their jurisdictions and budgets. Competition for these scarce bureaucratic resources should then put pressure on retrograde ministries and agencies to bring their procedures and processes into line with those of the successful commissions. Something like a bureaucracy-wide procedure and process law would then become possible.

Since Indonesia's economic crisis burgeoned in 1998, demands by the IMF and WB for the privatisation of state-owned enterprises and other publicly held assets have been much more muted than their demands for deregulation. In fact, and in defiance of their reigning ideology, the IMF and WB sponsored the largest nationalisation in Indonesian history: the Indonesian Bank Reconstruction Agency, or IBRA. The multilateral donors may have feared that extensive privatisations would topple unstable governments and that fire-sale prices attached to valuable state assets (companies whose stock was trading at prices commonly associated with *options* on such stock) would result in too large a windfall for domestic and foreign elites. But for the *third* entry point, the IMF and WB are now clearly gearing up their privatisation campaign. The Indonesian government must sell many state assets to avoid default on its multilateral loans and avoid inflation-provoking budget deficits. Much privatisation will thus happen anyway and IMF and WB inattention to the legal framework for this process - and the appalling failures of the more or less 'law-less' institutions the IMF and WB helped to create since 1998, such as IBRA and the Jakarta Initiative - offer opportunities for significant administrative law reforms.

The need for a carefully planned program of privatisation is clear. Asset sales must be spaced and timed to maximise the revenues government gleans from capital markets, which are 'thin' so far as Indonesia is concerned. IMF and WB mandates are unhelpful here. They are essentially contracts of adhesion which entitle government to a series of badly-needed loans if, for example, state assets X, Y and Z are sold off by month A. Such mandates create a windfall for low-bidding buyers when month A draws near since government (following IMF/WB templates) has so far been unable to organise itself to promote a speedy decision making; and sometimes because lawsuits provoke further delays. Such IMF/WB mandates do not add up to a coherent and consistent scheme for divesture. Rather, an imaginative and accountable process (to forestall corruption, etc.) should be created under administrative law to replace the donors' failed expedients. Such a law could then serve as a model for government putting other revenue and expenditure arrangements in order, especially through improved and elite-proofed tax collection efforts.

From a moral perspective, Indonesian state assets - state-owned enterprises (SOEs) and recently-nationalised private companies held by IBRA, and the like - are a sacred trust, a public patrimony. They represent a coerced postponement of citizens' private consumption (forced savings) to pay off the multilaterals' loans. These 'moral' assets should not be dissipated at speed, merely for the benefit of elites or to satisfy multilateral donors' whims. Enough 'success stories' are needed early in the process to help disarm Indonesia's critics. Reforms should create enough legal growth points to serve as foundations for more thorough reforms.

To the extent possible for a country now too indebted for the multilaterals to allow it to fail, Indonesia can often act on (if not declare) its independence from IMF/WB privatisation mandates. Slower and more careful balances could then be struck by Indonesians to increase economic efficiency while raising revenues to repay multilateral loans *and* to meet the pressing needs of the poor. In particular, a balance must be struck between breaking up state-owned enterprises or nationalised private companies prior to privatisation to forestall competition policy problems in the future on the hand; and, on the other, obtaining higher revenues now by recouping the premium (hopefully) gleaned by selling a state asset with its significant 'market power' intact.

For the foreseeable future, Indonesia's will remain a 'mixed' (private- and public-sector) economy (Booth 1995: 302). It is neither possible nor wise to privatise everything and quickly. Unaccountable but privatised enterprises have few advantages over unaccountable public enterprises. They are run by the same type of enterprise bureaucrats and in much the same ways. The solution is to promote accountability through the ongoing Companies Law revisions and, ideally, under a new Public Enterprise Law as well (Brietzke 2000). This would rationalise the chaos in another body of Indonesian administrative law that is plagued by gaps, vague grants of discretion and the absence of enforceable performance criteria.

Getting the public-sector economy under control would increase government's revenues through increased efficiency and perhaps forestall demands from economic nationalists and populists to 're-organise' the public sector (their code for merging state enterprises into inefficient and anti-competitive megaliths). A more vibrant public sector would also erode justifications for rapid and total privatisation. It would add value to state assets prior to the privatisation of some at a later date. Government would be able to regulate from within, through 'yardstick' state-owned enterprises, located in industries thought vital to (vague) 'national security' interests.[10] Some countries have also had success with a tactic rarely used in Indonesia: competitively-bid management contracts for SOEs.

Two other entry points, social welfare policies and decentralisation, also revolve around things that are going to happen anyway; and around increased efficiency achieved through 'downsizing'. This pursuit of efficiency should have 'spread effects' into other areas of administrative reform. The *fourth* entry point concerns 'safety net' policies that serve the poor and even include a few modest subsidies designed to build political support within the middle class. Such policies respond to forceful political demands and also help to reduce the uncertainties that hamper development and democratisation alike. An acute shortage of the resources needed to fund such worthy projects creates opportunities to build efficiency concerns and policy direction into administrative reforms: how can scarce resources be allocated to accomplish as much as possible of what really needs doing; and how can bureaucratic incentives and organisations be redirected toward this end? In other words, how can subsidies be kept out of elite hands? Citizens would presumably prefer such an approach over the conventional Indonesian solution of throwing more bureaucrats (but usually not more money) at a problem.

For the *fifth* entry point, some kind of decentralisation is now vital to maintaining a modicum of Indonesian national unity and human rights protections. The Economist (2000), citing Larry Siedentop, claims the only secure basis for self-government requires that the link between a 'moral liberty' and a 'moral equality' be maintained. In this regard, federalism combines the advantages of large and small states, with fewer of their disadvantages and less of a need for coercion – provided that a moral and cultural unity is maintained at the centre. Italians see European federalism as short-circuiting a hopeless political system. Spain views it as a means to modernisation and respectability. Smaller states see it as a means of restraining the larger ones. Some Indonesians see all of these hopes reflected in decentralisation.

10 Jayasuriya (1999: 13-14) states that German private law was premised on a separation of state and society and a depoliticised economy rather than a privatised one. North (1995: 25) comments, "Privatisation is not a panacea for solving poor economic performance". Polities shape solutions by defining and enforcing the rules of the game and through changed institutions and belief systems.

However, whether decentralisation becomes a policy of substance or of pretence remains to be seen. Asked why he robbed banks, the American Willy Sutton in the 1930s replied: "Because that's where they keep the money". 'Where they keep the money' will undoubtedly be the key to an Indonesian decentralisation and the Germans have a huge 'comparative advantage' in advising on the many, messy details that must be resolved concerning the finance of decentralisation. They are also a good model for the Indonesians: Germany successfully decentralised an authoritarian police-state, one akin to the *beamtenstaat* that the Dutch bequeathed Indonesians and that Soeharto strengthened into a 'command capitalism' (Lindsey 2000a).

Decentralisation offers opportunities for a significant downsizing of bureaucracies and of the administrative, police, and military resources they deploy from the centre, so as to match reduced bureaucratic tasks. Wahid's partial 'victories' over the now-downsized Ministry of Cooperatives and the disbanded Ministry of Public Information are instructive. But if decentralisation is not carefully managed, it will mean little more than jobs in the provinces for cashiered bureaucrats from the centre (provided their ethnic and religious affiliations pass muster). Instead of an enhanced regional, local, and individual autonomy, decentralisation can mean a deeper entrenchment of local elites, or local replications of the centre's control, corruption, and other inefficiencies. Yet optimists will hope for a comparative decentralisation: different experiments in different localities will serve to identify the most efficient and effective bureaucratic arrangements that are suited to local conditions.

Conclusions

Indonesian reform is for Indonesians to decide. My speculations are offered as food for thought from a sympathetic outsider. It seems clear that the quality of democratisation is deeply dependent on the quality of development, and vice versa. Both require something that most states do poorly and some not at all: resolving a long series of interrelated collective action problems.

From the quasi-dialectical perspective on the state adopted in this Chapter, Indonesian nationalists and most IMF/WB transnationalists consider only part of a very complex story: pragmatically, the state is the solution and the problem in roughly equal measures. Administrative law reforms should therefore seek to advance the state remedy and repress the state mischief, wherever this is imagined to be possible. At the same time, incumbent Indonesian elites are using their unreformed 'black' state to delay, deflect or negate these and other reforms (Lindsey 2000b and 1999: 187).

The outcome of this epic battle is still in doubt but the black forces often prevailed over the Wahid regime. To overcome such successes by predatory elites, Jayasuriya (this volume) stresses the need for durable domestic *coalitions* for reform. Creative support of these coalitions by foreign and multilateral donors is also required, rather than the donors imposing reform agendas from outside by force of loans. Jayasuriya's coalitions seem to require a democratically-feasible *consensus* over the nature, pace and sequence of reforms. They also require the political entrepreneurship (*leadership*) to implement this consensus and to foster a 'cultural system', where the reformist whole is an inspiration greater than the sum of its micro-reform parts.

This chapter is unabashedly state-centric. For survival if nothing else, the democratically elected Indonesian government must seize as much of the 'black' state as it can from incumbent elites and do so as quickly as possible. Such state fragments are poorly disciplined and increasingly lack anything like a monopoly over the legitimate means of coercion. Thus the only way to defeat the more experienced and less scrupulous predatory and multilateral elites is to strengthen the captured parts of the state through democratic and developmental reforms like those outlined here. The aim would be to turn the authoritarian into the morally authoritative, something that large numbers of Indonesians will want to support.

Arrived at in this fashion, the 'public interest' is indistinguishable from successful outcomes to group conflicts. Government winning this 'war', while minimising violence and staying on a democratic and reformist track whenever possible, is a usefully pragmatic definition of good governance in Indonesia. A great deal of politics is required.

Democratic politics are, sadly, still a scarce resource, especially under the short time horizons imposed by predatory elites. If reformers dissipate opportunities, or use them to become the kinds of elites the reformers were empowered to replace, *reformasi* will become just a slogan for 'defensive modernisation' that allows predatory elites to survive more or less intact. If the reformers move quickly and creatively, there is still time to recover lost ground.

References

Advocates Draft Law, (2000), (translated MS on file with author).

Bastone, Sue and Brietzke, Paul, (2000) 'Neither Quick Nor Easy: A Review of Duncan and Lindsey (eds), Indonesia after Soeharto', 2(1) *Australian Journal of Asian Law* 88-95.

Bates, Robert, (1995), 'Social Dilemmas and Rational Individuals: An Assessment of the New Institutionalism', in John Harriss, Janet Hunter and Colin M Lewis (eds), *The New Institutional Economics and Third World Development*, Routledge, London and New York, 27.

Booth, Anne, (1995), 'The State and the Economy in Nineteenth and Twentieth Century Indonesia', in John Harriss, Janet Hunter and Colin M Lewis (eds), *The New Institutional Economics and Third World Development*, Routledge, London and New York, 283.

Borosage, Robert, (2000), 'The IMF, Peddling Misery', *Washington Post*, 22 September, A25.

Bourchier, David, (1999), 'Magic Memos, Collusion and Judges With Attitude: Notes on the Politics of Law in Contemporary Indonesia', Kanishka Jayasuriya (ed), *Law, Capitalism and Power in Asia: The Role of Law and Legal Institutions*, Routledge, London, 233.

Brietzke, Paul, (2000), 'Companies Law in Indonesia', 2(2) *Australian Journal of Asian Law* 193-216.

Brietzke, Paul, (1999), 'Democratization and Administrative Law', 52 *Oklahoma Law Review* 1.

Brietzke, Paul, (1983), 'Administrative Law and Development', 26 *Harvard Law Journal* 645.

Brietzke, Paul and Timberg, Thomas, (1999), 'An Economic Reform Agenda for Indonesia?', 31 *Law and Policy in International Business* 1.

Burgess, John, (2000), 'Giving the World Bank an Outsider's View', *Washington Post*, 27 September, E01.

Clark, David, (1999), 'The Many Meanings of the Rule of Law', Kanishka Jayasuriya (ed), *Law, Capitalism and Power in Asia: The Role of Law and Legal Institutions*, Routledge, London, 28.

Duncan, Drew and Lindsey, Timothy (eds), (1999), *Indonesia After Soeharto: Reformasi and Reaction*, Centre for Asian-Pacific Initiatives, University of Victoria, BC.

The Economist, (2000), 'What Europe Needs', 19 August, 83.

Gillespie, John, (2001), 'The Political-Legal Culture of Anti-Corruption Reforms in Vietnam', in this volume.

Gillespie, John, (1999), 'Law and Development in "The Marketplace", Kanishka Jayasuriya (ed), *Law, Capitalism and Power in Asia: The Role of Law and Legal Institutions*, Routledge, London, 118.

Harriss, John, Hunter, Janet and Lewis, Colin M (eds), (1995), *The New Institutional Economics and Third World Development*, Routledge, London and New York.

Harriss, John, (1995), 'Introduction: Development and Significance of NIE', in John Harriss, Janet Hunter and Colin M Lewis (eds), *The New Institutional Economics and Third World Development*, Routledge, London and New York, 1.

Jacobini, HB, (1991), *An Introduction to Comparative Administrative Law*, Oceana, New York.

Jayasuriya, Kanishka (ed), (1999), *Law, Capitalism and Power in Asia: The Role of Law and Legal Institutions*, Routledge, London.

Jayasuriya, Kanishka, (1999), 'Introduction: A Framework for the Analysis of Legal Institutions in East Asia', Kanishka Jayasuriya (ed), *Law, Capitalism and Power in Asia: The Role of Law and Legal Institutions*, Routledge, London, 1.

Jones, Leroy, (1999), Policy and the Potential Impact of Privatization in Indonesia (PEG/USAID Consultants' Report, MS on file with author).

Khan, Mustaq, (1995), 'State Failure in Weak states: A Critique of New Institutionalist Explanations', in John Harriss, Janet Hunter and Colin M Lewis (eds), *The New Institutional Economics and Third World Development*, Routledge, London and New York, 71.

Klitgaard, Robert, (1991), *Tropical Gangsters*, Basic Books, New York.

Lev, Daniel, (1999), 'Comments on the Course of Law Reform in Modern Indonesia', in Drew Duncan and Timothy Lindsey (eds), *Indonesia after Soeharto: Reformasi and Reaction*, Centre for Asian-Pacific Initiatives, University of Victoria, BC, 88-106.

Lindsey, Timothy, (2000a), 'Black Letter, Black Market and Bad Faith: Corruption as Rational Response and the Failure of Reformasi Hukum' (MS on file with author.)

Lindsey, Timothy, (2000b), 'From Soepomo to Prabowo: Law, Violence and Corruption in the Preman state' (Draft No 2, MS on file with author).

Lindsey, Timothy, (1999), 'Corruption as a Rational Response in the Aspal state: The Failure of Reformasi Hukum', in Drew Duncan and Timothy Lindsey (eds), *Indonesia after Soeharto: Reformasi and Reaction*, Center for Asian-Pacific Initiatives, University of Victoria, BC, 176-188.

Mydans, Seth, (2000), 'Indonesian Commanders Losing Control of Troops', *New York Times*, 22 August: A3.

Myrdal, Gunnar, (1968), *Asian Drama*, vol 2, Penguin, Hammondsworth.

National Economic Research Associates, 1997, Governance and Regulatory Regimes for Private Sector Infrastructure Development, ADB REJA 5 785-REG (MS on file with author).

North, Douglas, (1995), 'The New Institutional Economics and Third World Development', in John Harriss, Janet Hunter and Colin M Lewis (eds), *The New Institutional Economics and Third World Development*, Routledge, London and New York, 17.

Paul, James, (1989), 'Rural Development, Human Rights and Constitutional Orders in Sub-Saharan African', 1989 *Third World Legal Studies* 57.

Pearlstein, Steven, 2000, 'The World Bank Re-Thinks Poverty', *Washington Post*, 13 September, E01.

Pierce, Richard, et al, (1985), *Administrative Law and Practice*, Foundation Press, Mineola, NY.

Seidman, Ann and Seidman, Robert, 1998, 'Project Proposal: The Nepal Legal Framework' (MS on file with author).

Seidman, Ann and Seidman, Robert and Abeysekere, Nalin, (2000), 'Legislative Drafting for Democratic Social Change: A Manual for Drafters' (Pre-publication MS on file with author).

Sims, Calvin, (2000), 'Scandals Sully Indonesian Leaders Reform Image', *New York Times*, 8 November, A10.

Smith, Rogers, (1988), 'Political Jurisprudence, the "New Institutionalism" and the Future of Public Law', 82 *American Political Science Review* 89.

Soegih Arto, (1999), 'Letter to the Editor', Jakarta Post, 23 December, 4.

Supreme Court Draft Law, 2000, (translated MS on file with author).

Thompson, Fred, (2000), 'Public Economics and Public Administration', <www.willamette.edu/~fthompso/ECON&PA.html>.

Tjiauw, Sen; Dedi Hermawan; and M Husni, (1999), 'Terbelit Gurita Bali Gate', FORUM Keadilan, no 33, 21 November 1999, 32-33

Chapter 8

Legends of the Fall: An Institutional Analysis of Indonesian Law Enforcement Agencies Combating Corruption[1]

Ibrahim Assegaf

Introduction

Historically, legal reform in Indonesia has usually been seen as a simple matter of legislative change, while the problems always lie in the implementation and enforcement - which are, in turn, usually explained away as a result of insufficient or flawed legislation. From a political perspective, legislative reform is appealing as it is relatively expeditious and tangible, thereby enabling the authorities to claim political achievement, but in its speed and convenience lie the roots of its problems - hasty drafting and substance held hostage to political convenience.[2] Unfortunately, this 'instrumentalist' approach has for three decades consistently left the agencies given the task of combating corruption inadequately equipped for their

1 An earlier version of this chapter was presented as a discussion paper at the Asia Law Centre, University of Melbourne, 26 April 2001. Rival G Ahmad, Bani Pamungkas and Ishaak Meeran, researchers at the Centre for Indonesian Law and Policy Studies (*Pusat Studi Hukum dan Kebijakan Indonesia*), have contributed to the research for this chapter.

2 Shortly after the fall of Soeharto's regime in 1998, the MPR (*Majelis Permusyawaratan Rakyat* or People's Consultative Assembly) as the highest state authority issued a decree instructing the government to pursue investigation of alleged corruptors (including former President Soeharto and his family) and to create a government free from corrupt practices by requiring public officials to disclose their wealth. Based on this decree, the DPR (*Dewan Perwakilan Rakyat* - People's Representative Council) and the government enacted Law No 28 of 1999 on Good Governance (*Pemerintahan yang Bersih dari Korupsi, Kolusi dan Nepotisme*) - the 'Good Governance Law'. Finally, the Parliament and the government enacted Law No 31 of 1999 on Eradication of Corruption (the 'Anti-corruption Law'), supposedly to remove inadequacies in the previous laws. Because very few alleged corruptors have been prosecuted (let alone sentenced) under the Anti-corruption Law, it widely regarded as inadequate and the government has commenced efforts to amend it.

task. Their consequent failures have left them alienated from the law reform process and have cemented popular cynicism about the anti-corruption movement, thus strengthening the hand of the corrupt.

As the previous paragraph suggests, the idea of an Indonesian anti-corruption agency is not new. Although it is now often forgotten, the Soeharto New Order government responded to public pressure to combat corruption by creating three ad hoc agencies to advise the government or coordinate the law enforcement agencies on corruption issues or cases. There were proposals for the government to establish a permanent agency responsible for prevention of corrupt practices since the early days of the New Order (Andi Hamzah 1984: 146), however, it was not until 1999 that an agency along these lines, the KPKPN (*Komisi Pemeriksa Kekayaan Pejabat Negara* or Commission to Investigate State Officials' Wealth), was established. Around the same time, popular opinion began to demand a more powerful body, one that could impose punitive measures (*Kompas* 1999). Responding to this new popular mandate, the amended Anti-Corruption Law of 1999 (Art 43) authorised the establishment of a Commission to Eradicate Corruption (the 'Commission'). Some critics have asked whether a new body is really necessary, as there are already many agencies tasked with combating corruption. Others argue that the Commission has little prospect of success, as similar agencies established in the past produced no tangible result.

In this chapter I will firstly identify the various existing traditional law enforcement agencies involved in combating corruption and examine why they have been unsuccessful. I will then argue that a separate and independent agency is, in fact, needed to combat corruption. Simply rejuvenating the existing agencies will not be enough. Past and existing anti-corruption agencies will be examined, together with reasons for their failure. Specific problems faced by the existing anti-corruption agencies will also be identified, as challenges for future agencies. Finally, selected issues surrounding the planned establishment of the Commission will be discussed.

The traditional agencies

Before discussing whether and why a separate agency is needed, it is important first to identify the traditional agencies with preventive, investigative or punitive powers in respect of corrupt practices.

Financial supervision

There are two main agencies responsible for financial supervision, the Supreme Audit Board (*Badan Pemeriksa Keuangan* or BPK) and the Finance and Development Audit Board (*Badan Pemeriksa Keuangan dan Pembangunan* or BPKP. BPK is an independent external auditor, separate from the government, whose function is to audit the implementation of the state budget and state-owned companies. It presents its reports and findings to the parliament (DPR) [3] (Art 23(5) of the Constitution and its elucidation; Law No 2 of 1973).

BPKP, on the other hand, is the government's internal auditor, set up under the aegis of ministries in charge of finance and development and subject to the supervision of state officials. BPKP conducts the same sort of audits as BPK, but reports to the President.[4] The exception to this is where it finds an indication of corruption, particularly through its special audit unit, in which case it must report its findings directly to the Attorney General.[5]

As mentioned, the KPKPN (*Komisi Pemeriksa Kekayaan Pejabat Negara* or Commission for Investigation of State Officials' Wealth) was set up in 1999. This Commission had primary responsibility for conducting, reviewing and verifying disclosure of state officials' wealth. KPKPN also has investigative powers, but these are limited to the purposes of verification.[6]

Bureaucratic officials supervision agencies and mechanisms

Almost all levels of the government have a branch responsible for the supervision and discipline of officials. In addition, superiors are responsible for directly supervising (*pengawasan melekat* or '*waskat*') and disciplining the conduct of their subordinates. It is worth noting that this mechanism in fact undermines stern measures against corruptors. If a superior finds subordinate taking actions classified as corruption, the former could impose sanctions, without recourse to the criminal law.[7]

Public complaint agencies

Since the 1970s, the government has operated a post office box (PO Box 5000) through relevant ministries under supervision of the Vice President. The public can lodge complaints regarding the services and conduct of public service agencies or government institutions and officials by sending them to this address.

In 2000, President Wahid established the KON (*Komisi Ombudsman Nasional* or National Ombudsman Commission), an independent commission

3 In this chapter, reference to parliament means either the DPR (*Dewan Perwakilan Rakyat* or People's Representative Council) or the MPR (*Majelis Permusyawaratan Rakyat* or People's Consultative Assembly), as the context indicates.

4 Presidential Decree No 31 of 1983.

5 Presidential Instruction No 15 of 1983, Art 19(1).

6 Good Governance Law, Arts 12, 17. If the KPKPN finds preliminary evidence that corrupt practices had occurred it refers them to relevant agencies (Art 18).

7 Art 29 Law No 8 of 1974 on Public Officials (as amended) and Arts 6-8 of Government Regulation No 30 of 1980. See also Pusat Studi dan Kebijakan (2001: 15).

designed to improve public participation in supervising the conduct and services of officials.[8]

Law enforcement agencies

The main law enforcement agencies are the police force, which is responsible for the investigation of corruption cases; and the *Kejaksaan Agung*, or Attorney General's Office (AGO), which is responsible for (further) investigation and prosecution of such cases. Both agencies have separate units to handle corruption cases. The police force has a Directorate for Crimes of Corruption, while the AGO has a specific Crime Division to investigate and prosecute corruption cases, respectively.

Why a separate agency?

Clearly, an institutional framework for combating corruption is already in place in Indonesia, covering almost all aspects or prevention, detection and punishment. Theoretically, these agencies should be adequate to combat corruption. However, they have manifestly failed and corruption, far from decreasing, is becoming rampant. Why have these traditional law agencies been unsuccessful? The reasons are detailed below, together with an argument for establishing a single, new anti-corruption agency to attempt what they have failed to achieve.

Corruption in existing agencies

Corruption in Indonesia is so systemic that it has plagued all levels and elements of the judiciary: the police force as primary investigator, the AGO as prosecutor; the courts (International Commission of Jurists 1999)[9] and even lawyers (Pusat Studi dan Kebijakan 2001: 131). It is obviously impossible to eliminate corruption if the very law enforcement agencies with responsibility for handling corruption cases have become centres of corruption.[10]

8 Presidential Decree No 44 of 2000 concerning the National Ombudsman Commission. It is interesting to note that within two months as of its inception, KON received a total of 200 complaints, the majority of which involved the judicial institutions (Anton Sujata nd: 4). Unfortunately, few of the clarifications (7 out of 191) sought by KON received responses from the relevant agencies (Elvy Yusanti 2000).

9 Corrupt practices in Indonesian courts are rated among the highest in several developing countries: see Daniel Kauffmann in *Governance and Corruption, New Empirical Frontiers for Program Design* quoted in Lubis (1998).

10 Corrupt practices also take place in various supervisory agencies, which are responsible for the prevention of corruption, namely the audit agencies as well as the various internal control agencies. Further, some reports suggest that growth of corruption prevention agencies parallels the growth of corruption.

This can be best seen as a three-level food chain. At the first level, the alleged corruptors feed the police and the prosecutor (or, alternatively, the police and prosecutors devour the alleged corruptors) in the investigation process during which the police or the prosecutor are required to decide whether corruption has actually occurred and commence further investigation (*penyidikan*).[11] If the case advances to prosecution and trial in the court, the second stage, prosecutor will play a significant role in deciding the charge (*dakwaan*), which will be filed against the alleged corruptors.[12] Eventually, the process reaches the courts, at the top of the food chain. The judges decide whether the alleged corruptors are guilty or innocent and, if guilty, what the proper sentence should be. Lawyers representing the alleged corruptor act as a corruption brokers throughout the process.

Incompetence of traditional agencies

Since the 1970s, the poor performance of the traditional law enforcement agencies - in terms both of political will and competence - has been seen as the prime cause of the failure of anti-corruption measures (Badan Pemeriksa Keuangan dan Pembangunan 1999: 321-323; Andi Hamzah 1984: 53). From 1977 to 1981, the AGO investigated a total of 1,170 alleged corruption cases and managed to prepare 76 per cent (1,011 cases) of those cases for prosecution. The AGO won 86 per cent of those prosecutions (875 cases). During the same period, however, the Attorney General managed to recover only 9 per cent of the losses to the state arising from the same cases (Andi Hamzah 1984: 13-16).

Despite the change in political climate and mounting public pressure to eradicate corruption, these levels of poor performance have not only continued but have, in fact, worsened. The Attorney General's annual report to parliament of 28 March 2000 revealed a dismal performance by the AGO in investigating and prosecuting corruption cases from 1999 to 2000: less than 20 per cent of cases were resolved. While the central AGO had completed investigations of approximately 30 per cent cases, a number of regional offices competed no investigations at all. The recovery rate of the states' assets lost through corruption was even worse: less than 0.05 per cent

11 Indonesian criminal law recognises a two-tier investigation process, *penyelidikan* and *penyidikan*. In the former, the police investigate the reports in order determined whether a crime has indeed occurred. If so, then the process continues to the second stage (*penyidikan*), where the investigators (the police or the prosecutors) collect the related evidence to support the allegation for purposes of prosecution, including legal actions such as searches, detention, seizure and prohibiting suspects from leaving the country.

12 If the prosecutor is not confident that he had been able to present sufficient evidence and convince the court, he can file for *nolle prosequi* or 'no indictment' (*dakwaan bebas*). The court must then free the prosecuted.

or 1.9 million rupiah was recovered out of an estimated 3 trillion rupiah lost by the state.[13]

The police force and the courts also performed very poorly. According to a report published by its own Directorate of Investigation, police completed investigations of only 32 per cent of reports filed on corruption during 1996–2001.[14] The courts likewise made a large number of controversial judgments in corruption cases, either releasing alleged corruptors or handing down lenient judgments.[15]

Lack of leadership: A need for core unit

Although there are many agencies involved in fighting corruption, no one agency is actually in charge or performing a coordination role. On the contrary, there is distrust amongst the different agencies; and even sharp disagreements over their various jurisdictions. Agencies in charge of supervising the conduct of government officials are reluctant to expose irregularities to investigators for fear of turning the irregularities into a commodity (Badan Pemeriksa Keuangan dan Pembangunan 1999: 131). The police and the AGO have, for example, long been engaged in on-going disagreements over who has the authority to investigate (*menyidik*) corruption cases, each claiming exclusive the legal authority to do so (Badan Pemeriksa Keuangan dan Pembangunan 1999: 387-388).

It is apparent that there is an urgent need for a core unit to lead and coordinate all efforts against corruption. Although the role of this unit could, in theory, be fulfilled by existing agencies, in practice it would be very difficult given the history of disagreements between the agencies and their lack of effective power and authority - to say nothing of inadequate human resources. A single, powerful anti-corruption agency could, therefore – in principle at least – be better placed to play a role as core unit than existing agencies.

The question thus arises: should Indonesia prioritise the establishment of the Commission before reform of the existing agencies? A recent study

13 This figure might be grossly understated. The Attorney General is now investigating alleged manipulation of bank liquidity credits provided by the central bank to ailing banks. The damages from these manipulations amount to approximately 60 billion rupiah were categorised not as losses caused by corruption but rather as 'civil case damages'. This is due to the system of classification of cases within the AGO, in which the liquidity credits cases are processed by the state civil suits division (JAMDatun) and not the corruption division (JAMPidsus).

14 Data obtained personally from *Direktorat Tindak Pidana Khusus, Data Tindak Pidana Korupsi yang Ditangani* 1996–2001 (not a publication).

15 For example, the Bank Bali accused (*terdakwa*) were all freed by the court. This could also be the fault of the prosecutors who in some cases did not ask for any indictment, opting not to proceed (*dakwaan bebas*). There are, nonetheless, some 'success stories', such as the sentencing of Bob Hassan, an influential crony of Soeharto, even if his sentence is widely considered lenient.

suggests that in a country where corruption is so endemic and systemic and governance quality is still weak, an anti-corruption commission is not relevant (Bhargava and Bolongaita 2001: 14). The study further suggests that the agency might itself become a centre of corruption. The study contends that priorities should be directed towards creating a government based on 'rule of law' and strengthening public participation in, and accountability of, government institutions rather than creating yet another weak and tokenistic Commission (Bhargava and Bolongaita 2001: 14).

While enhancing public participation and accountability should indeed be prioritised, it is difficult to imagine enhancing the rule of law in Indonesia as a 'stand alone' issue. Rule of law implies proper enforcement of the law but, in Indonesia, law enforcement - perhaps more than any other aspect of law - has been severely plagued with corruption. How can one expect proper law enforcement (particularly in combating corruption) if the law enforcement agencies themselves engage in corrupt practices and have, in fact, institutionalised corruption within their structures and work culture?

Overhauling the existing agencies is a daunting task. Such an exercise would require nothing less than reforming the entire civil service, including the recruitment and retention of credible and professional individuals; the creation of a merit-based promotion system; and the restructuring of salaries. This would be a long-term and costly process. In the interim, however, the problems continue. The need to institute the rule of law is pressing and this makes it necessary to revert to short-term measures, while not ignoring the long-term goals.

A number of countries have opted for short-term measures, usually by establishing anti-corruption agencies to combat corruption, particularly with regards to law enforcement agencies. This stems from the realisation that many corrupt individuals have links to the existing political establishment and would therefore be safeguarded if they were prosecuted by the existing agencies. Therefore, many governments have chosen to use an organisation with minimal links to the existing law enforcement institutions. Hong Kong is an excellent model for Indonesia. Corruption was rampant in the 1960s and 1970s, as a result of a police force which had become a centre for corruption. The government created the Independent Commission Against Corruption (ICAC) and gave it authority to investigate corruption, an area that had previously fallen under the jurisdiction of the police. ICAC successfully led Hong Kong in combating corruption.

Why previous anti-corruption agencies have failed

Contrary to general public belief, there have already been several agencies created to combat corruption or at least to intensify measures in the fight against corruption.

Corruption Eradication Teams (Tim Pemberantas Korupsi)

Two such teams were established under the same name, the first in 1967 and the second in 1982. The 1967 team was authorised to coordinate investigations of alleged corruptors.[16] Although the members were mostly *ex-officio* law enforcement agencies (including the military), the team did include prominent figures from the media in its initial stage, so as to establish the team's credentials as a transparent and independent agency. However, from its foundation to the end of its operations in 1982, the findings of this team were never made public.

In 1982, a team under the same name and with the same functions was established. Its members included all law enforcement agencies: the police; the Attorney General (including the Chairman of *Operasi Tertib* - see below); the Chief of the Supreme Court; and a number of ministers involved in law enforcement and supervision of state employees. However, the team lacked an implementing regulation and none was ever issued.

Commission of Four (Komisi Empat)

Responding to public pressure in the 1960s and 1970s to intensify attempts to combat corruption, the Commission of Four was established and chaired by the former Vice President, Mohammad Hatta, then adviser to the President.[17] The main objectives of this Commission were to conduct reviews and assessments of policies to combat corruption and to advise the government on necessary policy changes (Andi Hamzah 1984: 53).

Shortly after being appointed, the Commission of Four continued the probes initiated by the BPK into Pertamina (the state-owned oil and gas company); Telkom (the state-owned telecommunication company); and Bulog (*Badan Urusan Logistik*, the National Logistics Agency). The Commission submitted its report to the government, detailing its findings and recommendations on a variety of issues, including Pertamina, Bulog, illegal logging and general good governance principles (Badan Pemeriksa Keuangan dan Pembangunan 1999: 333). However, the government never disclosed the Commission's reports or followed up its recommendations. After the Commission had been operating for a mere six months, the government dissolved it.[18]

Operasi Tertib (Opstib)

Opstib was actually a multi-faceted operation designed to crack down on anti-government dissent. However, *Opstib* also inspected government agencies in an attempt to identify irregularities statistically. This operation was perhaps the most successful anti-corruption agency, as it processed

16 Presidential Decree No 228 of 1967, 2 December 1967.

17 Presidential Decree No 12 of 1970; and Presidential Decree No 13 of 1967, 31 January 1970.

18 Presidential Decree No 50, 16 July 1970.

1,127 cases involving 8,026 persons within a period of about four years (see table). However, these cases involved mostly petty corruption cases by lower ranking officials, against whom only administrative sanctions were issued. Only 34 major corruption cases were submitted to the Attorney General (Andi Hamzah 1984: 15).

The Joint Investigating Team to Eradicate Criminal Acts of Corruption (Tim Gabungan Pemberantas Tindak Pidana Korupsi)

Under the recently amended Anti-corruption Law, the *Tim Gabungan Pemberantas Tindakan Korupsi* (TGPTK or Joint Investigating Team, also known as JIT) functions as a coordinator for the investigation and prosecution of corruption cases which are difficult to prove.[19] The Attorney General created JIT and it reports to him.[20] It is composed of members of the police force, prosecutors, government officials and members of the community.[21] JIT has limited authority. Investigations and prosecutions are carried out by members or task forces of the police force and the AGO.[22] It is intended as an 'embryo' of the Commission and was intended to dissolve once the Commission is operational. During the period of its operation,[23] JIT was able to complete investigations leading to prosecution of 11.4 per cent of the total reports submitted to TGPK.[24]

JIT faced both external and internal obstacles. Internally, few members could dedicate sufficient time and energy to JIT, as they were active in their own positions and professions (Djajadi 2001, Attachment: 4). Likewise, as JIT relied heavily on the AGO, its discretion was restricted, and there were disagreements between JIT and the Attorney General. The latter reportedly refused to permit JIT to investigate corruption of banking liquidity credits, an issue which clearly fell within the criteria of cases to be handled by JIT.[25] Externally, JIT faced strong resistance from the courts, principally in the form of a refusal to recognise JIT's investigative powers (considered below). Believing that the corrupt judiciary is the main obstacle to eliminating corruption, JIT had intentionally focused on investigating corrupt practices

19 Art 27 amended Anti-corruption Law; and Art 11(1) of Government Regulation No 19 of 2000.

20 Art 4 of Government Regulation No 19 of 2000.

21 Art 5 of Government Regulation No 19 of 2000.

22 Art 11 (2)-(5) of Government Regulation No 19 of 2000.

23 JIT commenced its operation June 2000 and was (in theory) dissolved on 8 July 2000.

24 The remaining 88.6% had insufficient evidence and therefore could not be investigated further: Djajadi (2001, Attachment: 3).

25 Personal communication, April 2001. Most of these disagreements evolved around alleged corruption in bank liquidity credits. The Attorney General refused to hand over these cases to JIT, although banking crimes are usually considered 'difficult to investigate and prosecute' and thus within the jurisdiction of the JIT: See Art 27 and its elucidation, amended Anti-corruption Law.

involving judges and court staff, but it proved almost impossible to obtain access to Supreme Court Justices and staff - even though more than half of the cases handled by JIT in fact involved justices or staff. Likewise, in the first months of its operation JIT did not receive funding for facilities or operational expenses – not even salaries for its members (Tim Gabungan Pemberantas Tindakan Korupsi et al 2001).[26]

It is worth now summarising why previous agencies have failed. First and foremost, there has been no real political will from the government to ensure these agencies function properly. Successive governments have showed no real desire to combat corruption, but appear to have created agencies as temporary measures to stem public anger. This is evident from the fact that the findings and recommendations of these agencies, if any, were never properly followed up.

Secondly, the agencies were provided with minimal authority. They were generally:

(i) established to coordinate the activities of existing law enforcement agencies. This may have stemmed from the government's perception that the traditional agencies have failed due to a lack of coordination or communication. This perception is correct but is not the main reason for their (collective) failure;
(ii) designed to assist traditional agencies in advising on or formulating anti-corruption policies or strategies; and/or
(iii) at the most, designed to assist traditional agencies in investigating corruption cases.

In each scenario, implementation – once again – remains in the control of the traditional agencies themselves, despite the fact that they were often the targets of investigations.

Thirdly, corruption, even within law enforcement agencies, has become so systemic that it will be extremely difficult to eradicate, unless a clean judicial process (understood in the broadest sense of the word, to include investigation, prosecution and adjudication) can be created.

Current context: Challenges for the future agency

If the Commission is established, it will not be operating in a vacuum. The current situation clearly dictates certain pre-conditions for its success.

Lack of political will and support

In the past, the government's lack of political will was the main cause of the failure to eliminate corruption. This continues to the present, with governments still consistently failing to take stern action against major corruptors.

26 JIT did, eventually receive more than adequate funding from the government. The salaries of its members were, in the end, much higher than any other state officials. The same applied for its infrastructure and operational funding.

Not only do Indonesian governments lack the political will to take punitive measures in combating corruption but they also fail to provide political support for existing anti-corruption agencies.

This is evident in almost all state institutions concerned with law and was clearly demonstrated by the recent decision on judicial review issued by Supreme Court (considered below), which effectively nullified the regulation on which the JIT operates and thus stripped it of its authority to investigate and prosecute. The government - be it the President's office, the Minister of Justice and Human Rights or the Attorney General - issued no political statement whatsoever, much less expressed support for JIT.[27]

Full government support is absolutely critical for the proper functioning of any anti-corruption agency. In particular, the Commission needs this support to perform its supervisory and coordinative roles *vis a vis* the traditional agencies, without which full cooperation might not be forthcoming.

Improper planning and budget

During Abdurrahman Wahid's presidency, several new institutions were established to support existing agencies, principally the National Ombudsman Commission and National Law Commission. These institutions were impromptu products of the President, apparently aimed at increasing his profile on legal reform. However, due to improper planning and budgeting, they were not provided with adequate financial support and relied on funding from international donors. This was also the case with a number of other institutions, such as the Commission for Investigation of State Officials' Wealth (KPKPN), which were given a mandate through legislation but lacked even the most basic government support - even payment of salaries or operational budget were delayed for more than a year.[28]

The Commission similarly suffered from improper planning. Although the amended Anti-Corruption Law mandated the establishment of the Commission in mid-2001, *Propenas* (*Program Pembangunan Nasional* or National Development Program)[29] and the implementation of the 2001 *Repeta* (*Rencana Pembangunan Tahunan* or Annual Development Plan), which is part of the 2001 state budget (*Anggaran Pendapatan dan Belanja Negara*),

27 According to members of the Team, who met senior government officials seeking political support, the officials blamed other agencies that drafted the Law for creating an inadequate legislative scheme and, in fact, refused to commit any support at all. Personal communication April 2001.

28 Law No 28 of 1999 concerning Clean Government Free from Corruption, Collusion and Nepotism, required the KPKPN to be operational by May 2000. However, as members' appointments were delayed, the KPKPN operational budget was also delayed until late 2000.

29 Law No 2 of 2000 concerning National Development Plan.

failed to include allowance for its establishment.[30] This omission will prejudice the establishment and operation of the Commission, because:

(i) *Propenas* and *Repeta* determine the legislative agenda for enactment by 2004; and

(ii) the *Repeta*, as part of the state budget, lists the various programs and their parameters, including budgetary items, for all state or government agencies. It is unclear whether there can be retrospective modifications to these plans and budgets.

Judicial resistance: The Three Judges case

In the past, the courts' poor attitude towards the investigation and prosecution of corruption cases was overshadowed by the impotence of traditional law enforcement agencies. However, in recent years, the courts' resistance to investigating and prosecuting alleged corruptors - particularly those within the court apparatus - has become more apparent as recent reforms begin to force cases to hearing. The clearest example of this is JIT's investigation into two active and one former Supreme Court justices and its aftermath.

Once the judges were aware that they were under investigation, their legal counsel brought a *pra peradilan* (pre-trial hearing) application under Art 77 of the Code of Criminal Procedure before the District Court, claiming that:

(i) the alleged corrupt acts took place before the new Anti-Corruption Law establishing the JIT came into force and, therefore that JIT has no authority to investigate; and

(ii) JIT has no power to investigate in any case, as the existence of JIT itself contravenes the Code of Criminal Procedure.

The District Court accepted these arguments and, in a judgment typically devoid of reasoning, simply declared that JIT had no authority to investigate the case. This decision triggered a public debate, as under the Code of Criminal Procedure, *pra peradilan* jurisdiction is limited to illegal seizure or detention, while in this case JIT had only investigated and had not taken any other action (and certainly not seizure or detention) in respect of the suspect judges.

Also, JIT, as an institution, has no investigative powers or authority. These functions were, in fact, performed by its members, who were police and prosecutors, in their own right, rendering the second limb of the judges' argument irrelevant.[31] Incredibly, there was no appeal. It is hard to understand why that the Attorney General (as the only party that can do so) did not appeal this decision by way of cassation 'in the interests of law' pursuant to Art 259 of the Code of Criminal Procedure but simply assigned a separate AGO's unit for 'further investigation' of the matter. Whatever the

30 Law No 34 of 2000 concerning State Budget.

31 Art 11 of Government Regulation No 19 of 2000.

reason for this decision, however – and allegations have made of undue influence from the judiciary – the result was that the Court's findings stood.

Counsel for the judges then submitted a petition for judicial review (that is, review of the validity of a (non-statute) regulation pursuant to Law No 14/1970) to the Supreme Court. They sought a declaration that Government Regulation No 19 of 2000 – which forms the basis of JIT's operations – was void. The Supreme Court again accepted the judges' application and held the regulation to be invalid, ordering the government to revoke it within 90 days, failing which it would automatically be deemed revoked by law.[32] In its published reasons, the court found that the content of Government Regulation No 19 of 2000 expands the powers of the JIT as set out in the Anti-corruption Law; and that this expansion conflicts with Code of Criminal Procedure. Interestingly, last year the Supreme Court took an opposite position in a similar case, refusing an application for judicial review petition in respect of the Government Regulation on the Indonesian Banking Restructuring Agency. In that case, the Court held that although the regulation contradicts the Banking Law, the banking crisis justified the issue of the regulation. The Court even went so far as to state that the Regulation should be enacted in statutory form.[33]

The presiding panel of judges was chaired by Justice Paulus E. Lotulung,[34] who appeared to have a significant conflict of interest when hearing the case. He had previously been assigned by the Association of Indonesian Judges (*Ikatan Hakim Indonesia* or *Ikahi*) to 'accompany' the judges being investigated and, if necessary, to take any action as a legal adviser (*penasehat hukum*).[35] The decision for judicial review, like the earlier *pra peradilan* decision, was not appealed. JIT nonetheless met informally with Supreme Court justices and requested that the decision, particularly the issue of Lotulung's conflict of interest, be reconsidered. They were unsuccessful.

The significance of this case goes far beyond JIT, as it provides clear evidence for the courts' continuing strong resistance to anti-corruption

32 See <http://www.hukumonline.com/hukumonlinespesial_det.asp?id=2404> for the complete text of the decision.

33 See Supreme Court Decision of 1 December 1999. It is worth noting that JIT argued this point at a later meeting with the Supreme Court to seek reconsideration of the decision. Justice Lotulung, who was present to 'defend' his decision, did not respond to the argument (confidential personal communication, April 2001).

34 Lotulung is perhaps the most knowledgeable judge in the Supreme Court and had previously been revered by pro-reformers and even seen as the most suitable candidate for the Chairman of the Supreme Court prior to Justice Bagir Manan's appointment.

35 This is evidenced by a letter issued by Ikahi dated 18 August 2000, which also assigned Justice Toton Suprapto, a Deputy Chairman of the Supreme Court and now Chairman of the Ikahi, as an advisor to the three suspect judges. See <http://www.hukumonline.com/ hukumonlinespesial_det.asp?id=2340> for complete text of the letter.

initiatives. The case therefore suggest that the Courts well might jeopardise the role of a future anti-corruption agency. This resistance prompted the JIT to appeal to President Wahid to create a new specialist Corruption Court to stand independent of the general court system. However, Wahid failed to take any clear position on the proposal and its fate remains unclear.[36] Without such an institution or an unlikely revolution in judicial attitudes, the prospects for the Commission must remain poor at best

The Corruption Eradication Commission (*Komisi Pemberantasan Korupsi*)

Corruption is seen as an extraordinary crime and therefore calls for extraordinary measures. This attitude justifies the broad power and authority of the Commission, which in some respects deviates from general principles of the Indonesian Criminal Code and the Code of Criminal Procedure. This section will not describe all aspects of the Commission, but rather highlight and discuss some pertinent issues arising from the Draft Law on the Commission (the Bill), which the government has now submitted to the DPR for deliberation.[37]

Powers and authorities

Under the amended Anti-corruption Law,[38] the Commission has the power and authority to supervise and coordinate corruption cases, including their investigation and prosecution.[39] The present Bill envisages that the Commission can:

(i) receive reports and conduct investigation and prosecution independent of traditional agencies; and
(ii) receive reports and instruct investigation and/or prosecution, as is already done by the traditional agencies; or
(iii) take-over corruption cases handled by other agencies, if these agencies are unable or unwilling to handle those cases properly.

The Bill provides criteria for the grounds on which such a take-over can occur (including unwillingness or lack of seriousness on the part of the

36 The earlier version of the draft law on the Commission required the establishment of an Anti-Corruption Court. The relevant provisions were later removed, to be inserted in a separate draft. Following this event, JIT, with several NGOs, organised a seminar and prepared a draft for the establishment of an independent and separate court to handle corruption cases (Tim Gabungan Pemberantas Tindakan Korupsi et al 2001).

37 The amended Anti-corruption law states that the Commission should be established by August 2001. A faction within the Parliament has prepared and submitted a competing draft. It is not yet clear which one will be the working draft.

38 Law No 31 of 1999 concerning Eradication of Corruption Crimes.

39 Art 43 of the Anti-corruption Law.

police force or AGO in pursuing the case) and allows the procedure to be further regulated by a decree of the Chairman of the Commission.[40] There are strong criticisms of these provisions and these are now summarised.

First, the Commission might be blamed for the failures of traditional law enforcement agencies because of its monitoring and supervision roles (De Speville 2001).

Secondly, many critics, including De Speville (2001: 69) take the view that because the take-over mechanism under the Bill is weak and unclear, it will only lead to endless bickering with other traditional agencies, ultimately paralysing the Commission.[41] The Draft Law attempts to prevent the Commission from being swamped by the vast number of corruption cases, many of which are now handled by traditional agencies. In 2000, AGOs throughout Indonesia had to deal with approximately 595 corruption cases.[42] The Commission will quickly collapse if it is forced to deal with all these cases. Therefore, the Commission should be able to focus only on major cases that it deems important. Nevertheless, the current take-over mechanism as it stands does not make clear which agency will have the final say in deciding whether the case should be taken over by the Commission. Nor does it provide a settlement mechanism if there is any disagreement between the Commission and the other agencies. In addition, it is still unclear whether the Commission can take-over an ongoing prosecution. This is obviously critical if institutional cover-ups are to be prevented.

Thirdly, the Commission's investigation *and* prosecution roles contravene the traditional concept of separation between investigative and prosecutorial functions into separate agencies (De Speville 2001). Some critics suggest that the Commission should only handle investigations and leave the prosecutions to the AGO, as occurs in Hong Kong's ICAC. However, it should be noted that the AGO itself is corrupt and incompetent, unlike in Hong Kong, where the ICAC was meant to circumvent only the police force. Therefore, unless a clean and able prosecution can be ensured, proper investigation will achieve little. This line of argument eventually leads to the third criticism: the question of how the Commission can, in any case, win prosecutions before corrupt and resistant courts.

40 Arts 8 and 9.

41 If such provisions are to stay, De Speville contends that it would be difficult to argue that the police or the Attorney General is either unwilling or lacking seriousness. Therefore, he suggests that the Commission should have an absolute discretion and authority to take over the case if it deems necessary. Lobby Loqman has further suggested that the Commission take over the entirety of investigation and prosecution of all corruption cases, so that the police and the AGO no longer have the authority to do so.

42 See Attorney General's Report. This figure includes cases filed during 2000 and unfinished 1999 cases.

The Commission as core unit and entry point

The Commission is envisaged as an entry point, the core unit, in efforts to eradicate corruption. This is significant, as past failures were often caused by absence of leadership and coordination amongst traditional agencies, be it financial supervision or supervision of state officials and law enforcement agencies. Under Arts 6 and 7 of the Bill, the Commission has the power of coordination and supervision. The Commission can provide guidance to or cooperate with other relevant agencies, review the performance of those agencies and, if necessary, take independent action. It will be interesting to observe how the other agencies will cooperate with the Commission, given their history of institutional arrogance. In any event, strong political support from the government is a pre-requisite to implement this provision and, as mentioned above, this has been in short supply.

Structure, organisation

Article 3 of the Bill envisages the Commission as a state entity, independent and separate from the power structures of the executive, legislative and judiciary. This stems from perception that one of the reasons for the failure of traditional agencies is that they are inferior to the formal branches of government and their subsidiary organs, thereby making the agencies prone to intervention.

Structurally, the Commission will be under the leadership of a three-member Board. One of the Board Members will serve as Chairman.[43] The President will nominate candidates for members of this Board to the Parliament, which will then choose three, one of whom will be appointed as Chairman. The President will then officially appoint the Board members. Once constituted, the Board will appoint all other members of the Commission.[44] A Commission member can be removed from office only if he/she violates stipulated prohibitions[45] or if he/she commits crimes, including corrupt practices.[46] These provisions are intended to limit partisan and interest-based politics and ensure the efficiency of the Commission. Previous commissions have frequently become targets of partisan and interest based politics by the Parliament and the President, as, for example, in the case of the KPKPN (as mentioned above) or have become large and inefficient organisations. The aim here is to keep the Commission relatively small and efficient.

Article 14 of the Bill stipulates that the Commission will have an office in Jakarta with jurisdiction over the entire Indonesian archipelago. It says -

43 Arts 16(1) and18(1).

44 Art 21. This process must be done openly and transparently (Art 22).

45 Namely, meeting suspects or other related parties other than in compliance with the law, handling cases in which he/she has conflict of interest, or serving as an officer or in another profession: Arts 27 and 28.

46 Arts 23, 24(1) and 27. Art 24(2) states that vacant positions will be filled through the same procedure as an appointment.

nothing about regional offices, although earlier versions required the establishment of regional offices in all provinces. The removal of this requirement was due to concerns that, if the Commission were too widely spread and cumbersome, conflicts over areas of jurisdiction would be inevitable. Instead, it is now intended that investigations and prosecutions of regional cases will be done by the Commission in cooperation with local authorities.

Article 18 of the Bill stipulates that the Commission has three departments: prevention, enforcement and intelligence. The enforcement department is further divided into units of investigation (*penyelidikan dan penyidikan*) and prosecution.

Finance and budget

Financing the Commission is an important issue because, without a realistic budget, it may end up like the other traditional agencies, that is, financially constrained and forced to resort to corrupt measures itself. In principle, like any other state/governmental agency, the Commission will be financed through the state budget. In addition, the Commission can keep up to 10% of recovered assets. Many critics have attacked this provision, claiming that it could lead to the Commission only handling 'fat' cases. It is also important to note that the Bill does not indicate whether retention of assets requires approval. It is therefore likely this 'contingency' provision will cause problems in practice.

Public accountability

The Commission is accountable to the public through performance appraisals and financial audits. It must publish quarterly reports and disclose information to the public when required. The Commission must also file periodical reports to the Parliament and the President (Art 15). Although public accountability is ideal, this must be done in such a way that it does not contravene the confidentiality of investigations or prosecutions. This issue is not addressed at all and De Speville (2001) considers that this can diminish the Commission's integrity, stressing that the performance audit will automatically require disclosure of investigated files.

Article 19 of the Bill stipulates that the Board's supporting units will include internal control and public complaints units. It is unfortunate that these are simply required without elaboration. The detail is left to the Board's discretion, which is to say the determination of the structure, duties and powers of the watchdog is left to the watched! This is an issue that must reconsidered because it clearly increases the risk of the Commission becoming a centre of corruption.

Table 8.1
Indonesian Anti-Corruption Agencies

Institutions	Members	Result
Corruption Eradication Team, (1967 – 1982), under the Attorney General's control	Chairman: Attorney General Soegih Arto Advisers: Minister of Justice, Army and Police Chief of Staff. Members: Sutopo Juwono, Sudomo, Saleh Basarah, Soebekti, Deputy Attorney Generals P. Abdurrasjid and Kusnun.	Not available.
Commission of Four (January – July 1970)	Adviser: Mohamad Hatta (former Vice President) Chairman: Wilopo Members: Anwar Tjokroaminoto, Herman Johannes, JJ Kasimo Secretary: Sutopo Juwono.	In the six months of its operation, it found irregularities in and recommended counter-corruption measures to the government in relation to Pertamina, *Bulog, Telkom* and several logging companies. None of these findings or recommendations were followed up by the government.
Anti-Corruption Committee (June – August 1970)	Members included student activists, namely Akbar Tandjung, M. Setiawan, T. Mutis, J. Kendang, Imam Waluyo, Tutu Surowijono, Agus J. Batuta, M. Surachman, Alwi Nurdin, Lucas Luntungan, A. Nababan, Sjahrir, Amir Karamoy, E. Pesik, Vitue, Mangadang Napitupulu and Chaidir Makarim.	Not available.
Operasi Penertiban (July 1977 -March 1981	Minister of Finance, Commander of Kopkamtib (security/intelligence organisation) and the Attorney General, assisted by regional officials and the Head of Police.	Processed 1,127 cases involving 8,026 persons, mostly petty corruption cases involving lower rank officials.
Corruption Eradication Team (1982)	Members: Minister of Finance JB Sumarlin, Commander of Kopkamtib Sudomo, Chair of the Supreme Court Mudjono, Minister of Justice Ali Said, Attorney General Ismail Saleh, Police Chief Awaludin Djamin.	The necessary implementing regulation was never issued.

Conclusion

With the failure of traditional agencies, and their reluctance to reform so obvious, the Commission is seen by many as the last hope for a law enforcement agency that will really fight corruption. The Commission must not, however, be seen as the only means to this end. Existing law enforcement agencies must undergo reform at the same time and the Courts, in particular, should be a major focus of such efforts. The Commission should only be seen as a short-term 'shock' measure, to initiate the beginnings of a restoration of the rule of law.

Many critics have questioned whether this latest Commission will be able to function as intended to combat corruption, or whether it will itself become a centre of corruption, as its legislation seems to allow. Others have questioned whether there is any genuine desire on the part of government to eradicate corruption. Such a radical break with the last four decades of Indonesian political history is now, however, a critical necessity given the strength of popular demands for real action against KKN. If the Commission fails, as many activists predict it will, the political situation will rapidly turn bad and deteriorate into crisis. No Indonesian would want that to happen again.

References

Andi Hamzah, (1984), *Korupsi di Indonesia: Masalah dan Pemecahannya*, Gramedia, Jakarta.

Attorney General, (2000), *Evaluasi Program Kerja Kejaksaan Agung 2000*, 28 March, Jakarta, unpublished speech presented before the DPR.

Badan Pemeriksa Keuangan dan Pembangunan (BPKP), (1999), *Strategi Pemberantasan Korupsi Nasional*, Pusat Pendidikan dan Latihan Pengawasan BPKP, Jakarta.

De Speville, Bertrand, (2001), 'Public Debate on Draft Law regarding Anti-Corruption Commission', Jakarta, 7 April 2001, unpublished paper.

Djajadi, Iqbal, (2001), 'One day Seminar on Performance Review of JIT', delivered at Seminar, 'Kinerja JIT', 25 July, Jakarta, unpublished paper.

Elvy Yusanti, (2000), 'Komisi Ombudsman Bantah tak Dipercaya', Satunet.com, 23 June, <http://satunet.com/artikel/isi/00/06/23/ 18761.html>.

International Commission of Jurists, (1999), *Ruler's Law: Mission to Indonesia*, ICJ, Chatelain, Switzerland, October.

Kompas, (1999), 'MTI Minta Dibentuk Secepatnya', 1 July, <http://www.kompas.com/kompas%2Dcetak/9907/01/utama/mti01.htm>.

Lubis, T Mulya, (1998), 'Reformasi Hukum Anti Korupsi', presented at conference 'Towards Indonesia Free from Corruption', Depok, 18 September, unpublished paper.

Pusat Studi dan Kebijakan (PSHK), *Potret Buram Pemberantasan Korupsi*, Jakarta, unpublished paper.

Pusat Studi dan Kebijakan, (2001), *Advokat Indonesia: Mencari Legitimasi*, PSHK, Jakarta.

Tim Gabungan Pemberantas Tindakan Korupsi, Pusat Studi dan Kebijakan, Lembaga Independensi Peradilan and Masyarakat Transparensi Indonesia, (2001), *Naskah*

Akademis dan Rancangan Undang-undang tentang Pengadilan Khusus Tindak Pidana Korupsi, July, unpublished manuscript.

Vinay Bhargava and Emil Bolongaita, (2001), *Cara Mengefektifkan Program dan Kebijakan Nasional Anti Korupsi: Sebuah Kerangka Analitis*, presented at a Distant Learning Course organised by the World Bank, 18 June, Jakarta, unpublished paper.

Chapter 9

Corruption and the Outsider: Multinational Enterprises in Vietnam

Elizabeth Maitland

Introduction

> Corruption is taking place every day and every hour, at all places, all the time. (Vietnamese President Tran Duc Luong, quoted in *Far Eastern Economic Review* 2001: 70).

After many years of imposed isolation from non-Soviet bloc trade and investment, Vietnam's embrace of economic reform in the mid-1980s presented multinational enterprises with the alluring prospect of untrammelled commercial territory. A large population, numerous natural resources and a strategic geographic position abutting the East Asian miracle economies led many to tout Vietnam as the newest Asian tiger. By the mid-90s, flows of foreign investment averaged US $2 billion a year but disquiet at the slow pace of reforms and escalating problems of corruption coloured foreign press articles on the opportunities awaiting foreign companies in Vietnam (The Economist 1995, 1999, 2000; Edwards 1999; Stier 1999; Cleary 1995; Diaz 1995; Vatikiotis 1994). The Asian financial crisis of 1997 triggered a severe and prolonged reduction in FDI flows, undermining the ability of the economy to meet investment employment creation targets in a country with approximately 37 per cent of the population living in poverty and a million new participants in the workforce annually (World Bank 2000: 1). Both within and without, corruption is now viewed as a key constraint on economic growth and an impediment to revived participation by foreign firms in Vietnam.

Vietnam exhibits many of the characteristics that political scientists and economists have argued are conducive to corrupt practices and, by knock-on effects, to slower economic growth. Prescribing cures for countries afflicted by high-levels of distortion to resource flows requires an understanding of the conditions that produce and enable such behaviour to become entrenched. Yet, cross-country studies that empirically test such conditions are rare. Equally neglected has been analysis of why corruption emerges, compounded by confusion surrounding the different types of corruption and the impact on economic performance.

This chapter extends existing models of corruption by drawing on New Institutional Economics to incorporate an explicit role for the institutional framework, or incentive set, that shapes behaviour by government officials, private individuals and firms. The second half of the chapter presents an application of the model to Vietnam, highlighting conditions that promoted corrupt activity targeted at multinational enterprises (MNEs). For evidence of corruption, the chapter draws on media reporting in various secondary sources, including the English-language Vietnamese press and business news journals.

'Modelling' corruption

Within the economics literature, much attention has focused on determining the effect of corrupt practices on the pace and level of economic development, the impact on wealth distribution, and the conditions that produce and sustain greater or lesser levels of corruption.[1] Defining corruption as 'the abuse of public office for private gain', economists typically model the phenomenon as a classic, but two-stage agency problem. At one layer of analysis, corruption is specified as a bargaining process, whereby a public official (the principal) and an individual or firm (the agent) negotiate a payment for the illicit sale of a public resource (a licence or permit). The second agency relation casts the public official as the agent of the top-level of government, focusing attention on the conditions that foster corrupt behaviour.

Many economists have viewed corruption benignly. Authors have variously argued that bribes improve economic welfare by enabling firms and individuals to overcome bureaucratic delays and by providing incentives for government officials to work harder (see for example, Leff (1964); Huntington (1968); Beck and Maher (1986); and Lien (1986)). Corruption is promoted as an efficiency-enhancing practice when government policy produces second-best outcomes in resource allocation – particularly through over-regulation of economic activity. The ability of officials to price discriminate between bidders for government permits or licences imitates a competitive process, such that the permit is allocated to the highest value-user. Similarly, bribe-taking may function as a *de facto* tax, surmounting weaknesses in government expenditure. Bribes equate to a wage premium for public-sector employees, supplementing inadequate official incomes and 'incentivising' appropriate effort in the provision of government services. Accelerated approval time through bribery also lowers

1 Very extensive reviews of the economics literature on corruption can be found in Rose-Ackerman (1999) and Bardhan (1997). The overlap between rent-seeking activity and corruption is discussed in Khan and Jomo (2000).

the costs of over-rigid bureaucracies, 'greasing the squeaky wheel' (Bardhan 1997: 1332).

Corruption as an efficiency-enhancing practice arguably holds only in highly stylised models that overlook the costs of efforts to avoid detection and punishment for corrupt activity. Drawing on models of industrial organisation to analyse 'markets' for corruption, influential work by Shleifer and Vishny (1993) and Rose-Ackerman (1999) argued such costs critically affect the distortionary impact of corruption. Context matters because discovery costs are a function of competition between political groups and the scale of entry barriers to corruption markets.

Shleifer and Vishny (1993) demonstrated their arguments using a basic model of a public official able to restrict the quantity of a government good 'sold' to private agents. The official can charge a bribe on top of the government price for the good (labelled corruption without theft); or 'hide' the sale, such that the buyer price is equal only to the bribe (corruption with theft). By introducing various complicating variables, such as the need to obtain multiple government goods to operate a business, entry barriers to the pool of bribe-takers were shown to affect the level and type of corrupt activity. Where public officials can freely enter the corruption market (that is, there are no restrictions on the ability of officials to bribe private individuals to obtain government goods), the bribe burden on private individuals stretches to infinity, deterring investment and retarding economic growth.

A strong state able to erect entry barriers to corruption markets produces fewer distortions in resource allocation than a weak state unable to restrain the multiplication of independent bribe-takers intent on maximising their individual rent stream. In the latter case, collusion between public officials or agencies imposing bribes on private agents is less *in*efficient than conditions of perfect competition in corruption markets. In all cases, the need to minimise the risk of exposure renders corruption more deleterious than taxation as payment for government produced goods.

Rose-Ackerman (1999) emphasised the importance of incorporating the 'demand' side of corruption markets, particularly where the bribers exercise monopoly power. In cases such as mafia-dominated states, the 'return' to bribe-takers includes a non-monetary component of avoiding retribution from the dominant group. Hence, the persistence of corruption may not rest with the state's ability to control entry of bribe-takers to corruption markets. Rather, the power of organised crime may prevent the state controlling the pool of bribe-*givers*, whose intimidatory practices 'create' a supply of bribe-takers.

Resolving the debates on the costs and benefits of corruption is impeded by the difficulties of assembling comprehensive and rigorous data-sets. Utilising subjective perceptions data for a cross-section of countries, Mauro (1995) analysed the impact on economic growth of corruption and a series of institutional variables, such as the level of red-tape, judicial integrity, political stability and the degree of social homogeneity. Mauro's empirical estimates found perceptions of corruption were strongly and negatively associated with the investment rate. The negative association held irrespective of the level of red tape, providing little support for benign views of corruption overcoming the inefficiencies of lumbering bureaucracies. The strong association between corruption and investment rates appeared to operate through a broad-brush impact on total investment, rather than corruption inducing inefficient investment choices. Discerning the factors fostering high levels of corruption uncovered an association between greater ethnolinguistic diversity within a country and heightened corruption. Mauro speculated this was linked to bureaucrats favouring members of their own social group, such that more homogenous societies were able to achieve Shleifer and Vishny's (1993) notion of joint-bribe maximisation, with its less-deleterious impact on economic performance.

Following Mauro's lead, Treisman (2000) explored potential sources of corruption utilising perceptions data for a large cross-section of countries. A series of regression models tested explanatory variables from political stability, democratic governance, state-market intervention and legal system (common, civil, religious); to ethno-linguistic homogeneity, religious affiliation, colonial heritage, level of development, openness to trade and raw material endowments. The strongest influence belonged to the 'dead hand of the past'. Countries that had been democracies since 1950 and, more particularly, former British colonies (and Britain) were perceived to be significantly less corrupt, even when controlling for economic development and openness to trade. Political instability was not a significant determinant of high levels of perceived corruption, nor was the country's current status as a democracy.

Building on findings from La Porta et al (1999) that countries with French or socialist legal systems exhibit inferior government performance, Treisman (2000: 438-39) hypothesised that British colonial heritage and prolonged experience of democratic rule proxied complex traditions placing the rights of the individual alongside, rather than subordinated to, the interests of the state. Legal culture was pivotal. Countries with common law systems but no history of British rule had higher perceived corruption, while countries with just British heritage were still associated with lower perceived corruption (Treisman 2000: 422-24). As La Porta et al (1999: 232) argued:

> A civil legal tradition ... can be taken as a proxy for an intent to build institutions to further the power of the state...[t]he English common law tradition is entirely different in that its development starting in the 17th century has been shaped by Parliament and the aristocracy at the expense of the Crown, and hence it has reflected to a much greater extent the intent to limit the power of the sovereign... As a result of this influence, the judges who made common law "put their emphasis on the private rights of individuals and especially on their property rights"... There is also more emphasis on restraining the government and on protecting the individual against the government.

Context clearly matters. Corruption, whether in response to large-scale government inefficiency or more exclusively individual greed, feeds on decisions shaping the incentive set. Individual public officials face a series of decisions, balancing the costs of discovery, which may occur in the distant future, against largely immediate benefits. Arguably, the forces raising the possibility and penalties of discovery evolve slowly within societies. The key findings of the few empirical cross-country studies appear to emphasise the importance of multiple bodies able to check the abuse of power by individual government agencies.[2] Tirole (1996) posited that inter-generational persistence of corruption may be linked to the difficulty of resuscitating collective reputation, once a potentially one-off event - war, for example - triggers corrupt activity. For following generations, inherited reputation may diminish the incentives for behaving honestly.

The task for economists is to incorporate the setting, or 'rules of the game', into theoretical models, as well as empirical tests. Corruption is not a simple bargaining process in which the bribe-taker and bribe-giver negotiate an 'efficient' outcome disembodied from the surrounding political, economic and social environment. The following section leverages the emphasis placed by various authors on the importance of context through a New Institutional Economics (NIE) model of corruption that explicitly specifies property rights systems and the incentive set for corruption. Viewing corruption through a property rights lens casts light not only on differing levels of corruption across countries, but also, through a more refined definition of corruption, the conditions that promote different types of corruption. The latter strength of the model potentially enables identification of the vulnerability to corrupt practices of individual multinational enterprises (MNEs) in specific locations.

A new institutional economics model of corruption: The importance of context

Uncertainty of ownership is a powerful disincentive to acquiring knowledge and skills. Where corruption undermines incentives to invest in new capabilities, development will slow and, potentially, retreat. Defining ownership requires measurement and delineation of assets, while enforcement rests on the presence of a credible threat discouraging violation of rights. Historically, economies of scale in the use of violence have favoured the emergence of a single agent - the state - with formal powers to define and enforce property rights systems. Property rights encompass the right to earn income and to contract over the terms of asset use with other parties and the right permanently to transfer the asset to another party, as well as user rights, such as the right to physically alter or destroy an asset (Eggertsson 1990).

Specifying corruption as a re-assignment of property rights under the aegis of state sovereignty reveals two types of corruption: 'greasing the

2 Multinational lobbyists, such as Transparency International, in particular, tout the need for an independent press and judiciary.

wheel', including bribes to speed or gain a government permit, and 'theft by stealth', where bribes are paid to re-assign rights to select interests.

In Type I corruption ('greasing the wheel'), the individual or organisation paying the bribe 'agrees' to a partial rights transfer to the public official. The bribe represents the transfer of part of the income stream (rent) on the asset or assets the individual seeks to exploit but is prevented from doing so by some aspect of government regulation. While a firm's competitive position may be enhanced by obtaining a government permit, only their right to earn income, rather than the full set of property rights, is impinged upon. Examples of Type I corruption are frequently cited in economic studies. The pervasive system of industrial licensing in India from the late 1960s to late 1980s epitomised this form of corruption. The need for businesses to obtain licences to alter any aspect of their activities, including to expand output or even alter product design, created extraordinary levels of corruption, as firms sought to speed licence applications through the rigid bureaucracy of the 'licence raj' (Bhagwati 1993; Encarnation 1989; Krueger 1974).

Type II corruption is far more insidious, but rarely recognised in existing economic models. 'Theft by stealth' is distinguished by the payment of bribes to achieve the transfer of full or partial rights from the initial owner *without* consent. This form of rights re-assignment falls into three sub-categories: (a) the transfer of private property rights to new private owner(s); (b) re-assignment from public to private ownership; and (c) from private to 'public' ownership. Correspondingly, the manifestations of Type II corruption are many and often difficult to discern. A firm paying a bribe to obtain a permit to utilise toxic-fume emitting technologies represents one such case. Under government environmental policy, the use of the technologies in question may be fully legal and the bribe is a straight-forward example of 'greasing the wheel' to speed permit clearance.[3] Alternatively, the bribe may form Type II(b) corruption, whereby the rights of the public to a clean environment are transferred to the private firm through the issue of a 'false' permit.

At any point in time, the property rights system is a function of the distribution of power within a society. The politically-advantaged benefit from a redistribution of property rights, providing an incentive for interest groups, including public officials, to engage in predatory rent-seeking behaviour (Eggertsson 1990; Libecap 1989, 1993). Much of the work in new institutional economics has considered the definition and enforcement of property rights as a political process, subject to high degrees of divisiveness (North and Weingast 1990; Libecap 1989, 1996). As Coase (1960) demonstrated, the initial assignment of property rights affects economic outcomes. Valuable rights will not always find their highest value use for transaction costs (or the costs of search, negotiation and enforcement of

3 This does not presume that the technology is safe, merely that it meets government standards, which may either be set by law or reflect the prevailing state of scientific knowledge.

agreements) may be so high as to prevent voluntary re-allocation. The classic example of the Coase theorem is of a polluting factory affecting the air quality of adjacent housing. Cooperation and coordination among home owners are likely to be affected by 'freeriders' seeking to benefit from clean air without having to incur the 'costs' of engaging in negotiations with the factory.[4] Contiguously, valuable rights may find their way to the individuals or organisations with the greatest lobbying capabilities.

An understanding of property rights systems requires an understanding of the institutional web or rules of the game that structure human interaction in a particular setting. The institutional environment defines the organisations – as the players – that will be viable and is modified by them.[5] Political, economic and social groups emerge in response to the opportunities created by institutions and, in turn, mould changes in the rules of the game in a complex process of institutional evolution (North 1990). Change may be in the form of new legislation or gradual shifts in social attitudes towards, for example, racism or slavery, with the effectiveness of each new institution heavily dependent on its enforceability within the society.

Functioning either as formal or informal constraints, institutions limit the choice set of individuals to induce cooperation and coordination (or limit non-cooperative behaviour) between members of a society. Formal institutions encompass political, judicial and economic rules, such as legislation, common law decisions and government competition and welfare policies, while informal constraints are the conventions or codes of behaviour in a society (North 1981; 1990; 1991). Although competition for scarce resources forces economic agents to invest in skills and knowledge to survive, it is the full institutional framework that dictates the pay-off for such investment (North 1990). Numerous empirical studies have revealed societies do not always produce institutions that support sustained economic growth (Greif 1989, 1992, 1993; Greif, Milgrom and Weingast 1994; Landa 1994; Libecap 1996).

With respect to corruption, Shleifer and Vishny's argument that "[c]ountries with more political competition have stronger public pressure against corruption" (1993: 610) holds only with an implicit assumption that 'the public' does not discriminate on the basis of who (or what) is the victim of corruption. Local norms may support corruption against certain groups,

4 When transaction costs are zero, negotiations between the factory and residents will determine the allocation of the rights to 'air', depending on the relative valuations of air as a resource by residents and the factory. Irrespective of the initial position of whether residents have the right to clean air in their neighbourhood or the factory has the right to pollute, the problem of social cost, as defined by economists, thus disappear (Coase, 1960).

5 Organisations range from political bodies (such as the organs of government, regulatory agencies and political parties) through economic groups (including firms and trade unions) to social bodies (such as churches and educational groups).

particularly when in favour of others. MNEs are just one case in point. Others include different ethnic, religious and socio-economic groups.

Embedding the agency relations between the public official, the bribe-giver and the 'state' is a crucial missing step in existing economic models of corruption. While Shleifer and Vishny (1993: 600) recognised the importance of political competition and concentration of authority as determinants of corruption, their analysis is comparatively static at best and takes as given the conditions that enable the corrupt official to have effective property rights over the government good in question. 'Neutral' technical language disguises behaviour deeply embedded in cultural, social, political and religious systems. Abuse of public office extends beyond existing models of corruption, which consider only the shift of assets from public to private ownership, neglecting the more complex forms of corruption detailed above.

Remedies for diminishing corruption or minimising the exposure of individuals or firms to corrupt practices will differ according to the institutional setting and the type of corruption in question. Even in the most developed countries with strong systems of checks and balances on abuse of office, political competition will not restrain corruption if based on socially-sanctioned manipulations against particular groups. The motivation for, and form of, manipulations are subject to high degrees of information asymmetries between the government agent in question and 'the victim', determined by the surrounding context.

A priori, reducing levels of Type I corruption, where the practice is driven by bribe-takers, requires attention primarily be given to raising the costs of discovery for public officials. Potential measures include raising public-sector wages (where out of line with private-sector skill rates) and increasing the effectiveness of monitoring. However, such techniques are less effective in tackling Type II and Type I corruption, where bribe-*givers* drive the abuse of public office. The incentives shaping such practices emanate not just from weaknesses in the structure of political and state organisations. Rather, the wider institutional set of the society is 'problematic'.

The transitional economies of the former Soviet bloc provide a contemporary laboratory of 'exogenous' shocks to systems characterised by high, but allegedly stable, patterns of corruption, resulting in perceptions of rampant corruption and constrained economic performance. In Vietnam, the process of liberalisation has shifted the status quo: existing barriers to markets for corruption have been dismantled, permitting freedom of entry for a wider pool of bribe-takers. The radical shift in rules (the incentive set) has wrought responses from organisations and individuals. A key question is whether the shift in the supply curve for corrupt practices resulting from the change to the incentive set will ultimately have a negative effect on Vietnam's economic development.

The following section applies the notions of Type I and Type II corruption to Vietnam. As the World Bank (2000: 61) noted in its recent handbook on fighting corruption in Vietnam, "there is scant quantitative evidence on the extent and main sources of the problem". Although the following analysis is preliminary, it critically identifies the tensions producing the different types of corruption against MNEs.

Vietnam, corruption and *doi moi*

Doi moi, or the reform program of economic renovation, was formally adopted by the Sixth National Party Congress of the Communist Party of Vietnam (CPV) in 1986. The program was explicitly aimed at overhauling the "bureaucratic centralised state subsidy system" in favour of a multi-sectoral economy (Vo Nhan Tri and Booth 1992; Plummer 1995). In December 1987, the first *doi moi* law pertaining to foreign investment was passed, effectively re-opening the country to Western companies. However, Vietnam's embrace of economic liberalisation has been clouded by myriad structural legacies of poverty, uneven regional and industrial development, and mismatched political and economic systems.

As the 1990s progressed, corruption was an increasingly visible 'side-effect' of *doi moi*. Mid-decade, the Political and Economic Risk Consultancy described Vietnam as "in contention for the Imelda Marcos golden shoe award for outstanding achievement in the category of corrupt activities" (quoted in Schwarz 1996b: 18). The need to combat corruption emerged as a recurring theme in official pronouncements and policy platforms. At the Eighth Plenum of the Central Committee of the CPV in January 1995, General Secretary Do Muoi bemoaned the rising corruption and deteriorating morality of state officials. In a blunt report to the National Assembly, the Prime Minister observed:

> The state of corruption plus incapabilities, red tape and domineering behavior, and lack of a sense of discipline among numerous officials in various state machines at all levels and branches ... have ... jeopardized the renovation process and brought discredit to the Party's leadership and State management (Goodman 1995: 95-96; omissions in original).

Combating corruption was again a major theme of the Sixth and Seventh Party Plenums in 1998 and 1999, producing a number of ordinances and decrees including the Ordinance against Corruption (March 1998) and its related implementing regulations decreed under CP64/98-ND-CP. A complaints hotline established by the Prime Minister in 1998 received within a year roughly 50,000 calls alleging corruption and government inefficiency (World Bank 2000). In a November 1999 address to the National Assembly, the Prime Minister listed corruption as a top priority for the coming year and an anti-corruption campaign was launched in May 2000.

Examples of Type I corruption abound, with customs officials displaying a particular predilection for extracting bribes. A representative example is that of a customs office in the southern part of Vung Tau, where, in an apparent effort at bureaucratic streamlining, inspectors agreed to pool all bribes above US $45. When the scheme was uncovered, the inspectors' 'mutual fund' was reaping US $20,000 per month (Schwarz 1996b: 18). A Taiwanese investor company was reportedly so frustrated by corrupt customs officials failing to 'fulfil' the activities they had been bribed to undertake that it tried to sue for breach of contract (The Economist 2000).

For foreign firms, their potential exposure to Type I corruption has been considerable. Local People's Committees possess powers to investigate, survey, classify and carry out zoning and land-use planning, enforce rules and regulations, carry out registration functions, inspect the land, and resolve land disputes. All foreign investment projects also require approval by the local committee. Quoting anonymous foreign business executives, the *Vietnam Investment Review* provided tentative evidence that the far-reaching inspection powers of various state bodies were enabling corrupt activity:

> "We are frequently forced to receive inspection delegations from various authorities. They often unnecessarily interfere with our business operations, sometimes threatening us and demanding bribes" said a textile company official in Hanoi. (Duc Hung 1998)[6]

Evidence of Type II corruption has also appeared in media reports on the experiences of foreign firms in Vietnam. In articles published four years apart, *The Economist* has twice reported the availability of 'neatly-bound' photocopies of foreign firms' business proposals, first in a bookshop in Hanoi and, later, throughout Vietnam (The Economist 1995; 1999: 48). In such cases, the transfer of rights from the MNE is twofold: first, having paid[7] a corrupt official(s) to leak copies of the proposals, the bookseller profits from the sale of the MNE's intellectual -and, potentially, technological property - as embodied in the proposals. Secondly, buyers of the proposals can erode the rent stream on the MNE's exploitation of its distinctive resources and capabilities by establishing activities in competition based on the 'revealed' know-how.

MNEs are exposed to similar threats of Type II corruption through, for example, requirements to submit import plans for each year of operation; any amended import plans during a year; and annual plans for exports and domestic contributions. As with investment licence applications, such import and export plans reveal confidential information from which production levels and raw materials can be calculated and, more critically, components identified, as well as new product and geographic areas of operation.

Press reports indicate a complex form of Type II corruption involving an Australian mining company, Westralian Sands, which entered into a joint venture with a state-owned enterprise of the Ha Tinh province People's Committee. Westralian Sands became embroiled in a bitter dispute with its partner and government officials over machinery, the importation of which the Australian partner allegedly failed to notify customs and its local partner. The Vietnamese partner was reported to have sought to take control of the joint venture's revenues and, ultimately, the enterprise itself, by co-operating with officials to harass the Australian parent and its staff.

6 Quote from on-line edition.

7 The word 'paid' is employed in its most general sense, such that the bribe may take forms other than monetary payment.

Australian expatriates were arrested by the local People's Committee for failing to have properly obtained visas. The Australian firm counter-argued that the source of the dispute lay in its discovery that the government-appointed general-manager of the JV was covertly selling the mine's ilmenite to a Japanese buyer in direct breach of the joint venture agreement (Baker 1995; Cleary 1995; Diaz 1995; Schwarz 1995; O'Flahertie 1996).

However, delineating the difference between Type II corruption and the activities of a government pursuing economic and social policies is difficult. The dispute between the large consumer-goods multinational Proctor and Gamble (P&G) and its local partner, a subsidiary of the Industry Ministry's Vietnam Chemicals Corporation, provides a good illustration of the problem. The dispute was triggered by P&G's desire to increase its current licensed investment to enable it to stem losses and regain profitability. Hampered by a lack of cash, the local partner was unable to increase its equity share in the joint venture but rejected P&G's counter-offer to take over full ownership of the alliance. Within a climate of strong attacks on P&G and other consumer goods MNEs for alleged unfair marketing tactics against local companies, the Central Bank of Vietnam ordered a freeze on the loans of the joint venture, forcing P&G to default on its borrowings. One possible interpretation of the reported events is that P&G fell victim to Type II(b) corruption: the local partner sought to free-ride on the competitive advantages of P&G and 'paid-off' officials in several government agencies to ensure access to P&G's rent stream on the distinctive resources and capabilities it had transferred to Vietnam.

In formulating legislation and policy, central governments must carry on a multiple-level bargaining process not only with pressure groups but also with lower levels of government, foreign governments and multilateral agencies. It is a 'game' complicated by incomplete and imperfect information as to the costs and benefits for the country, let alone the motivations of those involved. Distortions to the property rights of the foreign firm may be based on ideological grounds, resulting in a form of transfer of the private rights of the MNE to public ownership. In Vietnam, foreign companies are charged a premium relative to domestic firms for basic utility services, such as water, electricity and telecommunications, as well as for housing, advertising and wages for local labour.[8] Commenting on the US firm, 3M, *The Economist* (2000: 65) reported that the:

> [P]aper that 3M imports to make Post-It Notes faces an arbitrarily high tariff as 'office' products (40 percent duty) rather than 'adhesive-backed paper' (ten percent). This makes it more expensive than the same Post-It Notes smugglers bring in from Thailand.

8 The Ministry for Planning and Investment, which oversees foreign investment, reported that electricity charges for foreign firms were 25 per cent higher in Vietnam than in regional countries, while postal and telecommunications charges were four to five times higher (Ha Thang 2000: online).

Equally, ideological opposition may also function as a convenient screen for Type II(a) corruption, whereby the public official accepts a bribe to ensure the transfer of private rights to a select interest group. Disentangling the source of difficulties for MNEs and determining whether a firm has fallen victim to corruption or a legitimate exercise of state power is obscured by Vietnam's long-run history of animosity to outsiders, the state's ideological commitment to maintaining the economic pre-eminence of the state-owned sector and the sheer scale of transformation being undertaken by Vietnam.

Corruption versus state policy

While economic necessity forced the adoption of the *doi moi* reform program by the CPV, the embrace was an unwilling one and has been resisted by many state organisations. Overlaying Vietnam's re-opening to foreign firms is a political ideology and rhetoric of continued xenophobia and officially-sanctioned differential treatment of foreign firms relative to domestic enterprise. All are embedded in an historical tradition of hostility to outsiders. Woven into traditional culture and myth are tales of heroic resistance to far-stronger invaders (Jamieson 1993). Across Vietnam's history, territorial and cultural turbulence has informed a fierce nationalism symbolised by a rhetoric of a "tradition of resistance to foreign aggression" (Chapuis 1995; Keyes 1995; Pelley 1995; Jamieson 1993; Post 1989; Marr 1971; Chesneaux 1966). Nationalism and resistance to foreign interests has, in fact, been a hallmark of the Communist Party of Vietnam.

Vietnam's history is one of colonisation and internal conflict. From at least 200 BC successive waves of Chinese colonisers were interspersed with fraught periods of fragmentation under rival clans. It was not until 1802 that national unification under a single Vietnamese ruler was achieved - and it was to prove little more than a brief interregnum before the arrival of French colonial administration in the 1860s.[9] Although small groups within Vietnam (Indochina) benefited from French occupation, for the majority the colonial experience was one of misery; disintegration of societal village structures; and growing protest movements (Marr 1971, 1981; Chesneaux 1954 (1966); Jamieson 1993).[10] Amidst the shifting alliances of the Second

9 The brevity of national unification and the highly fractious nature of the historical record led Marr (1971: 7) in the opening line of the first chapter of his inquiry into Vietnam anti-colonialism during the period 1885-1925, to ask: "What did it mean to be Vietnamese in the nineteenth century, just before the French colonial period?"

10 For example, during the 1920s somewhere between 100,000 and 200,000 were either deceived or press-ganged into working on the rapidly expanding commercial estates in rubber-growing regions. As Marr (1981: 6-7) noted, "[c]onditions were abysmal, including endemic malaria, contaminated or insufficient food and water, long hours, the docking of wages, and vicious punishments. Consequently the turnover rate due to death, escape and non-renewal of contracts was extraordinarily high, as indicated by the fact that the rubber plantation work force never exceeded 41,000 in any one year."

World War the communist-led Viet Minh emerged as the dominant revolutionary force, drawing legitimacy and power from its ties with Allied forces. During August of 1945, the Viet Minh seized power in the North of the country, declaring the founding of the Democratic Republic of Vietnam. For nine tumultuous years, the Viet Minh battled the French for control of the Northern provinces of Vietnam, as the colonists vainly attempted to restore their authority. In 1954, an internationally brokered cease-fire agreement divided the country at the latitude 17°N, creating the communist Democratic Republic of Vietnam to the north and the increasingly US-backed State of Vietnam to the South.

During the 1950s and 1960s, a surge of Vietnamese language works with historical subjects were published in the communist Democratic Republic of Vietnam. While many were translations of primary historical materials, others were secondary, interpretative publications. Pelley (1995: 233) argued they comprised a 'new history' aimed at cultivating among "the Vietnamese an understanding of the national past that revolved around the central thematic of resistance to foreign aggression". During the war between North and South Vietnam, historians redeployed rhetoric to 'interpret' current events.

> Since August of 1964 … the American imperialists have widened the war in Indochina and used their navy and air force to invade the Democratic Republic of Vietnam, but the People's Army of the North has dealt them a decisive blow … All the progressive countries of the world have voiced support for our cause and day by day they watch our sacred war unfold … At no other moment has the history of our Ancestral Land been so glorious (Tràn Huy Liêu, June 1965; as quoted in Pelley 1995: 236).

A language of 'resistance to foreign interests' continues to characterise government and CPV statements in the *doi moi* era. The official 'campaign against foreign evils' launched in December 1995 by the signing into law of Decree 87/CP epitomises the rhetoric of xenophobia and hostility towards foreign firms. Two years earlier, in 1993, party and state officials had been warned to limit their association with foreigners to business only and not to engage in social intercourse (Pike 1994). Under the campaign against foreign evils, attempts were made to enforce earlier decrees on the use of non-Vietnamese language signs and advertising boards and requirements for all signs to include and accord priority to Vietnamese. For foreign companies, the campaign created significant confusion, with the removal of advertising signs for foreign companies such as Kodak, Pepsi and Heineken occurring unevenly across the country.

The Decree was accompanied by inflammatory language from senior figures. In a speech on 30 June 1996, Le Minh Huong, a vice-minister of interior and soon to be member of the Politburo, declared:

> Hostile forces are trying to carry out peaceful evolution, and make ill use of loopholes in our management and conditions … to plant their people deeper into our internal organs (quoted in Schwarz 1996a: 14; omission in original).

Although enmeshed in factional posturing within the CPV, the campaign against foreign evils underlined the inherent contradiction within the reform process: the simmering tension between a nation seeking foreign aid and technology while clinging to a rhetoric of independence, self-reliance and freedom from foreign firms.

The most recent government attempt to pass foreign investment legislation amendments through the National Assembly, in mid-2000, was similarly characterised by ambivalence, as well as strident opposition, towards foreign firms. Reporting on the debates, Ha Thang (2000: 1) noted "unclear perceptions of the role of foreign investment in the economy by many delegates", while the Minister for Planning and Investment conceded some "foreign-invested companies have purposefully made losses in order to drive out their local partners…[and] criticised some executives employed by foreign-backed firms for being irresponsible and not active enough in protecting Vietnamese rights in businesses" (Duong 2000: 1).

This unease and hostility towards foreign interests is embedded in a social and political system unaccustomed and ill-adapted to private ownership. Vietnam has not embraced unfettered market capitalism and the government remains committed to maintaining the leading role of state-owned enterprises (SOEs) in the economy (Thayer 1991). The Seventh Congress of the CPV in June 1991 emphasised that key industries would remain under central control. The 1992 Constitution and the Eighth Party Congress in June 1996 reaffirmed the pre-eminent position of SOEs. State monopolies were formally retained in key strategic industries, such as defence, aviation, railways, energy, post and telecommunications. The importance of SOEs to individual ministries reluctant to forego further resources and status beyond that already lost through the adoption of market based planning further underpins the ideological commitment to SOE economic prominence.

A cobweb of regulations and financial market distortions slant the playing field in favour of SOEs. In 1995, SOEs drew nearly 70 per cent of the volume of credit available from the four state-owned banks, which collectively provided 84 per cent of the total credit available in the economy (Le Dang Doanh 1996: 18), Similar figures have been quoted for the year 1999 (Nguyen Manh Hung 2000: 99). The World Bank (2000) cited official estimates as showing 60 per cent of SOEs were loss makers or marginally profitable at the end of 1997, with total SOE debt by end-1999 at 126 trillion *dong* (roughly US $9 billion) equivalent to 32 per cent of GDP. Largely excluded from formal credit markets, domestic private sector firms have been forced to rely on cash holdings or borrow from informal sources at interest rates as high as four to seven per cent per month (Riedel 1997: 64).

Heavy government intervention in markets impedes the growth of private-sector firms. By the mid-1990s, SOEs accounted for 87 per cent of all firms' assets in the economy, despite representing only 23 per cent of registered domestic companies and being characterised by very low profit ratios (EIU 1995: 18; Le Dang Doanh 1996: 17). At the end of the decade, private enterprises accounted for less than ten per cent of GDP (World Bank et al 2000). Correspondingly, foreign firms face an environment not only characterised by unease with private ownership, but also one in which they potentially represent the only competitors to powerful SOEs in an institutional setting of extreme flux.

The protracted development of institutions and organisations suitable to a market economy fuels the scope for abuse of public office for private gain. The dismantling of central planning has both magnified the ability of individual ministries and government agencies to resist the imposition of central will and devolved decision-making the allocation and use of resources away from state planners at the top, particularly within the Politburo of the CPV. Middle-level cadres within the government and SOEs have become "the main actors in the process of law-making and law implementation in their areas" (Vasavakul 1996: 47). The scope for administrative discretion is significant, given extensive gaps in the legal framework (Bui Kim Chi 1996). Each piece of formal legislation is the product of very extensive and intensive consultations across ministries, such that enacted laws exhibit varying degrees of inconsistency. Correspondingly, legislation is subject to differing interpretations, applications, and numerous clarifying documents.[11] The flexibility in legal interpretation and application fosters what the Australian Ambassador to Vietnam described as "a gap between top-level pronouncements and delivery down the line" (Boyd 1995: 5). Similarly, the World Bank (2000) elliptically noted the "need for institution-building that will gradually establish the rule of law as the basis of government-business relationships".

Foreign firms entering such an environment encounter three very strong sets of incentives encouraging corruption. First, public officials – particularly at the provincial and local levels – possess high degrees of autonomy and discretionary decision-making power over the operations of MNEs. Secondly, official wages are very low, averaging about US $25 per month (World Bank et al 2000). Finally, the introduction of economic reforms constitutes a significant threat to the beneficiaries of the previous system. The shock to the status quo is both ideological and pecuniary and invokes a compensatory response that exposes MNEs to high risk of Type II corruption, as well as to 'legitimate' actions of government policy that induce highly discriminatory treatment of economic actors.

11 The clarifying documents take a number of forms. Laws passed by the National Assembly are the highest form of legal instrument and, when not in session, its Standing Committees pass ordinances. Decrees, usually accompanied by more detailed regulations, are passed by the government to implement laws or ordinances. Individual ministries then issue circulars as guidelines to how the ministry should administer a law, ordinance or decree.

Consequences

The recognition of corruption as a key constraint on economic performance has led to the introduction of a range of measures to achieve greater transparency and procedural clarity in administrative decision-making. Various decrees have sought to force all high-ranking government employees and government officials to declare their property interests, bar family members of senior officials from positions in related enterprises and prohibit officials from receiving gifts from outside parties. Further administrative reforms have included designing procedures for filing complaints against officials and stronger penalties for corrupt officials. With respect to foreign firms, the scope for bribery has also been reduced through alterations to the number of permits and licences required in addition to the initial investment licence, and clarification of the rights of local people's committees to conduct inspections.

However, analysis of the surrounding environment for foreign firms in Vietnam presents an unsettling picture. As with all institutions, enforcement is critical to achieving changes in administrative practice. Yet, the highly evolutionary nature of the legal framework in Vietnam incorporates a lack of judicial expertise and judicial independence. Gillespie's (1993: 143) caution that "written laws and regulations can only be regarded as general guidelines, establishing the rough ambit of bureaucratic discretion" should resonate strongly against expectations of rapid change.

Secondly, Type II corruption is supported by an atmosphere of mistrust, which is at the very least tacitly approved by the highest levels of the state. Within an environment of long-run historical animosity towards outsiders, and an apparently unyielding ideological commitment to maintaining the prominence of the state sector, ambivalence towards protecting the competitiveness of foreign firms seems set to continue. For Vietnam, the risk is that both increasing evidence of Type II corruption and an appearance of unease and discriminatory treatment towards foreign firms may drive out existing FDI, as well as repel potential new sources. Not only does Vietnam require fresh sources of technology and capital accumulation to achieve its ambitious economic targets, but it also lacks the capacity to use facilities and workforces abandoned by exiting MNEs.

The ambiguity of Vietnam's transition also fuels corruption against local private enterprise, highlighting the degrees of 'outsider' status. From a 1995-1997 survey of 259 privately owned manufacturing firms in Hanoi and Ho Chi Minh City, McMillan and Woodruff (1999) found not only that entrepreneurs could not rely on the courts for help, but also that managers:

> [m]aintained good relations with the local authorities, not only for help in obtaining licences and permissions quickly, but also because the local authorities sometimes intervene in disputes in discretionary ways. One case (case #5) said he has good relations with the district People's Committee, and the committee would help him if someone tried to cheat him. Most managers, however, said they do not appeal to the authorities to help solve disputes. As

> one put it (case #9), the local authorities "just create problems for us rather than supporting us" (McMillan and Woodruff 1999: 641.)

The climate of state-'sanctioned' discrimination against particular groups exerts many significant constraints on economic performance. Ambivalence not only directly feeds into 'official' discrimination that limits the capacity of local private enterprise to develop, but also implicitly supports corruption targeted against them. Foreign firms are both directly repelled by growing evidence of corruption and by the failure of the economy and the system of governance to transform sufficiently quickly. A pressing question for Vietnam is what path the government and political system will take in the unfolding economic reform.

Conclusion

For all foreign companies, inadequacies in the legal framework, the pre-eminent position of SOEs in the economy, corruption and the long history of hostility to foreign interests present strong barriers to successful entry and participation in the country. However, the changes expected of Vietnam are staggeringly complex and have been asked of few countries in such a short period of time. Even China has not undertaken such radical steps. The liberalisation and re-opening of the Chinese economy has occurred far more slowly. Weaning state enterprises from the central budget (off the state purse) is difficult. The required reforms encounter not only a lack of skilled managers, with respect to output and pricing decisions, product adaptation and general risk management, but also a tangled web of political and economic structures that threaten the power and wealth of entrenched interests, as well as providing new and particularly lucrative avenues of rent-seeking to officials far down the governance hierarchy.

The process of liberalisation has shifted the status quo in Vietnam, permitting entry by a wider pool of bribe-takers and bribe-givers. Transitional Vietnam exhibits many of the characteristics that political scientists and economists have argued are conducive to corrupt practices and, by knock-on effects, to slower economic growth. Applying the extended model of corruption presented in this chapter to Vietnam reveals the tensions that render MNEs 'easy targets' in an institutional setting historically hostile to 'outsiders'. By incorporating an explicit role for the 'rules of the game', the model identifies the specific vulnerability of MNE's property rights to their competitive advantages in Vietnam. However, the universality of the model enables its application across development levels, style of government and in cross-country studies. Although the ranks of the most corrupt countries are allegedly dominated by developing nations, corrupt practices pervade all societies.

References

Baker, Russell, (1995), 'Handle this Tiger Cub with Care', *The Bulletin*, 18 July: 75-77.

Bardhan, Pranab, (1997), 'Corruption and Development: A Review of Issues', 35(3) *Journal of Economic Literature* 1320-1346.

Bhagwati, Jagdish, (1993), *India in Transition: Freeing the Economy*, Cambridge University Press, Cambridge.

Boyd, Susan, (1995), 'Australia and Vietnam - Already a Close Relationship', 2(3) *Asialine* 4-6.

Chapuis, Oscar, (1995), *A History of Vietnam: From Hong Bang to Tu Duc*, Greenwood Press, Westport and London.

Chesneaux, Jean, (1966), *The Vietnamese Nation: Contribution to a History*, translated by M Salmon, Current Book Distributors, Sydney.

Chi, Bui Kim, (1996), 'Providing Legal Services in Vietnam: A Practitioner's Viewpoint', in S Leung (ed), *Vietnam Assessment: Creating a Sound Investment Climate*, Institute of Southeast Asian Studies, Singapore, 107-114.

Cleary, Paul, (1995), 'Vietnam: A Minefield for Foreign Investors', *Australian Financial Review*, 15 July, 15.

Coase, Ronald H, (1960), 'The Problem of Social Cost', 3 *Journal of Law and Economics* 31-44.

Diaz, Tina, (1995), 'Vietnam a Minefield of Risks for Foreign Resource Groups', *The Australian*, 2 June: 28.

Doanh, Le Dang, (1996), 'Economic Developments and Prospects', in S Leung (ed), *Vietnam Assessment: Creating a Sound Investment Climate*, Institute of Southeast Asian Studies, Singapore, 6-20.

Duc, Hung, (1998), 'PM Acts to Stamp Out Official Corruption', *Vietnam Investment Review*, Hanoi.

Duong, Phong, (2000), 'Some Foreign Partners were Unfair, says Minister', *Vietnam Investment Review*, Hanoi.

The Economist, (1995), 'Foreign Firms in Vietnam: Uncle Ho's Ghost', 9 December, 75-76.

The Economist, (1999), 'Vietnam and America: No Trade', 23 October, 48.

The Economist, (2000), 'Goodnight Vietnam', 8 January, 65-66.

Edwards, Adrian, (1999), 'Big Risk, Low Returns', *Far Eastern Economic Review*, 26 August: 12.

Eggertsson, Thrainn, (1990), *Economic Behavior and Institutions*, Cambridge University Press, Cambridge.

EIU, (1995), 'Vietnam: Country Report', Economist Intelligence Unit, London.

Encarnation, Dennis J, (1989), *Dislodging Multinationals: India's Strategy in Comparative Perspective*, Cornell University Press, Ithaca.

Gillespie, John, (1993), 'The Evolution of Private Commercial Freedoms in Vietnam', in CA Thayer and DG Marr (eds), *Vietnam and the Rule of Law*, Australian National University, Canberra.

Goodman, Allan E, (1995), 'Vietnam in 1994: With Peace at Hand', 35(1) *Asian Survey* 92-99.

Greif, Avner, (1989), 'Reputation and Coalitions in Medieval Trade: Evidence on the Maghribi Traders', 49(4) *Journal of Economic History* 857-82.

Greif, Avner, (1992), 'Institutions and International Trade: Lessons from the Commercial Revolution', 82(2) *American Economic Review* 128-133.

Greif, Avner, (1993), 'Contract Enforcement and Economic Institutions in Early Trade: The Maghribi Traders Coalition', 83(3) *American Economic Review* 525-548.

Greif, Avner, Milgrom, Paul and Weingast, Barry R, (1994), 'Coordination, Commitment and Enforcement: The Case of the Merchant Guilds', 102(4) *Journal of Political Economy* 745-776.

Ha, Thang, (2000), 'Adjusted FDI Law Emerges from Debates', *Vietnam Investment Review*, Hanoi.

Jamieson, Neil L, (1993), *Understanding Vietnam*, University of California Press, Berkeley.

Kahn, Mushtaq H and Jomo Kwame Sundaram, (2000), 'Introduction', in MH Kahn, Jomo KS (eds), *Rents, Rent-Seeking and Economic Development: Theory and Evidence in Asia*, Cambridge University Press, Cambridge, 1-20.

Keyes, Charles F, (1995), *The Golden Peninsula: Culture and Adaptation in Mainland Southeast Asia*, University of Hawaii Press, Honolulu.

Krueger, Anne O, (1974), 'The Political Economy of the Rent-Seeking Society', 64(3) *American Economic Review* 291-303.

Landa, Janet, (1994), *Trust, Ethnicity and Identity: Beyond the New Institutional Economics of Ethnic Trading Networks, Contract Law, and Gift Exchange*, The University of Michigan Press, Ann-Arbor.

Libecap, Gary D, (1989), *Contracting for Property Rights*, Cambridge University Press, Cambridge.

Libecap, Gary D, (1993), 'Politics, Institutions and Institutional Change: Comment', 149(1) *Journal of Institutional and Theoretical Economics* 29-35.

Libecap, Gary D, (1996), 'Economic Variables and the Development of the Law: The Case of Western Mineral Rights', in LJ Alston, T Eggertsson, DC North (eds), *Empirical Studies in Institutional Change*, Cambridge University Press, Cambridge, 34-58.

Marr, David G, (1971), *Vietnamese Anticolonialism 1885-1925*, University of California Press, Los Angeles.

Marr, David G, (1981), *Vietnamese Tradition on Trial, 1920-1945*, University of California Press, Berkeley.

Mauro, Paolo, (1995), 'Corruption and Growth', 110 *The Quarterly Journal of Economics*, August, 681-712.

McMillan, John and Woodruff, Christopher, (1999), 'Dispute Prevention Without Courts in Vietnam', 15(3) *Journal of Law and Economics* 637-658.

Nguyen, Manh Hung, (2000), 'Vietnam in 1999: The Party's Choice', 40(1) *Asian Survey* 98-111.

North, Douglass C, (1981), *Structure and Change in Economic History*, WW Norton, New York.

North, Douglass C, (1990), *Institutions, Institutional Change and Economic Performance*, Cambridge University Press, Cambridge.

North, Douglass C, (1991), 'Institutions', 5(1) *Journal of Economic Perspectives* 97-112.

O'Flahertie, Susan, (1996), 'Is Vietnam Worth the Risk?', *Asian Business Review*, June, 24-32.

Pelley, Patricia, (1995), 'The History of Resistance and the Resistance to History in Post-Colonial Constructions of the Past', in KW Taylor and JK Whitmore (eds), *Essays into Vietnamese Pasts*, Southeast Asia Program, Cornell University, Ithaca.

Pike, Douglas, (1994), 'Vietnam in 1993: Uncertainty Closes In', 34(1) *Asian Survey* 64-71.

Plummer, Michael G, (1995), 'The Emerging New Tiger: Economic Reform and Development in Vietnam', 6(3) *Journal of Asian Economics* 307-310.

Porta, Rafael La, Lopez-de-Silanes, Florencio, Shleifer, Andrei and Vishny, Robert, 1999, 'The Quality of Government', 15(1) *Journal of Law and Economics* 222-279.

Post, Ken, (1989), *Revolution, Socialism and Nationalism in Viet Nam*, Vol 1: 'An Interrupted Revolution', Aldershot, Dartmouth.

Riedel, James, (1997), 'The Vietnamese Economy in the 1990s', 11(2) *Asia-Pacific Economic Literature* 58-65.

Rose-Ackerman, Susan, (1999), *Corruption and Government : Causes, Consequences and Reform*, Cambridge University Press, Cambridge.

Schwarz, Adam, (1995), 'The Honeymoon is Over', *Far Eastern Economic Review*, 13 July, 60-64.

Schwarz, Adam, (1996a), 'Vietnam: Safety First', *Far Eastern Economic Review*, 11 July, 14-16.

Schwarz, Adam, (1996b), 'Vietnam: Enemy No 1', *Far Eastern Economic Review*, 11 July, 18.

Shleifer, Andrei and Vishny, Robert W, (1993), 'Corruption', 108 *The Quarterly Journal of Economics*, August, 599-617.

Stier, Ken, (1999), 'Trouble in "Nam"', *Asian Business*, December, 36-39.

Thayer, Carlyle A, (1991), 'Political Developments in Vietnam: From the 6th to 7th National Party Congress', *Vietnam 1991: An Update*, Canberra.

Tirole, Jean, (1996), 'A Theory of Collective Reputations', 63(1) *The Review of Economic Studies* 1-22.

Treisman, Daniel, (2000), 'The Causes of Corruption: A Cross-National Study', 76(3) *Journal of Public Economics* 399-457.

Tri, Vo Nhan and Booth, Anne, (1992), 'Recent Economic Developments in Vietnam', 6(1) *Asia-Pacific Economic Literature* 16-40.

Vasavakul, Thaveeporn, (1996), 'Politics of the Reform of State institutions in the Post-Socialist Era', in S Leung (ed), *Vietnam Assessment: Creating a Sound Investment Climate*, Institute of Southeast Asian Studies, Singapore, 42-68.

Vatikiotis, Michael, (1994), 'Romance Meets Reality', *Far Eastern Economic Review*, 22 September, 72-77.

Womack, Brantly, (1997), 'Vietnam in 1996: Reform Immobilism', 37(1) *Asian Survey* 79-87.

World Bank, Asian Development Bank and UNDP, (2000), *Pillars of Development*, Hanoi.

World Bank, (2000), *Fighting Corruption in Vietnam*, World Bank, Washington.

Chapter 10

The Political-Legal Culture of Anti-Corruption Reforms in Vietnam[1]

John Gillespie

Introduction

The proliferation of corruption in Vietnam following *doi moi* mixed-market reforms in 1986 was perceived as a national calamity by the Communist Party of Vietnam (CPV) (Huong Xuan 1996). A consensus gradually emerged among party leaders that bureaucratic profiteering was detrimental to economic reforms and challenged party legitimacy. Moral rectification campaigns relying on revolutionary zeal, backed by criminal laws borrowed from the Soviet Union, held bureaucratic corruption in check under the command economy, but proved less effective in the post-*doi moi* mixed-market economy. Economic reforms prompted the search for alternative anti-corruption measures that reduced malfeasance without unravelling sociopolitical structures.

Lacking home-grown solutions, the CPV and Government of Vietnam (Government) turned to the United Nations Development Program (UNDP) for assistance in developing anti-corruption strategies. Largely conceived and funded by the UNDP, a Public Administration Reform (PAR) program was developed to circumscribe public and private orbits with legal rules and procedures. Drawing from Western (predominantly American) anti-corruption strategies, PAR presupposed a separation of party and state and legally-definable public and private duties (Government of Vietnam 1994: 2-6; Nguyen Nien 1996).

Legislative reforms under the PAR program are clustered around the recently enacted Ordinances on Anti-Corruption 1998 and Public Employees 1998. The former established bureaucratic behavioural standards, while the latter aimed to professionalise the public service. The Penal Code 1995 was also amended to extend violations of public duty to banking and environmental offences. Public duty definitions of bureaucratic corruption are used

1 The author thanks the Australian Research Council for financial assistance and numerous Vietnamese officials and lawyers for their invaluable assistance.

in these statutes to criminalise behaviour that consciously deviates from formal duties and accepted norms for private advantage (Shihata 1997).

Reforms designed to streamline procedures and abolish licences and permits have achieved limited successes in reducing and constraining bureaucratic powers - and, by extension, the opportunities for corruption (Gillespie 2001a). More typically, however, reforms have either failed to curtail discretionary powers; or have simply displaced them from one regulatory arena to another. Admittedly organisational changes are incomplete and take time to change decision-making patterns, but the party's and state's response to PAR intimates that political-legal institutional structures and cultures may prove formidable barriers to law-based anti-corruption reforms.

Despite acknowledging that the criteria used to define bureaucratic corruption differ between countries, PAR assumes that everywhere corruption is the abuse of powers separating public and private interests. From this perspective, corruption is only possible where state interests, defined by laws and conventions, override private and political party interests. In societies where interests outside the state are paramount, state-centred notions of corruption break down. This chapter explores whether law-based anti-corruption reforms are capable of defining and controlling abuses of power in Vietnam's binary party-state.

Foreign sources of public administration reform policy

By the late 1980s and early 1990s, some party reformers in Vietnam were urging broad-reaching administrative and legal reforms. State apparatuses conceived to implement central planning were manifestly unsuited to controlling abuses of bureaucratic power in a mixed-market economy. Reformers were familiar with bureaucratic corruption, since it permeated the command economy. Credible official sources estimated that, by the start of *doi moi* reforms, approximately forty per cent of state-production passed through non-state distribution channels (Vo Van Kiet 1986: 9). The de facto privatisation of state distribution did not excite high levels of official opprobrium, because it primarily benefited party cadres and reinforced existing sociopolitical structures.

In the new mixed-market economy, the state could no longer simply suppress private markets to curb corruption, but the structural changes required to introduce alternative anti-corruption measures lay beyond the experience of party leaders. Even so, party leaders mostly resisted broad-ranging administrative reforms (Porter 1993: 151; Vietnam Economic Review 1995: 50-51) until inefficiencies and corruption could no longer be ignored (Thu Linh 1993: 3). Reluctantly, they turned to the UNDP to "learn from the knowledge, practical experiences and modern scientific tools of public administration currently available in the world" (Doan Trong Truyen 1996: 92).

A symposium in 1993 co-sponsored by the UNDP and the Vietnamese Office of Government and Institute of National Administration explored ways of more effectively organising public institutions to check bureaucratic corruption (Phan Van Khan 1993: 1-3; Nguyen Khanh 1995: 3-6). The Government in May 1994 launched the PAR program (UNDP Programme Support Document 1995).

Though it is often difficult to identify the origin of transplanted laws and precepts, the PAR program clearly evinces its Western roots. Vinyu Vichit-Vadakan (1996: 128-129), the senior policy adviser to the PAR program, publicly acknowledged that UNDP anti-corruption reforms were based on World Bank policies, which in turn rested on Western (primary American) anti-corruption strategies.

Despite following different trajectories, Western anti-corruption reforms share common assumptions about the proper relationships between political parties, state bureaucracies and society. Structural tensions generated by the triangular relationship between capitalism-democracy-society (Girling 1997: 150-154) and the liberal democratic principle of separate party and state, produced law-based anti-corruption reforms designed to minimise political patronage, cronyism and bribery. Laws were drafted to quarantine bureaucrats from political patronage, but not from liberal political values and ideology.

Anti-corruption reforms in 19th century America, for example, relied on education and training to produce moral and competent public employees infused with capitalistic values. Moral virtue was considered protection enough from the temptations of political patronage. Later, when morality alone failed to check corruption, structural reforms aimed to make bureaucrats more responsive to the public interest, instead of political or personal interests (Goodnow 1967: 127-129). Selecting efficiency and rationality as the ultimate objectives, scientific managers in the 1930s approached corruption as a problem of organisational design rather than moral failing.

Echoing these Western sociopolitical concerns, the PAR program in Vietnam advocated bureaucratic training and meritocratic recruitment and promotion to counter political patronage. However, its overriding objective was taming the bureaucratic juggernaut with laws. PAR programs, for example, have attempted to streamline administrative procedures, close licensing gateways, and enhance accountability through citizen complaint procedures and administrative courts. Underpinning efforts to constrain bureaucratic discretion is the perception that bureaucrats are self-interested wealth-maximisers actively seeking corrupt opportunities (Rose-Akerman 1978). PAR reforms derive this gloomy contention from the public choice theories promoted by the UNDP and World Bank (Mueller 1989).

In summary, PAR programs presuppose democratic, multi-party states that separate party and state, promote 'rule of law' ideology and possess institutions capable of policing boundaries between public and private rights. They further assume a political culture fashioned in the image of self-interested, bureaucratic, wealth-maximisers actively seeking corrupt opportunities (Badson 1996: 101). Anti-corruption laws, as a consequence, attempt to separate party and state, lock bureaucrats out of the market place and, through privatisation, expose state organisations to market competition (Rose-Akerman 1978: 221-225; Buchanan and Tubock 1965: 281). Above all else, PAR anti-corruption programs presume that the more bureaucracies diverge from Weber's bureaucratic ideal, the less control the state has over corruption.

Transplanting legal change

Anti-corruption reforms in Vietnam form part of the broader debate concerning the efficacy of law-reform through legal transplantation. At issue is whether laws arising out of, and serving the sociopolitical needs of one society, can induce similar effects in other societies. Even though transplanted law is widely used to induce anti-corruption reforms in East Asia, the literature does not discuss the sites of interaction between donor and host country laws and legal institutions, much less seek explanations for the uneven reception of transplanted anti-corruption laws.

The implicit assumption underlying PAR anti-corruption reforms is that laws are transplantable because they have de-coupled from their social moorings. Proponents of legal transplantation argue that a long-term process of social differentiation and internationalisation means that laws reflect the legal traditions of governing elites rather than extrinsic social, political and economic factors.[2] Globalising forces are also credited with accelerating legal decoupling, by creating one international legal dialogue comprised of a collection of regional sub-variations (Paul 1995: 614; Teubner 1997: 79). In its extreme form, some multilateral donors postulate a future where a single transnational jurisdiction emerges as national legal systems wither away (Cappelletti et al 1986: 1). It is a small step from this vision of global equivalence and conversion to the supposition that legal transplants no longer convey national culture from one society to another but rather function as a series of technical adjustments between legal systems.

Others deterministically contend that since laws are cultural artefacts that mirror the 'felt needs' of society, they are unlikely to induce the same behaviour in different societies (Von Savigny 1975: 30-8, 152-3; Kahn-Freund 1974: 24-28). Put differently, there is much 'law' beyond legal rules and the transplantation of statutory and doctrinal rules does not necessarily transfer the 'whole law' (Legrand 1997: 119; Seidman and Seidman 1994: 46). Rules, it is argued, lie on the surface of legal systems and do not accurately represent deeper underlying sociopolitical dynamics.

2 Alan Watson (1999: 346-350) is one of the most influential proponents of law reform through legal transplantation. His voluminous writings and shifting interpretations of the relationship between law and society make it difficult, however, to confidently state his position on legal transplanting. For a good discussion of Watson's shifting interpretations, see Ewald (1995: 498-502).

Confounding deterministic explanations, legal history shows that certain legal transplants *do* take root in foreign legal terrain. Although successes are largely limited to borrowing between Western countries (Evens-Jones 1998: 230-233; Watson 1985, 1987: 537-560, 1993: 95), some Western legal transplants function in East Asia (Wellons and Pistor 1997: 35-50).

In considering the uneven reception of transplants, Otto Kahn-Freund (1974: 27) opined that the laws "designed to allocate power, rule-making, decision making, above all, policymaking power" remain deeply embedded in social institutions, and are unlikely to transplant easily. But he also acknowledged that "there are degrees of transferability" (Kahn-Freund 1974: 6). His discourse concerning transferability is scattered in fragments throughout his writings and requires compilation and synthesis with neo-Marxist, comparative law and sociological theory to form a coherent hypothesis (Gillespie 2001a). Kahn-Freund did, however, identify three sites of interaction between imported laws and host country sociopolitical structures:

(i) At a macro-sociopolitical level, legal coupling is strongly influenced by law-making mechanisms and the congruence between the ideological content of transplanted laws and host country politico-legal ideologies. Here ideology signifies categories of meaning to understand social reality. His postulation that ideology profoundly determines the success of legal borrowing is demonstrated in an analysis of the role of ideology in Vietnamese anti-corruption reforms (Gillespie 2001b).

(ii) The effectiveness of transplanted law is also profoundly influenced by its compatibility with host country power structures and legal cultures (epistemologies). Although both ideology and political-legal culture influence modes of thought, political-legal culture encompasses non-abstract cultural processes, such as habits and organisational structures (Silbey 1992; Macaulay 1987).

(iii) Certain laws require specific configurations of state and non-state interest groups, such as market-support organisations (for example banks, lawyers, accountants, unions, political parties, markets and family-based commercial structures) to function effectively.[3]

This discussion applies Kahn-Freund's second proposition concerning the congruence of donor and host country power distribution and legal cultures. The principle inquiry is whether transplanted anti-corruption laws act as technical additions to otherwise structurally- and culturally-developed state institutions. If this presumption is proved, Kahn-Freund's proposition infers that transplanted principles are unlikely to re-engineer existing party-state and public-private boundaries.

The term political-legal culture is used in preference to legal culture, because it broadens the discussion to include power structures that shape

3 The analysis of anti-corruption transplants in Vietnam from the perspective of non-state institutions is a work in progress undertaken by the author.

the political order that dominates Vietnam's legal system. As Daniel Lev recently observed:

> [F]or all that culture has long been taken for granted as a formative influence on law, it does not explain all that much, in fact, and often diverts attention from more critical influences (Lev 2000: 74).

Political-legal culture is taken to mean "a specific way in which values, practices, and concepts are integrated into the operation of legal institutions and the interpretation of legal texts" (Bell 1995: 63-101; Macauley 1987; Silbey 1992). Put more broadly, it is the historically conditioned, deeply-rooted attitudes that influence the way bureaucrats use law to find reality. Political-legal culture encompasses epistemological assumptions regarding rationality, efficiency and merit, which in turn shape understandings of the relative importance of party and state policies and rules and, in particular, the boundaries separating state and private orbits.

Imagining the Vietnamese state

Drafted to minimise corruption in Western, liberal democracies, PAR anti-corruption laws presupposed coherent and functionally distinct political parties and state organs. Most nation states have created approximations of Western politico-legal institutions, such as parliaments, courts, and executive agencies. For example, Vietnam imported a Soviet institutional structure comprising a National Assembly, President, government (executive), People's Courts, and People's Procuracy. Soviet state institutions were in turn originally based on European models adopted by Czarist Russia (Butler 1988: 25-26; Sacco 1988). Though sharing institutional commonalities, the fact that the Soviet state functioned differently from Western Europe and the Vietnamese state differed from the Soviet template, suggests that states are more than structurally-equivalent institutional configurations.

Conventional definitions invest states with the sole authority, with the backing of force, to make and implement binding rules for all people within a given territory. According to this formula, Vietnam uses different institutional configurations to implement party policy, but otherwise functions like Western states. Others believe that state models comprised of impersonal superstructures overlying society are incompatible with observed reality. As Theodore Lowi wrote, "one can look in vain for the state. What one generally sees are rules ..." (Lowi 1987: 1070). Still others add that institutional rules operate through "the continuous and regulated activities of individuals acting as occupants of offices" (Poggi 1978; March and Olsen 1989: 17-22). They suggest that what makes state institutions distinctive are the rules, precepts and habits residing inside and outside formal structures that guide the distribution of state power. The next section briefly traces the main political-legal influences shaping the Vietnamese state.

Historical patterns

Constructed from different systems of knowledge, the new overlaying the old (McKinley 1979: 306; Rambo 1987: 121-122), state-building everywhere is a product of historical processes. It is argued that in a myriad of permutations the new overlaying the old, foreign influences—Chinese, French colonial, socialist, contemporary East Asian and Western—have created striated sociopolitical institutions in Vietnam. Imported laws and institutions have been superimposed over indigenous Vietnamese cultural precepts and habits.

The imperial state

Vietnamese imperial institutions were closely modelled on the Chinese state (Woodside 1971: 66-96, 112-126). Especially after the adoption of Confucianism as the state ideology by the Le Dynasty in the 15th century, the Vietnamese state organised around three pillars: emperor, Confucian ideology and bureaucracy (Wolters 1979: 447-488; Smith 1973: 16-21). As the Son of Heaven (*Thien Tu*), emperors and, by extension, the mandarinate, represented the embodiment of moral virtue. They were Confucian 'superior men' (*quan tu*).

Since most mandarins lacked large estates and bonded labourers, they justified their privileges by claiming Confucian moral supremacy. Woodside (1999: 23-24) writes that assertions of moral superiority as the 'first knowers' or 'first apprehenders of principles', invested mandarins with mystical clairvoyant powers and a duty to instruct those who were slower to understand. From their position of moral superiority, only emperors and mandarins were permitted to relate Confucian principle to reality. Confucian ideology both legitimised, and furnished the moral basis for, personal rule. It stressed that social integration could only come through hierarchical social patterns: the emperor at the pinnacle, followed by mandarins, village notables and family heads.

The state ruled by conflating political and religious/moral authority in government teachings: a process that inhibited the development of doctrines separating and specialising state power (Woodside 1999: 23-24). Specialisation of state institutions, such as legislators and courts was further contained by the tendency to analogise the state to the family. Since the emperor was the head of the bureaucracy (outer court) and the imperial household (inner court), a clear distinction between public and private functions was difficult. Bureaucrats routinely interfered in the imperial household and in turn, members of the imperial household interfered in bureaucratic matters. By functioning like an extended family, distinctions between state and society and public and private were obscured. The interests of rulers were synonymous with those of the state.

French colonial administration

France had transformed into a liberal, democratic state by the time it colonised the southern province of Cochin China in 1862 (Hooker 1978: 175-185; Marr 1971: 12-22; Nguyen The Anh 1985: 147-151). The remaining provinces of Annam (Central Vietnam) and Tonkin (Northern Vietnam) notionally continued under the leadership of the Nguyen emperors, subject to the overriding control of the French Resident Générale. Imperial edicts were ineffective unless endorsed by colonial officials.

The French were not interested in indiscriminately administering all inhabitants and maintained two parallel administrative and legal systems. Since the colonial system used law as the primary written record of government policy, implementation required a complex administrative and judicial system. Colonial power was concentrated in Resident Générales backed by an executive and courts lead by Frenchmen (Marr 1981: 24).[4] Without democracy there was no need for a legislature. The authoritarian colonial state used universal laws instrumentally to impose order, without providing counterbalancing liberal democratic institutions capable of defining and policing boundaries between public and private interests.

A tiny indigenous group (less than one per cent of the population) of Western-educated middle- and low-ranking government officials and businessmen mediated between the colonial leaders and the masses (Luong 1992: 80). Though Western philosophical and literary canon was read by the Francophone elite (some volumes were translated into Vietnamese), Western state institutions were associated with colonial repression by all but a few of the urban intelligentsia (Luong 1992: 85-86; Nguyen Khac Kham et al 1967: 228-249). Throughout the colonial period, rural Vietnamese (in Annam and Tonkin) continued to be governed by the mandarinate and village notables.

By the end of the colonial period, French influence in urban centres had reordered traditional patterns of social organisation with Western bureaucratic institutions and processes. Located on the periphery of the colonial administrative map, the corporate village structures that had once moderated the behaviour of mandarins and village officials degenerated, giving rise to unprecedented levels of corruption, nepotism and patron-clientism.

Socialist administration

The anti-colonial struggle, culminating in the declaration of independence in 1945, was lead by the *Dang Duong Cong San Dang* (Indochinese Communist Party) (ICP). As a revolutionary organisation, the ICP's main objectives were to replace the colonial state with revolutionary organs and a "struggle against feudalism" (Nguyen Khac Vien 1993: 198-199). Revolutionary

4 Approximately 60 per cent of the state budget supported Frenchmen, who held the top 20 per cent of the colonial posts.

ideology derived from the Soviet Union, and to a lesser extent China, emphasised the central role of the 'vanguard party' leading a class struggle, the Leninist principle of 'democratic centralism', and implementing policy through mass-mobilisation campaigns rather than bureaucracies (Marr 1995: 210-214, 225-232). Although, the Democratic Republic of Vietnam (DVR) established the trappings of a modern state, such as a National Assembly and Military and Civil Courts, other legal institutions - including State Economic Arbitrators and Procurators - were imported much later from the Soviet Union (Ginsburgs 1979: 190).

French legalism lingered for some years after independence, but by the 1970s had been largely displaced by the imported Soviet system. Not only were despised colonial institutions and legal norms targeted for reform, but many Francophile Vietnamese fled to the South in 1954 and overseas after reunification in 1975.

The relationship between party and state was never clear in the DRV. First there was the question of whether the party or legislators made the law. So few laws were passed by the early National Assembly, some commentators believe, that "even a semblance of legality became superfluous or just a formality" (Hoang The Lien 1994: 34). Secondly, the issue of party subordination to state law had little practical relevance, since there were few laws, while the voices raised in opposition to the party 'replacing law with viewpoint' were suppressed (Nguyen Huu Dang, 1956). Until comprehensive economic reforms were introduced under *doi moi* reforms, law and party policy were interchangeable and implementing agencies did not distinguish between legislation and party edicts. There was no real attempt to apply consistently, far less develop, a coherent body of rules circumscribing public and private orbits. Thirdly, the overlapping responsibilities between party committees or state administrators led Party Secretary, Le Duan (1978: 91) in 1978 to lament that the party was supposed to "lead the state, but not replace the state".

Following reunification in 1975, the revolutionary nature of party rule became increasingly irrelevant to the tasks of managing a modern state with a professional bureaucracy. Questions were raised during the Fifth and Sixth Party Congress as to whether revolutionary ideology should continue to dominate state institutions. As the party pondered these issues, the withdrawal of Soviet aid in 1989 forced the state to attract alternative sources of capital and engage with the non-communist world. External competition strengthened calls for a competent professional state bureaucracy. State-building raised questions of whether party leaders should obey laws, whether party organs should transfer supremacy to the legislature and, finally, whether the party should surrender control over government administration.

The 1992 Constitution appeared to eschew revolutionary tradition in favour of constitutional order. Party organs were required to operate within the framework of the law and the National Assembly was exalted as the paramount state institution. The Constitution did not clarify party-state relations. Evidently, the party was unable to decide whether to remain undifferentiated from the state and risk becoming submerged, or to detach and risk losing relevance and dominance (Thaveeporn Vasavakul 1997: 91-92). This unresolved tension continues to influence the configuration and implementation of anti-corruption laws in contemporary Vietnam.

Conceptualising the state through anti-corruption laws

Though resting on PAR conceptual principles, the distribution of power in Vietnamese anti-corruption laws reflects the ambivalent status of party and state. Article 1 of the Ordinance on Anti-Corruption 1998 defines corruption as taking advantage of 'responsible positions' (*vi tri co trach nhiem*) and 'state power' (*quyen luc nha nuoc*) to embezzle, accept bribes or otherwise obtain a personal benefit. These elements are elaborated in the Penal Code 1999, which describes corruption as "infringements upon the legitimate activities of [sic, party and state] agencies and/or organisations"[5] by those "taking advantage of position and power" for personal gain or 'violating the law'.[6] Superficially, these provisions accord with PAR public duty notions of bureaucratic corruption: the criminalisation of behaviour that consciously deviates from formal duties and accepted norms for private advantage (Ibrahim Shihata 1997). A closer reading of the Vietnamese law shows that 'legitimate activities' are violated by abusing powers and duties that are both regulated and unregulated by law.

As a corollary, corruption is comprised of several elements. Wrong-doers must hold 'responsible positions and state power' and take advantage of their 'positions and powers' in ways that infringe the 'legitimate activities' of party or state bodies, and either derive personal benefit and/or violate state law. Corruption is accordingly composed of two concepts – abuse of power and violating laws. This observation provokes a series of questions: what is, and who exercises, state power and what is the nexus between state power and law?

State positions

Anti-corruption laws provide that only those holding 'state positions' can act corruptly. Decree No 64/ND-CP Detailing and Guiding the Implementation of the Ordinance against Corruption 1998, Art 1, identifies "persons holding positions of power" as public employees (*vien chuc*), while the Ordinance on Public Employees 1998 (OPE), Art 1, defines public employees as "Vietnamese citizens who are on the State payroll and get paid from the State budget". This expansive definition not only encompasses those working in the state executive (such as ministries and people's committees/local government) but also extends to elected National

5 Penal Code 1999, Art 277.

6 Decree No 64/ND-CP Detailing and Guiding the Implementation of the Ordinance Against Corruption, 1998 Art 2.

Assembly delegates, army, police and teachers. Although CPV members are not specifically mentioned, the definition includes "people who are recruited, appointed or assigned regular tasks in political and sociopolitical organisations". Since the CPV and associated Fatherland Front mass-organisations are the only political organisations permitted in Vietnam, members of CPV standing committees and organs paid from the state budget are, by implication, state employees and hold 'positions of power'.

Rather like prerogative powers, those holding 'state positions' (*vi tri nha nuoc*) are invested with 'state power'. Abuse of 'position and power' (*vi tri va quyen luc nha nuoc*) depends on whether the 'legitimate activities' (*cac hoat dong hop phap*) attached to state positions have been violated. The term 'legitimate activities' is not defined and is sufficiently nebulous to encompass duties and obligations derived from sources other than law.

Mapping the sources of 'state power'

The legislative framework

Both the Constitution and the OPE 1998, Art 3, require those holding 'state positions' to "strictly abide by party-lines and policies and state policies and law". State laws establishing the legal architecture governing the powers and operational parameters of state organisations are non-specific and hortative. They are devoted to delineating areas of responsibility and creating reporting regimes for organisational hierarchies. Take, for example, the rules clarifying the powers and duties of Market Management Authorities (*ban quan ly thi truong*). Decree No 10 on the Tasks and Powers of Market Management 1995 established an organisation led by the Ministry of Trade and administered by market control authorities attached to provincial/city and district people's committees.[7] Market control authorities are required to "inspect and control" the market by enforcing "laws, regulations and policy regimes" (*phap luat va cac chinh sach, che do, the le*) and ordering commercial activities. "Laws, regulations and policy regimes" (*phap luat va cac chinh sach, che do, the le*) are comprised of legally enforceable instruments and sub-legal official instructions, letters or resolutions issued by the party politburo and ministries. Internal sub-legal documents prescribe the 'policy regimes' (*chinh sach che do*) that fine-tune the scope and nature of 'state power'.

For instance, Decree No 10 1995 requires market control authorities to 'manage' (*quan ly*) economic markets. Implementing regulations, rather unhelpfully, describe the purpose of market management as "organising the

7 Decree No 10 on the Organisation and Responsibilities of the Market Management Authorities 23 January 1995, sets out the organisational structure and function of the central and provincial authorities. Decision No 269 TM/QLTT (MoT) on the Organisation and Responsibilities and Rights of the Market Management Authorities 1995 and Decision No 35 Concerning Administration and Market Management Fines, Use of Firearms 30 March 1995 (Ministry of Trade) contains more specific duties and basic powers.

market ... to promote production development and expand goods circulation according to the law".[8] Numerous sub-legal documents issued by the party and state promote *y truong lanh manh* (healthy markets) as the regulatory ideal. Although preserving the state benefit (*loi ich cua nha nuoc*) is unquestionably the overriding regulatory objective, implementing rules and regulations contain few applicable standards or principles. As a result, the precise meaning of *y truong lanh manh* (healthy markets) is never fixed, and is flexibly adjusted through the 'policy regime' (*chinh sach che do*) to reflect protean party-state economic policies.

The rules governing inspection powers are similarly open-ended. Market control authorities are required to "observe the law and the working statute on market management".[9] General provisions concerning 'market management' and the assessment of penalties are contained in the Ordinance on the Handling of Violations of Administrative Regulations 1995, and the Decree on Administrative Penalties for Economic Violations 1996. Once again, numerous bureaucratic decisions and sub-legal circulars and official letters implement these higher level legal documents. Sub-legal documents determine the type of identification and firearms carried, uniforms worn and documentation used by market control authorities. They do not, however, convey practically applicable guidelines determining the scope and nature of 'state power'. The detailed nuances of 'state power' are conveyed through non-legislative conduits.

Party leadership of the state

Differentiating the party and state

If statutory rules delineating 'state power' are open-ended, what other sources of authority constrain bureaucratic discretion? The answer lies in the relationship between party and state.

From the inception of the DRV, party control over state organs generated confusion. The party applied the principle that leadership of society must be "direct, unified and detailed" (Porter 1993: 84-85). Reformers at the Fifth National Congress of the Communist Party of Vietnam in 1982, argued for a separation of the party from the day-to-day running of the government. Administrative reforms were intended to "overcome resolutely and definitely the long-standing confusion of functions between party and state organs".[10] Little was done, however, until the Sixth National Congress of the CPV in 1986 decided that:

8 Decision No 96/TTg Promulgating Regulations on the Responsibility and Relations of Coordination of Activities among State Management Agencies in the Management of the Market and the Fight Against Smuggling and Other Acts of Illicit Trade 1995 (Prime Minister), Art 7.

9 Decree No 10 on the Organisation and Responsibilities of the Market Management Authorities, 23 January 1995, Art 6.

10 Quoting Le Duc Tho at the Fifth Party Congress in 1982. Reproduced in Carlyle Thayer (1991: 23).

> [t]he management of the country should be performed by law instead of simply by moral concepts. … It is necessary to systematically supplement and perfect the legal system so as to ensure that state machinery organises and operates in accordance with the law (Truong Chinh 1986).

Under this proposal, the party would determine socioeconomic objectives, such as modernisation (*hien dai hoa*) and industrialisation, and the state would enact and implement laws to realise these policy goals.

The party-state nexus is not defined by law. Constitutional reforms in 1992 were designed to 'separate state functions' (*hoc thuyet tam quyen phan lap*) from party functions, but not depoliticise the state and bureaucracy (Nguyen Van Tai 1996: 7). Unlike their Western counterparts, Vietnamese policymakers never countenanced quarantining bureaucrats from direct party supervision and control (Than Duy 1998: 26-27). Party theorists explain that "the Party rules and uses the State as a tool to manage society. The Party must be the centre of political leadership, while the State is the centre of the political power" (Than Duy 1998: 26-27). The Party Statute provides that the CPV "leads the state and political and mass organisations through its political platform … and by its supervision and control". State bureaucrats are accordingly required to implement party policy transmitted by party and state organs. This 'lip and teeth' (*moi va sang*) party-state nexus raises some perplexing questions about the efficacy of legal definitions of corruption based on 'state power'.

Party resolutions

Until 1989 the party operated like a parallel government. VCP departments dealt directly with their counterparts in state organs (Nguyen Huu Tho 1989: 65). Following internal reforms, the party's daily work is now carried out by a series of committees (*uy ban*), commissions (*ban*) and offices (*van phong*). For example, economic policy formulation has been consolidated into the Economic Commission (*Ban Kinh Te Trung Uong*) (Sidel 1997a: 483-484). Informants indicate that the Commission develops detailed directives guiding the implementation of broad economic policies contained in Central Committee and Politburo resolutions. The internal operational guidelines on market management prepared by the Ministry of Trade, for instance, are based on internal policy directives compiled by the Economic Commission.

The OPE 1998, more generally, requires state employees to operate under the direct authority of party resolutions (OPE, Art 1). Article 4 places the work of state employees under "the uniform leadership of the Communist Party of Vietnam", while Art 6 requires state employees to "[s]trictly abide by the Party's lines and polices, and the State's policy and law…" Even "the management of public employees shall comply with the Vietnamese Communist Party's and State's regulations on assignment of sub-management" (OPE, Art 37). By differentiating party policy and state law, the OPE clearly signals that state employees must obey both sources of authority.[11]

In requiring, universal, authoritative and compulsory law, the doctrine of *nha nuoc phap quyen* (law-based state) introduced by the Seventh Party Congress in 1991 theoretically constrains party power within Constitutional institutions (Nguyen Duy Quy 1994: 32). Notions of legal equality compete, however, with deeply entrenched principles of 'socialist legality' (*phap che xa hoi chu nghia*) (Hoang Hao 1987: 24-28; Tran Duc 1987: 69-73). This Soviet concept provides that "law is the institutionalisation of Party lines and policies and a manifestation of the people's will" (Truong Chinh 1986). Its one purpose is to promote the party-line (Nguyen Dinh Loc 1999: 14-20). Even though the language of class-struggle is unfashionable, the Marxist-Leninist footprints of socialist legality criss-cross the legal system.

Despite efforts to 'routinise' party rule through legal instruments, statutory rules remain both hortative and unimplementable or narrow, prescriptive 'bureaucratic rules'. As a party commentator recently observed, since "all party directives and resolutions are still implemented by the people through their 'self-understanding' (*tu tim hieu*), the role of the state is somewhat blurred" (Nguyen Nham 1997). The legal system lacks secondary rules and jurisprudential principles capable of interpreting and circumscribing primary legal documents. In their place, party-state directives provide the operational standards and norms used by bureaucrats to link law with reality. For example, bureaucratic loyalty is evaluated according to political and professional yardsticks. However, informants indicate that political (*chinh tri*) and moral (*dao duc*) qualities (*pham chu*) are valued more highly than professional competence.

Some indication of the relative importance of party policy and state law is gleaned from the different standards of bureaucratic reporting. Agency heads must submit monthly reports reviewing "the execution of the Party's resolutions",[12] but report only twice yearly on the implementation of laws combating "red-tape, authoritarianism, corruption, harassment of the people and weakness in the implementation of tasks, plans and law ...".

Party leadership in state apparatuses

Recruitment and promotion

The party leads the state from the outside and inside. Internal party control over the state is provided by the *nomenklatura* system, which reserves key state positions for party members (Beresford 1988: 105-108; Sidel 1997b: 364). The *nomenklatura* ensure that 'state power' follows the party-line (Party

11 Decree No 97/ND-CP on the Disciplining and Material Responsibilities of Public Employees 1998, Art 3.

12 Decree No 71/ND-CP Promulgating Regulations on Exercising Democracy in the Activities of Agencies, Art 5.

Statute 1996, Art 42(20).[13] The Party Central Organising Committee (*Ban to chuc Trung uong*) compiles *nomenklatura* lists for central level positions, and party branches perform an equivalent function at provincial/city and village/district levels.

Legal justification for the *nomenklatura* system is weak. The Constitution contains vague principles confirming party leadership of state and society, while the Party Statute (which is not a legal instrument) entitles "the party to recommend qualified cadre for state agencies … for selection and employment" (Party Statute 1996, Art 41 (2)).

Some commentators speculate that the *nomenklatura* system has declined in importance since *doi moi*. They argue that the National Assembly rather than party organs now has the final say over the appointment of ministers. Even so, well-informed Western observers believe that the system fills enough key state positions to ensure that the party elite is the state elite (Dang Phong and Beresford 1998: 92-94). Using horizontal linkages intertwining party and state, party organs directly participate in state decision-making, prompting Nguyen Nham (1997: 3), a senior party commentator, to observe that "the role of the Party somehow 'encroaches upon' that of the state".

Under the PAR program, attempts have been made to professionalise the public service (OPE, Art 23). Recruits are expected to "possess good morals, meet professional criteria and pass recruitment examinations". There is insufficient information to ascertain whether meritocratic recruitment has eroded *nomenklatura* power, but this outcome seems unlikely. It is true that party recruitment emphasises talent and education in addition to Marxist-Leninist theory but recruitment procedures are evidently waived for senior state positions (Nguyen Phu Trong 1999: 8-9).

Party affairs sections (Ban Can Su Dang)

Although the *nomenklatura* system places party members in state positions, "[t]he party exercises its rule through party organisations and not through individual members" (CPV 1996: 6). Party affairs sections (*ban can su dang*) are the main conduits of party power in state organs. They are expected to "lead and motivate members in the organisation, to implement the party-line and polices" (Marr 1994: 8-9). Party affairs sections are formed at each level of state agencies.

At the central level, party affairs sections typically include ministers, vice-ministers and senior department heads (Dang Phong and Beresford 1998: 47-49). These bodies transform detailed policy directives received from central committee commissions and committees into subordinate legislation,

13 Informants believe the Vietnamese *nomenklatura* is modelled on the Soviet party recruitment system, but offer few details about its organisational form and the criteria used to compile *nomenklatura* lists. Informed Western observers believe, however, that the system allows the party apparatus to become deeply enmeshed in all levels of state decision-making.

sub-legal documents and *quan triet* (highly authoritative instructions). They also channel state information back to relevant central party organs. Returning to the example of market management, the party affairs section in the Ministry of Trade formulates subordinate regulations and guidelines creating the 'policy regime' (*chinh sach che do*) governing provincial/city level market control authorities. Party affairs sections at the provincial/city level implement and, where necessary, localise policy regimes.

Despite long-standing criticism that party affairs sections confuse lines of authority, eroding the prestige of state organ managers, the system remains entrenched (Le Quang Thuong 1996: 19; Nguyen Kim Dinh 1995: 57-58, 66). A senior party official recently opined "[n]o matter how big an economic unit is, if it is headed by a person who is not a party member, this does not mean that the unit lies outside party leadership" (Nguyen Huu Tho 1988: 7). In other words, even if the organisational head is not appointed through the *nomenklatura*, party affairs sections ensure compliance with the party line.

Democratic centralism

Democratic centralism (*tap trung dan chu*) is the organisational principle that binds central party organs, party affairs sections and party members (Doan Khue 1998: 6-9; Do Phuong 1995). The doctrine's main objectives are to place common interests above personal interests and the national interest above provincial interests and to make individuals responsible for collective decisions (Doan Khue 1998: 6-9; Tien Chouc 1999).

Democratic centralism aims to generate discipline and adherence within state organisations to party resolutions, instructions (*chu truong*) and hierarchical lines of personal authority. Party members are enjoined to strictly obey central party resolutions and the "monolithic thought and action" of the party-state (Khue Doan 1998: 6-9). It places the National Congress at the pinnacle of the party structure, followed by the central committee, politburo and provincial/city, district and xa/phuong party committees. Party affairs sections in state organs are required to "submit themselves to higher-echelon organisations" (Party Statute 1996, Art 9). "No party members should be allowed to distance themselves from the management of organisations" (CPV 1996: 3-6). The ultimate objective of democratic centralism is to create party affairs sections that owe allegiance to the central party before state organs.

Polycentric power-sharing

Far removed from monolithic *democratic centralism*, polycentric party power fragments among institutions and even between different departments in the same organisation. Although the permutations of party-state power-sharing are endless, commentators have identified several governing factors (Beresford 1988: 105-108, 118; Thayer 1991: 21-28). Party membership alone says little about personal attitudes to public morality. Marxist-Leninism and the thoughts of Ho Chi Minh are sufficiently nebulous to legitimise a vast range of precepts, attitudes and habits.

In this ideological and moral ether, organisational environments are potent shapers of social and moral attitudes. Especially in powerful ministries and people's committees, rather than dictating party policy, party affairs sections are influenced and even co-opted by institutional imperatives. For similar reasons, provincial party branches must negotiate rather than impose outcomes where the local party secretary chairs the people's committee. Power-sharing is more pronounced where senior party officials head economically weak state bodies like the courts and poor provincial people's committees. In these circumstances, bureaucratic policy is largely determined by the party viewpoint.

Polycentric power structures and party-state power sharing are inevitable corollaries of the extremely complex interaction between party organs, party affairs sections and state organisational structures (Thaveeporn Vasavakul 1997: 81, 114-117). Numerous calls to implement strictly democratic centralism underscore the fact that the party line is not monolithically followed by state organisations.

Party leadership through moral example

So far, the discussion has considered direct party leadership of the state through resolutions and democratic centralism. Political morality, however, provides an equality potent control system that is overlooked by the PAR program because it operates beyond the parameters of Western legalism. Nguyen Khac Vien famously observed that "[a]mong the great family of Communist Parties, the Vietnamese and Chinese have particularly exhibited more of a moralistic tone than Communist Parties elsewhere" (Nguyen Khac Vien 1974; Truong Chinh 1994: 563-568). He was of the opinion that in defining people as "a totality of their social relationships", Confucianism and Marxism shared similar frames of reference that transcended doctrinal differences. Belief in 'collective discipline' and the 'fulfilment of social obligations' provided a common platform that enabled neo-Confucian political morality to influence profoundly Marxist-Leninist party-state relationships.

Naturally, the heavenly authority of Confucianism could hardly differ more from Marxist-Leninist secularism and claims to 'scientific' legitimacy. Of equal importance, neo-Confucian morals conflicted with Marxist-Leninist principles of state ownership and class struggle (Marr 1981: 130-132). Transcending these differences, the party drew heavily upon the neo-Confucian principle of *chinh nhgia* (exclusive righteousness) to support assertions of Marxist-Leninist infallibility (Nguyen Khai Vien 1974: 45-52; Young 1979).

The associated neo-Confucian concept that 'superior men' are morally obligated to lead society strongly resonated in Ho Chi Minh's adaptation of Marxist-Leninism to Vietnamese conditions (Woodside 1971: 112-168). He exalted the party-state to 'a higher level' by making it responsible for the people's needs.

> If the people are hungry, it is the fault of the Party and the Government, if the people are cold, it is the fault of the Party and Government, if the people are sick, it is the fault of the Party and the Government (Thanh Duy 1997: 27-28).

Leadership by moral virtue is a consistent theme in his reception of Marxist-Leninism (Nguyen Duy Quy 1997: 16). "A brilliant example", he argued "is better than one hundred propaganda speeches" (Vo Nguyen Giap 1999: 8-9, 11). Leadership through revolutionary ethics became a pivotal tool of party rule.

By portraying the party-state as an infallible moral exemplar, contemporary writings echo neo-Confucian political theory. Nguyen Phu Trong, a member of the politburo, grandiloquently described the party as "the intellect, the honour, the conscience of our time, the party is the embodiment of the wisdom, quality, the quintessence of the nation" (Nguyen Phu Trong 1999). High-ranking party officials are, by implication, 'superior men' inhabiting a moral high ground that descends in all social directions. Party authority and legitimacy depend on the public believing assertions of moral rectitude. This linkage is constantly reinforced by commentators warning that corruption endangers party survival (Bui Dinh Bon 1994: 4; Editorial 1997: 1, 3).

A correlate of party-state infallibility is the notion that senior party members should educate and lead the state and society through exemplary virtue. Self-improvement is accordingly an obligation of every party member. Especially those in senior state positions are required to:

> constantly study and steel oneself to improve one's knowledge, working ability, political quality and revolutionary ethics; adopt a wholesome lifestyle; struggle against individualism, opportunism, departmentalism, bureaucracy, corruption, wasteful spending and other negative phenomena (Party Statute, Art 2(2)).

Once again, contemporary policies reflect neo-Confucianism, which held that education perfects human nature.

Ethical standards are maintained by first vetting the political background of party applicants and three generations of their extended families, and secondly, by inculcating political theory. Central Committee Resolution No 210 on Teaching Political Theory and Ideology to Cadres and Party Members 1970 established party theoretical training schools at district, provincial, and central levels. Depending upon party seniority, those aspiring for promotion are required to complete political training courses at the middle-level party schools or advanced degree courses at the Ho Chi Minh Political Academy (Nguyen Phu Trong 1999: 7-8). In addition to Marxist-Leninism and the thoughts of Ho Chi Minh, in-service training courses familiarise party members with the party viewpoint on state policies and laws. A willingness to study political theory is a pre-condition for promotion, while non-attendance is a ground for expulsion. Large numbers of party members take part in training courses (Nguyen Phu Trong 1999: 7-9).

Considerable importance is attached to ensuring that:

> [C]lean party members keep their purity. Those who are not clean must purify themselves. Those who degraded themselves should now realise their mistakes and be given assistance to correct themselves (Tien Chuoc 1999: 3).

A recent regulation issued by the Politburo designed to "enhance the political acumen and revolutionary ethics of cadres and party members and strengthen the militancy and leadership capabilities of the party to meet requirements on the new stage" prescribes appropriate moral values (Saigon Giai Phong 1999d: 2). In addition to prohibiting party members from criticising the party or state, members are required to follow state rules and party policies in allocating land and approving investment projects. They are forbidden from bribing state officials to acquit law-breakers; using state funds for entertainment and gambling; buying 'unlawful' lottery tickets; managing 'unhealthy' businesses such as karaoke bars and massage parlours; and "feasting in ways that damage the personality of party members". The resolution also forbids party members from organising holidays, lavish funerals, weddings, housewarming parties or other celebrations that exceeded the 'normal level' (*cap trung binh*).

Party morality is reinforced through 'self-criticism' (*tu phe binh*), a process involving criticism and confession of public and private transgressions. Since party members are expected to lead through moral example, little distinction is made between public and private morality. Attempts to differentiate public and private orbits with legislation have been largely unsuccessful. For example, the implementation of assets declaration legislation has been deferred "to prevent possible instability in agencies and organisations as well as indication of psychological negativity that might follow the declaration of assets by officials" (*Thoi Boa Kinh Te Saigon* 1998: 3).

Unravelling the party-state nexus

The dual systems of party leadership and accountability problematise conventional representations of the state. Constitutional theory rather vaguely requires party organisations to operate within the law. Party theorists distinguish party and state by rhetorically asserting that the party formulates policy, which the state implements. However, these explanations do not account for party affairs sections, democratic centralism and moral leadership.

That party organs deeply penetrate Vietnamese state institutions is beyond question. Whether the party's reach is sufficient to justify the compound term 'party-state' is less certain. The distinction is significant, because party directives in binary party-states emanate from within the state and do not constitute external (to the state) corrupt influences.

The relationship between party and state is complicated by the party's dual roles. In some circumstances the party functions as a type of political bureaucracy that formulates policy for the state. Like Western political parties, in this manifestation the party is functionally separate from, and frequently competes with state institutions. But this competitive role coexists with a revolutionary party that functions like a mass organisation, infiltrating, managing and controlling state institutions through resolutions, party affairs sections and the *nomenklatura* system. In this guise, the party "uses the state as a tool to manage society" (Nguyen Nham 1997). The party is in state institutions, but also above and around them.

The binary party-state lies beyond the explanatory power of Western, democratic notions of the state and challenges the presumption of separate party and state underpinning PAR anti-corruption reforms. Where the party functions as a political bureaucracy, laws are the primary locus of the 'legitimate activities' of public officials. In this legal space it makes sense to define corruption as the violation of 'state power' for personal gain, because 'state power' is based on, and circumscribed by law. Where the party functions as a revolutionary organ, the 'legitimate activities' of state officials are based on party resolutions, party interpretations of state law and direct personalistic rule through party affairs sections. In this revolutionary space abuses of 'state power' can arise from violating law, party-policy, personal party directions or a combination thereof. The transplantation of PAR anti-corruption reforms to a society regulated by legal and extra-legal 'revolutionary' state power presupposes an improbable voluntary submission of party political power to state law.

Punishing abuses of state power

One means of evaluating whether party power complies with state law is by observing the criminal prosecution of corrupt party officials. Two sets of rules and institutions are used to assess and punish abuse of 'state power': the Party Statute 1996 and party investigation and disciplinary committees, and state law and legal institutions. Party statutes penalise breaches of party rules and state law. Art 53 of the 1976 Party Statute, for example, emphatically stated that "party members violating state law must be subject to strict and unequivocal disciplinary measures taken by the party and the state, and not be condoned by anyone".

Despite subsequent constitutional reforms requiring party organisations and members to follow the law, the 1996 Party Statute, Arts 1, 9, rather indeterminately directs members to follow party resolutions and state law. Contrasting with its predecessor, it does not directly authorise state officials to investigate party members. Party members "manifesting poor attitudes towards organisational structures, deliberately opposing party instructions and resolutions and showing tendencies to breed factions within the party" violate party rules. They also violate state powers, because those holding 'state positions' are required by the OPE, Art 6(2) to follow the party line and policies. For similar reasons, breaches of the party line and hierarchical command structures (established under democratic centralism) also violate state power. Party members are further forbidden from breaching state law and must allocate state resources according to state regulations (Lao Dong 1999: 1).

Operating within party and state organs, inspection committees investigate behaviour that impedes the implementation of the party's political platform, resolutions, directives, and organisational principles (democratic centralism) (Nguyen Thi Xuan My 1997: 4-5). Their powers extend to breaches of public authority, such as "lines, policies, resolutions and directives", and breaches of personal morality like "declining virtue and lifestyle among cadre and party members" (Nguyen Thi Xuan My 1997: 4-6). The "Government and its party affairs sections take collective action and responsibility [sic] against corrupt cadre to ensure the principles of democratic centralism" (Vo Van Kiet 1996: 3). Sanctions include 'self-criticism', demotion or, in serious cases, expulsion from the party (Party Statute 1996, Art 35).

The Statute does not indicate whether party rules apply before, after, or in addition to, state laws. The relationship between internal party investigations and those conducted by state inspectors and procurators is similarly vague (Party Statute 1996, Arts 30-33). The case studies below intimate, however, that state prosecution is permitted only where party discipline strips party members of immunity.

Party rules versus state laws

According to the Penal Code 1999 and the Ordinance against Corruption 1998, anti-corruption provisions apply to public employees regardless of party membership or rank. Statistical evidence and case studies portray a reality significantly different from the statutory ideal. Over a two year period between 1994 and 1995, for example, 7,000 state officials (most of whom were party members) were prosecuted for corruption (Nguyen Tri Dung 1995: 5). Only 876 cases went to trial and the conviction rate was very low.

Consider the case of the Director and Deputy Director of the Education-Computer Science Service in Ho Chi Minh City, who were prosecuted under Art 226 of the Penal Code 1986 for accepting bribes totalling 100 million *dong* (approximately US $700) (Duy Quang Chu 1997). The Ho Chi Minh City, Court of Appeal dismissed charges, because the defendants returned the bribes to a public fund. This belated act of contrition did not, in the district procurators opinion, alter the fact that the People's Committee's seal was wrongfully applied for personal advantage, an unequivocal breach of the Penal Code. More generally, commentators report that "cases which initially handed down heavy convictions were later 're-tried' and convictions 'softened', implying bribery or favouritism to party members and civil servants" (Nguyen Tri Dung 1995: 5). Evidence of an uneven application of law to party cadre accused of abusing 'state power' is demonstrated in the following case studies.

Violations of dyke protection laws

The Hanoi Chief Architect's Office (*Van Phong Kien Truc Su Truong*) and local district people's committees are responsible for administering dyke protection laws that prohibit construction within twenty five meters of the Song Hong (Red River) dyke in Hanoi. In 1994 the *Dai Doan Ket* (Great Unity) newspaper accused Chief Architect officials of accepting bribes to approve the unlawful construction of houses and mini-hotels within the dyke precinct (Tran Quang Vu 1995a: 6). Despite widespread public notoriety, the practice continued with impunity. Eventually local officials stopped granting further approvals, but continued contravening dyke protection laws by legalising (*hop phap hoa*) non-conforming uses on the payment of small fines (Tran Quang Vu 1995b).

When the scandal began to implicate senior officials, the Prime Minister personally intervened. Countermanding the Chief Architect's legal-isation program, the Prime Minister ordered the demolition of unlawfully constructed buildings in the exclusion zone.[14] Of 1100 illegally constructed villas, only 200 were removed and a further 150 partially demolished (Vietnam News Agency 1995: 76). Allegations of favouritism were disingenuously dismissed by a government official, "[f]ortunately no high ranking officials have houses in the area and there were not many of their relatives there either" (*AFP* 1995). Others were less circumspect, suggesting an unusual degree of leniency where officials so clearly endangered the public (Viet Nam News 1995: 3).

Though substantially increasing the risk of flooding, the four senior officials dismissed for accepting bribes were initially reinstated. A subsequent media campaign led to their re-arrest and imprisonment (*Dai Doan Ket* 1995: 6). Notwithstanding evidence of direct involvement and the conviction of his deputy Tinh Hong Trien, Chief Architect Nguyen Lan and other senior People's Committee officials escaped prosecution.

The Tamexco case

In 1996 Pham Huy Phuoc, the director of Tamexco, a company owned by the Financial and Administrative Committee of the Ho Chi Minh City Communist Party Committee, was sentenced to death for misappropriating socialist property (US $27 million) (*AFP* 1996a; *AFP* 1997). This case is significant for the large sums involved and because the media openly speculated that the misappropriation was possible only with the knowledge of senior party officials. While confirming the death sentence for three directors, Chief Justice Pham Hung on appeal commuted the sentence of one director to life imprisonment. Although, the Penal Code 1986 allowed mitigation only where offenders 'render good service', the sentence was reduced because the director's father was an honoured party member and

14 Decision No 158/TTg. Emergency Measures Against Acts of Violation of the Ordinance and Protection of Dykes in Hanoi, 19 March 1995.

recipient of the 'Labour Hero Medal', one of the country's highest honours (*Vietnam Investment Review* 1997).[15]

Tran Minh Phung case

In Vietnam's largest corruption trial, Tran Minh Phung was charged in 1997 with fraudulently misappropriating socialist property (Nguyen Nhu Phong and Vu Cao 1998a: 1-3; Nguyen Nhu Phong and Vu Cao 1998b). Procurators alleged that Tran Minh Phung and business associates fraudulently borrowed money from state banks.

Overlooking compelling evidence of systemic bribery of state bank officials, no one was charged with abuse of 'state power' (Saigon Giai Phong 1999a: 1; Saigon Giai Phong 1999b: 2; Saigon Giai Phong 1999c: 1). Informants attribute this anomaly to concern that investigations might compromise those holding positions in the highest echelons of the party-state. According to this explanation, one political faction used Tran Minh Phung to damage the credibility of their rivals. Whatever the reasons, only relatively junior bank officials were charged, even though evidence accepted by the court demonstrated that only Cao Sy Kien, the Governor of the State Bank and member of the Central Committee of the CPV, possessed the authority to approve hundred million dollar loans.

Thang Long Water Park (Thuy Cung Thang Long)

Background

This case concerned the unlawful allotment (*giao*) of land to Van Tien, a small private company. The Hanoi People's Committee allotted Van Tien twenty-two hectares of valuable real estate in the prestigious West Lake district in Hanoi to develop as a waterpark. Media commentators identified numerous dubious aspects of the project (Dai Doan Ket: 1998).

Though it is usually difficult for private companies to obtain land use right allotments, Van Tien convinced authorities to grant it a large parcel of extremely valuable land. Increasing the land's value, the allotments were issued with landfill permits allowing expansion into West Lake.

Even more unusually, the company was granted *duoc phap* (transfer) rights over the allotted land, allowing subdivision and sale of land-use rights (*quyen su dung dat*) to domestic and foreign investors. The right to change the purpose of land-use rights is rarely given to State Owned Enterprises (SOEs), much less private companies, because it deprives the state of capital gain profits. Residential land is many times more valuable than commercial land. The company paid land compensation for site clearance at rates varying between 7,600–19,000 *dong* per square metre.

15 Art 51 of the Penal Code 1986 empowers judges to reduce sentences where defendants have "rendered good service", but does not extend exemptions to services rendered by relatives of the defendant.

These allotments were later sold for 2,750,000-3,500,000 *dong* per square metre, and at a public auction organised by the Hanoi People's Committee, for five million *dong* per square metre.

Van Tien was, moreover, permitted to use the land as capital contributions to joint ventures with foreign investors. Recent amendments to the Land Law 1998, Art 78(d) now permit this practice, but at the time only SOEs were accorded this privilege.

The central government subsidised the cost of preparing a feasibility study for the project (Dao Minh Khoa 2000: 3). Under the Law on the Promotion of Domestic Investment 1998, state subsidies for private ventures are granted only for projects of strategic significance or to private developments in remote areas.[16]

Van Tien was also exempt from paying land tax on the allotment during the construction period and profit tax for several years thereafter. These benefits are rarely (if ever) granted to private investors in urban entertainment projects and are usually reserved for investments in remote regions or socially beneficial but marginally profitable undertakings (Webster and Taussig 1999: 36-38). It was also awarded concessionary state loans, which are sparingly given to private enterprises.

Despite development costs of 100-200 billion *dong*, Van Tien was capitalised at a mere 1.4 billion *dong*, with declared assets of 4.2 billion *dong*. Police investigations subsequently revealed that the director of the Hanoi branch of the Bac A Bank, made false asset declarations. At the relevant times, Van Tien held only 115,000 *dong* in bank accounts (Bui Thanh and Nguyen Van Hai 2000: 4).

Project feasibility criteria routinely applied to similar private sector projects were not followed. For example, Le Tan Cuong (the director of Van Tien) lacked appropriate professional qualifications and practical experience in constructing and operating large entertainment facilities. Prior to the Thang Long project, Van Tien unsuccessfully applied to the Hanoi People's Committee to develop a small 'decorative garden and fish pond' on 6,972 square metres of leased land in Thuy Duong ward (*phuong*). Newspaper reports queried why authorities rejected the modest Thuy Duong proposal, but soon afterwards approved the Thang Long project requiring forty times more capital. They speculated that, instead of developing a waterpark, the project's real objective was subdivision and sale of unimproved land.

In sum, the project breached many of the procedural safeguards designed to exclude private companies from generating profits from unimproved residential land. What distinguishes this case from many others involving land allotment violations is its scale and the high value of land and concessions granted to Van Tien.

16 Law on the Promotion of Domestic Investment 1998, Arts 8, 12, 15, 16; Decree No 7/ND-CP Detailing the Implementation of the Law on Promotion of Domestic Investment 1998, Arts 27-38 (waterparks do not fall within any of the preferred investment areas).

Allegations of ministerial pressure (*suc ep*)

The newspaper articles first reporting the scandal in 1998, speculated that Hanoi People's Committee officials lacked 'state power' to approve large-scale category 'A' projects and were pressured (*suc ep*) by 'someone else' (Dai Doan Ket 1998). Athough carefully avoiding direct accusations of corruption, they observed that two Hanoi-based construction consultancy companies, Sena Corporation and CDC Construction Company, applied for the land allotments on behalf of Van Tien. The reports described these companies as *cong ty binh phong* (companies sailing against the wind), a popular euphemism for bodies backed by powerful party-state interests (Dai Doan Ket 1998). Again, without drawing explicit conclusions, the reports observed that the director of Sena Corporation is the son-in-law of a General in the Police Ministry and that Ngo Xuan Quang, the director of CDC, is the son of Deputy Prime Minister Ngo Xuan Loc, at the time responsible for planning and construction.

The newspapers implied that pressure (*suc ep*) to approve the project came from the ministerial level of government. They noted that, with the exception of Deputy Prime Minister Ngo Xuan Loc, most ministries criticised the project. Ignoring these important objections, Tran Xuan Gia (Minister for Planning and Investment) signed Official Letter No 498 1998 accepting the feasibility study and recommending project approval (Minh Tuan 2000).

Without providing details, newspapers described the involvement of the Police Ministry as *bao ke*, a term denoting punitive or physical intimidation (Dai Doan Ket 1998). The choice of language was deliberate. Also meaning high-level protection, the more benign *o du* (umbrella) is applied where officials use administrative rather than physical power to protect or promote favoured clients. Some commentators claimed that this case evinced *maphia* (mafia) links between state officials and private companies. They intimated that people's committee officials were intimidated from complaining about procedural irregularities.

Sanctions

On 26 March 1999 the Prime Minister issued Decision No 235/ QDBT-TTg revoking all decisions approving the Thang Long project and shortly afterwards dismissed Ngo Xuan Loc from his position as Deputy Prime Minister. Dinh Hanh was also dismissed as Vice Chairman of the Hanoi People's Committee. No action was taken against Tran Xuan Gia (Minister of Planning and Investment), Hoang Van Nghien (Chairman of the Hanoi People's Committee) or Nguyen Lan (Chief Architect). As previously mentioned, Nguyen Lan survived other land corruption scandals.

In April 2000, Ngo Xuan Loc was rehabilitated and appointed senior party adviser to the Prime Minister on planning and construction. This Central Party Committee position is considered just as important as Ngo Xuan Loc's previous role as Deputy Prime Minister.

Contrasting with the leniency shown to senior officials, criminal charges were filed against Le Tan Cuong, the director of Van Tien, for fraudulently appropriating socialist and private property (Dao Minh Khoa 2000: 3).[17] Senior officials in the Ministry of Planning and Investment Evaluation Department and the Hanoi People's Committee were charged with the less serious crime of neglecting responsibility.[18] With the exception of Nguyen Lan, those escaping prosecution were members of the Party Central Committee.

Press reports now exclusively focus on Le Tan Cuong's shadowy background. Articles vilify him for bribing a bank manager to overstate asset valuations, and for owning a notorious brothel operated in the Cung Dong Hotel (Dao Minh Khoa 2000: 3; Minh Tuan 2000). Earlier allegations of *bao ke* links between Sena and CDC Corporation and the Ministry of Police and Ngo Xuan Loc have disappeared from the narrative. In their place, Le Tan Cuong is now portrayed as the central protagonist responsible for devising the project and corrupting state officials.

Locating the case studies within party analysis of corruption

Two different explanations are given in party commentaries for the lenient treatment of party officials. Both maintain the constitutional fiction that party leadership operates within the framework of the law. Where they differ is in their interpretation of party intervention in the legal system.

One group argues, rather improbably, that state laws are the only measure of public duties and party interference is illegal and aberrant behaviour. They believe that corruption is defined, investigated and punished by state institutions applying laws and procedures that are strictly applied 'without deviation' to the "highest and the lowest levels" (*AFP* 1996b; *AFP* 1999). In a recent interview, the Chief Justice of the Supreme Court (Pham Hung) encapsulated this position. Responding to allegations that investigating officials are occasionally pressured to treat party officials leniently, he rather implausibly asserted, "I have not encountered any case in which the Political Bureau would interfere and refuse to grant permission to act" (Le Tho Binh and Vu Thuong 1997). When pressed whether there had ever been a case of political interference he replied, "[i]n principle, there certainly has been none. However, there might have been a few individuals who, for one reason or another, interfered". Interference is attributable to personal shortcomings where "the level of specialisation of cadre remains low" and some cadre lack "courage, objectivity, and impartiality". In short, most party theorists promote the constitutional image of an orderly law-based society regulated by a depoliticised, professional public service.

17 Penal Code 1986, Arts 134, 157 and 180.

18 Penal Code 1986, Art 220.

In the spirit of *chinh nhgia* (exclusive righteousness), others emphasise the party's wisdom and virtue and revolutionary mission to lead (Tien Chuoc 1999: 3; Nguyen Nham 1997). This narrative equates the party to a parent that has neglected the education and care of its children. It ascribes corruption to deviation from party policies and directives.[19] Three implications flow from this position.

First, party leadership rests on moral authority, which is undermined by malfeasant party members. Since senior party cadre are portrayed as moral exemplars, their prosecution damages party legitimacy more severely than action against middle- and junior-ranking officials. As inaction also erodes public confidence in party leadership, middle-ranking officials and entrepreneurs, like those in the case studies, are held accountable for state losses.

Secondly, state organisational rules, protocols and guidelines that interfere with the party's revolutionary mission to lead society constitute a type of corruption termed 'bureaucratism' (*quan lien*). Bureaucratism is a euphemism for otherwise lawful bureaucratic processes and organisational cultures that hinder or sabotage the use of the state as a dedicated instrument of party rule. PAR legal reforms clarifying the roles and responsibilities of public employees may induce bureaucratism if they impede the capacity of party affairs sections to lead the state. Those attempting to use laws to clarify party-state boundaries are denounced by some party leaders as 'demagogues' (Marr 1994: 8-9). Party injunctions routinely warn against 'imperialist' (*can thiep*) and 'reactionary' (*tai hanh dong*) arguments advocating separation of party and state.

Thirdly, the ultimate objective of anti-corruption measures is preserving party prestige. Laws are considered secondary indicators of corruption. In the binary party-state, corruption cases are primarily resolved to preserve party prestige and unity and only secondarily to uphold due process, objective and universal standards of 'truth' (Nguyen Huu Tho 1988: 7; Tien Chuoc 1999: 3).

Conclusion

Constitutional reforms have not unravelled the binary party-state. Deeply entrenched power structures and political-legal cultural attitudes treat the state as a dedicated instrument of party rule. By requiring public officials to follow the party-line, its morality and particularistic leadership, the political-legal culture has raised party paramountcy to the level of doctrinal principle.

Imported PAR notions of merit-based recruitment and promotion sit uncomfortably with the *nomenklatura* system that rewards and builds party loyalty. More importantly, PAR programs categorising and systematising

19 For rare admissions that lenient treatment of high ranking cadre is systemic, see Vo Van Kiet (1996: 3) and Le Van Khuyen (1996).

state powers and duties diminish the party's capacity to lead the state flexibly through edicts and party affairs sections. Personalism is considered a vital means of bridging party and state to induce uniform policy implementation and ensure party paramountcy. Far removed from PAR's preoccupation with legal and procedural compliance, corruption is dangerous in Vietnam where it compromises party-state prestige and unity, promotes decentralisation and unauthorised privatisation of public decision-making.

This observation returns the discussion to Kahn-Freund's proposition that incongruent power distribution structures are likely to impede legal transplantation. The capacity of PAR anti-corruption reforms to curb bureaucratic corruption is doubtful, since legalism occupies a comparatively small social space in Vietnam. Kahn-Freund's proposition also infers that institutional reform in Vietnam is an improbable vision of system change. PAR reforms require immensely complex systemic changes that reconfigure delicately balanced party-state power-sharing arrangements. The transferral of power from party to state - needed to induce sharp public-private legal boundaries - would unravel institutions built up over several generations. Each stage of reform is likely to induce political conflict over the direction and pace of change.

There is also a cultural dimension at work. Like their Confucian predecessors, party leaders distrust statutory norms, preferring leadership through moral virtue and mass campaigns. Moral rectification campaigns that reinforce party leadership are consequently preferred to legalistic anti-corruption reforms that destabilise particularistic lines of authority bridging party and state. Although, there is scope to develop party-sponsored morals that more clearly delineate the boundaries between public and private responsibilities, this long-term objective lacks state-society communication channels capable of manufacturing publicly accepted moral standards. It is doubtful whether public morality, which largely reflects Neo-Confucian village structures, can be artificially crafted by the party to serve a Marxist-Leninist state. Missing are the finely textured cultural precepts that would enable bureaucrats to apply anti-corruption mores to everyday life.

In the meantime, the continuation of the hybrid legal-personalistic system currently in place undermines both party and legal authority. Party paramountcy blurs legal distinctions between public and private duties, undermining the authority of state organs and statutory norms. PAR legal reforms designed to circumscribe public and private duties seem an unlikely short-term solution, since they will diminish party paramountcy. Even though existing anti-corruption laws are weak signposts of bureaucratic power, they create a legal architecture that censures party interference in the legal process. The resulting tension between legal certainty and party paramountcy forms part of a wider contest between universal legal norms promoted under the 'law-based state' doctrine; and party edicts, moral authority and discretionary decision-making underpinning 'socialist legality'.

What goes unremarked in the Vietnamese discourse is that anti-corruption laws are more than instruments for realising certain ends. They are cultural artefacts. As such, political and social matrices shape their capacity to induce behavioural change. Since party paramountcy is the primary objective of power distribution, transplanted notions of corruption are adjusted accordingly. It is a small leap to postulate the emergence of a bifurcated anti-corruption regime in Vietnam, whereby party paramountcy shields senior, but not middle- and junior-ranking, cadre from state prosecution. Whether dual standards of bureaucratic behaviour are sustainable in the long term depends on the capacity of the party-state to justify the doctrine of party paramountcy. In the interim, the prosecution of corrupt middle- and junior-ranking officials may have the unintended effect of re-engineering political-legal cultural assumptions regarding the boundaries of state power and the standards of bureaucratic rectitude.

References

AFP, (1995), 'Minister Denies Vietnam Leaders Involved in Dyke Scandal', unpublished press release, 23 March.

AFP, (1996a), 'Largest Corruption Case Hits Communist Party-Owned Firm', *FIBIS East Asia Daily Report* 96-084.

AFP, (1996b), 'Kiet Orders End to Lenient Corruption Investigation', unreported 15 March.

AFP, (1997), 'Eleven More Accused in Tamexco Case Appeal Sentence', *FIBIS East Asia Daily Reports* 97-032.

AFP, (1999), 'Vietnam Communist Party Vows to Stamp Out Corruption', *FIBIS East Asia Daily Report* 99-033, 2 February.

Badson, Bradley, (1996), 'Presentation to the Opening Session of the International Colloquium on Public Administration Reform', in *International Colloquium on Public Administration Reform*, UNDP, Hanoi, 100.

Bell, John, (1995), 'English and French Law—Not So Different?', *Current Legal Problems*, 63.

Beresford, Melanie, (1988), *Vietnam: Politics, Economics and Society*, Pinter Publishers, London.

Beresford, Melanie, (1993), 'Some Key Issues in the Reform of the North Vietnamese Industrial Sector,' Working Paper No 9, Australian National University, Canberra.

Buchanan, James, and Tubock, Gordon, (1965), *The Calculus of Consent: Logical Foundations of Constitutional Democracy*, University of Michigan Press, Ann Arbor.

Bui Dinh Bon, (1994, 'Concentrate Efforts on Successfully Resolving Urgent and Pressing Problems', *Quan Doi Nhan Dan*, 27 June, 1.

Bui Thanh and Nguyen Van Hai, (2000), 'Cong Ty "3 Khong" Va Nhung Cu Lua Cua Ti Phu Khong Tien' (The Company had the Fraudulent Behaviour of a Billionaire without Money), *Tuoi Tre* (*Youth*), 24 December, 1.

Butler, WE, (1988), *Soviet Law*, (2nd ed), Butterworths, London.

Capelletti, Mauro, et al, (1986), 'Introduction', in Mauro Cappelletti et al (eds), *Integration through Law: Europe and the American Federal Experience,* Walter De Gruyter, New York.

CPV, (1996), 'Political Report presented by the Seventh CPV Central Committee to the Eighth National Congress 28 June-1 July 1996' *Quan Doi Nhan Dan*, 30 June, 3, 6; translation *FIBIS East Asia Daily Reports* 96-134, 98.

Dai Doan Ket (Great Unity), (1995), 'Ve Vu Vi Pham Phap Lenh De Dieu O Nghi Tam-Nhat Tan (Ha Noi)', 1 April, 6.

Dai Doan Ket (Great Unity), (1998), 13 July.

Dang Phong and Beresford, Melanie, (1998), *Authority Relations and Economic Decision-Making in Vietnam: An Historical Perspective,* NIAS Publications, Copenhagen.

Dao Minh Khoa, (2000), 'Ket Thuc Dieu Tra Vu An Thuy Cung Thang Long' (Completion of the Investigation of the Thang Long Water Park), *Bao Cong An Nhan Dan* (People's Police Gazette), 26 February, 1.

Doan Khue, (1998), 'Scrupulously Implementing the Party's Fundamental Organisational Principles in Military Party Organizations', *Tap Chi Cong San,* January, 6.

Doan Trong Truyen, (1996), 'An Overview on Public Administration Reform in the Socialist Republic of Vietnam', in *International Colloquium on Public Administration Reform,* UNDP, Hanoi.

Duy Quang Chu, (1997), 'A Proposal of the Ho Chi Minh City People's Council: A Special Mechanism Needed for the City', *Lao Dong,* 10 July, 7.

Editorial, (1997), 'The Tasks that Need Concentrated Leadership for Fighting Corruption', *Quan Doi Nhan Dan,* 28 January, 1, 3

Evens-Jones, Robin, (1998), 'Receptions of Law, Mixed Legal Systems and the Myth of the Genius of Scots Private Law', 114 *Law Quarterly Review* 228.

Ewald, William, (1995), 'Comparative Jurisprudence (II): The Logic of Legal Transplants', 43 *American Journal of Comparative Law* 498.

Vietnam News Agency, (1995), 'Dyke Protection Law reportedly Violated', Radio Vietnam 10 November; *FIBIS* East Asia Daily Reports 95-222, 17 November, 76.

Gillespie, John, (2001a), 'Transplanted Company Law: An Analysis of Market Entry in Vietnam', in Fiona McMillan (ed), *International Corporation Law,* Hart Publishing, Oxford (forthcoming).

Gillespie, John, (2001b), 'Self-Interest and Ideology: Evaluating Different Explanations for Bureaucratic Corruption in Vietnam', 3(1) *Australian Journal of Asian Law* 1-36.

Ginsburgs, George, (1979), 'The Genesis of the People's Procuracy in the Democratic Republic of Vietnam', 5 *Review of Socialist Law* 187.

Girling, John, (1997), *Corruption, Capitalism and Democracy,* Routledge, London.

Goodnow, Frank J, (1967), *Politics and Administration: A Study in Government,* Russell and Russell, New York.

Hoang Hao, (1987), 'Phap Luat va Kinh Te' (Law and Economy), *Tap Chi Cong San,* December, 24.

Hoang The Lien, (1994), 'On the Legal System of Vietnam', 1(1) *Vietnam Law Legal Forum* 33.

Hooker, MB, (1978), *A Concise Legal History of South East Asia,* Clarendon Press, Oxford.

Huong Xuan, (1996), 'Nhu Nhoi Mot Quoc Nan' (Acute Feelings of a National Calamity), *Nhan Dan,* 4 February.

Ibrahim Shihata, (1997), 'Corruption: A General Review with an Emphasis on the Role of the World Bank', 5 *Dickinson Journal of International Law* 451.

Kahn-Freund, Otto, (1974), 'On Uses and Misuses of Comparative Law', 37 *Modern Law Review* 1.

Le Duan, (1978), *Phat Huy Quyen Lam Chu Tap The Xay Dung Nha Nuoc Vung Manh* (Develop the Right of Collective Mastery, Build a Strong State), Su That, Hanoi.

Legrand, Pierre, (1997), 'The Impossibility of "Legal Transplants"', 4 *Maastricht Journal: European Comparative Law* 111.

Le Quang Thuong, (1996), 'Mot So Van De Ve Cong Tac Dan Vien Trong Tinh Hien Nay', (Several Problems Concerning Cadre Work under the Current Situation), 14 *Tap Chi Cong San*, July, 18.

Le Tho Binh and Vu Thuong, (1997), 'Fighting Corruption: In Addition to Energy, Courage is Needed' *Tuoi Tre* (Youth), 8 April, 3.

Le Van Khuyen, 1996), 'The Party, State Should Take Drastic Measures to Eliminate the Root Cause of Bureaucracy and Corruption', *Saigon Giai Phong*, 23 May, 2.

Lev, Daniel, (2000), 'Comments on the Course of Law Reform in Modern Indonesia', in Timothy Lindsey (ed), *Indonesia: Bankruptcy, Law Reform and the Commercial Court*, Desert Pea Press, Sydney.

Lao Dong, (1999), 'SRV Party Issues Regulations "Banning" Members' Activities', *Lao Dong*, 11 June, 1; *FIBIS East Asian Daily Report* 1999-0617, 12 June.

Luong, HY, (1992), *Revolution in the Village: Transition and Transformation in North Vietnam, 1925-1988*, University of Hawaii Press, Honolulu.

Lowi, Theodore, (1987), 'The State in Politics: The Relation between Policy and Administration', in Seymour Haregot (ed), *Law-Making and Development*, Vol 2, International Law Institute, Washington, DC.

Macaulay, Stewart, (1987), 'Images of Everyday Life: The Lessons of School, Entertainment, and Spectator Sports', 21 *Law and Society Review* 1.

March, James and Olsen, Johan, (1989), *Rediscovering Institutions: The Organizational Basis of Politics*, Macmillan, New York.

Marr, David, (1971), *Vietnamese Anti-colonialism 1885-1925*, University of California Press, Berkeley.

Marr, David, (1981), *Vietnamese Traditions on Trial 1920-1945*, University of California Press, Berkeley.

Marr, David, (1994), 'The Vietnam Communist Party and Civil Society', unpublished paper 'Vietnam Update 1994 Conference: Doi Moi, The State and Civil Society', Australian National University, Canberra, 10 November.

Marr, David, (1995), *Vietnam 1945: The Quest for Power*, University of California Press, Berkeley.

McKinley, Robert, (1979), 'Zaman dan Masa, Eras and Periods: Religious Evolution and the Permanence of Epistemological Ages in Malay Culture', in A Becker and A Yengoyan (eds), *The Imagination of Reality: Essays in Southeast Asian Coherence Systems*, Greenwood Publishing Group, Westport CT.

Minh Tuan, (2000), 'Nhung Chuyen "Chua Noi" Thuy Cung Thang Long' (Disclosure Stories Concerning Thuy Cung Thang Long), *Dai Doan Ket* (Great Unity), January, 64.

Mueller, Dennis, (1989), *Public Choice II*, Cambridge University Press, Cambridge.

Nguyen Dinh Loc, (1999), 'Amending and Supplementing the Penal Code—A Must in the New Situation', 6(62) *Vietnam Law & Legal Forum* 14.

Nguyen Duy Quy, (1994), 'The Question of Building a State of Law in Vietnam', 1(2) *Vietnam Law and Legal Forum* 32.

Nguyen Duy Quy, (1997), 'Ho Chi Minh's Viewpoint on Socialism and the Path to Socialism in Vietnam', 5 *Vietnam Social Sciences* 15.

Nguyen Huu Tho, (1988), 'Phan Dinh Chuc Nang Giua To Chuc Dang va Nha Nuoc-Dieu Kien Dau Tien Thuc Hien Phap Luat' (Assignment of Functions between Party Organizations and the State-the Pre-Conditions for Observance of Laws), 5 *Tap Chi Cong San* 7.

Nguyen Huu Dang, (1956), 'It is Necessary to Have a More Regularized Society', 4 *Nhan Dan Van*, 5 November, translated by George Boudarel, (1990), 'Intellectual Dissidence in the 1950s: The Nhan-Van Giaia-Pham Affair', 13 *Vietnam Forum* 166.

Nguyen Huu Tho, (1989), 'Renovation of Mechanism – Pressing Needs of the Renovation Process,' *Tap Chi Cong San*, March; *FIBIS*, East Asia Daily Report, 086, May, 5.

Nguyen Khac Kham et al, (1967), 'Bibliography on the Acceptance of Western Cultures in Vietnam from the XVI Century to the XX Century', 54 *East Asian Cultural Studies* 228.

Nguyen Khac Vien, (1974), *Tradition and Revolution in Vietnam*, Indochina Resource Centre, Berkeley.

Nguyen Khac Vien, (1993), *Vietnam: A Long History*, The Gioi Publishers, Hanoi.

Nguyen Khanh, (1995), 'Administrative Reform in Action', 2(3) *Vietnam Law and Legal Forum*.

Nguyen Kim Dinh, (1995), 'The Bloc Party Organisation in the Party Organisational System', 10 *Tap Chi Cong San*, August, 57.

Nguyen Nham, (1997), 'Why is the Management of the State by Law Still Weak?', *Quan Doi Nhan Dan*, 13 June, 3.

Nguyen Nien, (1996), *Administrative Reform in Vietnam* (unpublished paper).

Nguyen Nhu Phong and Vu Cao, (1998a), 'Minh Phung Lam Giau va Sup Do The Noa' (Minh Phung- How did It Get Rich? How did It Collapse?), 61 *The Anh Ninh The Gioi* (The World Security Magazine), 13 February.

Nguyen Nhu Phong and Vu Cao, (1998b), 'Ways to Draw State Money', 63 *The Anh Ninh The Gioi (*The World Security Magazine*)*, 27 February, 1.

Nguyen Phu Trong, (1999), 'Effect a New Change in the Study of Political Theory of Cadres and Party Members', *Tap Chi Cong San,* November, 7.

Nguyen The Anh, (1985), 'The Vietnamese Monarchy Under the French Colonial Rule 1884-1945', 19 *Modern Asian Studies* 147.

Nguyen Thi Xuan My, (1997), 'Strengthen and Renovate Party Inspection Work', *Tap Chi Cong San,* August, 3.

Nguyen Tri Dung, (1995), 'Uphill Battle Against Graft', 17 *Vietnam Investment Review*, July, 4.

Nguyen Van Tai, (1996), 'On the State Ruled by Law and a Multipartisan Regime', 1 *Vietnam Social Science* 3.

Paul, Joel, R., (1995), 'The New Movements in International Economic Law', 10 *American University Journal of International Law and Policy* 607.

Phan Van Khan, (1993), 'Opening of the Third Session, National Assembly 9th Meeting: Government Report', *Nhan Dan*, 17 June.

Do Phuong, (1995), 'Party-State-Law', 1(5) *Vietnam Legal Forum* 3.

Poggi, Gianfranco, (1978), *The Development of the Modern State: A Sociological Introduction*, Stanford University Press, Stanford.

Porter, Gareth, 1993), *Vietnam: The Politics of Bureaucratic Socialism*, Cornell University Press, Ithaca.

Rambo, A, Terry, (1987), 'Black Flight Suits and White Ao-Dais: Borrowings and Adaptations of Symbolism of Vietnamese Cultural Identity', in *Borrowings and Adaptations in Vietnamese Culture,* Southeast Asian Paper No 25, Center for Southeast Asian Studies, University of Hawaii, 121.

Rose-Akerman, Susan, (1978), *Corruption: A Study in Political Economy*, Academic Press, New York.

Sacco, (1988), 'The Substratum in the Civil Law of the Socialist Countries', 14 *Review of Socialist Law* 65.

Saigon Giai Phong, (1999a), 'Minh Phung and Epco had the Risk of Going Bankrupt from their Establishment', 13 May, 1.

Saigon Giai Phong, (1999b), 'Companies Only Knew How to Borrow Bank Loans', 14 May, 1.

Saigon Giai Phong, (1999c), 'A Fraudulent Conglomerate on a Large Scale', 19 May, 3.

Saigon Giai Phong, (1999d), 'SRV Issues Regulation Banning Members Activities', 12 June, 3; *FIBIS East Asia Daily Report*, 1999-0617, 18 June.

Seidman, Ann and Seidman, Robert, (1994), *State and Law in the Development Process*, Macmillan, London.

Shihata, Ibrahim, (1997), 'Corruption: A General Review with an Emphasis on the Role of the World Bank', 5 *Dickinson Journal of International Law* 451.

Sidel, Mark, (1997a), 'Generational and Institutional Transition in the Vietnamese Communist Party', 37(5) *Asian Survey* 481.

Sidel, Mark, (1997b), *Vietnam: The Ambiguities of State-Directed Legal Reform*, Butterworths, Sydney.

Silbey, Susan, (1992), 'Making a Place for a Cultural Analysis of Law', *Law and Social Inquiry* 17.

Smith, RB, (1973), 'The Cycle of Confucianisation in Vietnam', in WF Vella (ed), *Aspects of Vietnamese History*, University of Hawaii Press, Honolulu.

Than Duy, (1998), 'Co So Khoa Hoc va Van Hoa Trong Tu Tuong Ho Chi Minh ve Nha Nuoc Phap Luat' (Scientific and Cultural Basis for Ho Chi Minh's Ideas of State and Law), 504 *Tap Chi Cong San* 26.

Thaveeporn Vasavakul, (1997), 'Sectoral Politics and Strategies for State and Party Building from the VII to the VII Congress of the Vietnamese Communist Party (1991-1996)', in Adam Fforde (ed), *Doi Moi: Ten Years after the 1986 Party Congress*, Political and Social Change Monograph No 24, Australian National University, Canberra.

Thayer, Carlyle, (1991), 'Renovation and Vietnamese Society: The Changing Role of Government and Administration', in Dean Forbes et al (eds), *Doi Moi: Vietnam's Renovation Policies and Performance*, Political and Social Change Monograph No 14, Australian National University, Canberra.

Thu Linh, (1993), 'Action on Government Reform', *Vietnam News*, April, 2.

Tien Chouc, (1999), 'Le Kha Phieu Interviewed on Corruption', *Lao Dong*, 30 June, 1.

Teubner, Gunther, (1997), 'Global Bukowina: Legal Pluralism in the World Society', in G Teubner (ed), *Global Law Without a State*, Dartmouth Publishing, Aldershot.

Thoi Boa Kinh Te Saigon, (1998), 'Assets Declaration: A Positive Anti-Corruption Measure', *FIBIS East Asian Daily Report* 98-246, 3 September, 2.

Tran Duc, (1987), 'Ve Cac Luat Kinh Te Trong Hoi Ly Qua Do Len Chu Nhia Xa Hoi' (Economic Laws in the Transition Period to Socialism), *Tap Chi Cong San*, May, 69.

Tran Quang Vu, (1995a), 'Xay Dung Nha Trai Phep, De Yen Phu va Tu Liem Ha Noi Bi Vi Pham Nghiem Trong: Lat Leo Trong 34 Giay Phep Lam Nha Tren De O Ha Noi Cua Ong Trinh Hong Trien' (Illegal Housing Construction, Serious Violation in Yen Phu Dyke: Some Actions on the 34 Housing Licences on the Yen Phu Dyke from Trinh Hong Trien), *Dai Doan Ket* (Great Unity), 6 January, 1.

Tran Quang Vu, (1995b), 'Xam Hai De O Ha Noi, Nhin Tu Goc Do Phap Luat' (Dyke Violations in Hanoi is Reviewed from a Legal Perspective', *Dai Doan Ket* (Great Unity), 6 March, 6.

Truong Chinh, (1986), 'Introduction to the Political Report', Part 4, *Vietnam News Agency*, 15 December.

Truong Chinh, (1994), 'Marxism and Vietnamese Culture', in *Truong Chinh Selected Writings*, The Gioi Publishers, Hanoi.

UNDP Programme Support Document, (1995, 'Public Administration Reform Programme', VIE/92/002, 9 June.

Vietnam, (1994), The Government of Vietnam National Programme on Public Administrative Reform, 26 May.

Vietnam Economic Review, (1995), 'Administrative Reform in Vietnam: An Urgent Requirement', March, 30.

Vietnam Investment Review, (1997), 'Hero's Son Saved from Firing Squad', *VIR On-Line*, 21 September.

Viet Nam News, (1995), 'Mercy Shown to Squatters', 2 November, 3.

Viet Nam News, (2000), 'Competition and Anti-Monopoly Laws Needed to Promote Healthy Business', 26 September, 6.

Vinyu Vichit-Vadakan, (1996), 'Reforming the Policy and Institutional Framework for a Market Orientated Economy', in *International Colloquium on Public Administration Reform*, UNDP, Hanoi, 124.

Vo Nguyen Giap, (1999), 'Ho Chi Minh Humanitarianism, Ethical and Cultural Thoughts: Some Comments', 2 *Vietnam Social Sciences* 3.

Von Savigny, K, (1975), *Of The Vocation of Our Age for Legislation and Jurisprudence*, translated by A Hayward, (reprint), Ayer Company Publishers, Manchester.

Vo Van Kiet, (1986), 'Report to the National Assembly on the 1987 Socio-Economc Development Plan', Hanoi Domestic Service, 26 December, 9; *FIBIS Asia and Pacific Daily Report*, 30 December.

Vo Van Kiet, (1996), 'Vo Van Kiet Speech on Corruption', *Nhan Dan*, 8 November, 1; translation *FIBIS East Asia Daily Service*, 96.

Watson, Alan, (1985), *The Evolution Of Law*, Johns Hopkins University Press, Baltimore.

Watson, Alan, (1987), 'Evolution of Law: Continued', 5 *Legal History Review* 537.

Watson, Alan, (1993), *Legal Transplants: An Approach to Comparative Law*, (2nd ed), University of Georgia Press, Athens GA.

Watson, Alan, (1996), 'Aspects of the Reception of Law', 44 *American Journal of Comparative Law* 335.

Webster, Leila, and Taussig, Markus, (1999), 'Vietnam's Undersized Engine: A Survey of 95 Larger Private Manufacturers', Private Sector Discussions No 8, Mekong Project Development Facility, Hanoi.

Wellons, Phillip A, and Pistor, Katharina, (1997), *Symposium on the Role of Law and Legal Institutions in Asian Economic Development: 1960-1995*, Oxford University Press, Oxford.

Wolters, OW, (1979), 'Assertions of Cultural Well-Being in Fourteenth Century Vietnam,' 10(2) *Journal of South East Asian Studies* 444.

Woodside, Alexander, (1971), *Vietnam and the Chinese Model*, Harvard University Press, Cambridge, Mass.

Woodside, Alexander, (1999), 'Exalting the Latecomer State', in Anita Chan et al (eds), *Transforming Asian Socialism: China and Vietnam Compared*, Allen and Unwin, Sydney.

Young, S, (1979), 'Vietnamese Marxism: Transition in Elite Ideology', 19 *Asian Survey* 770.

Chapter 11

The Vietnamese Courts and Corruption

Pip Nicholson

> Nothing much comes as a surprise. The anti-corruption chief was sacked for corruption, the deputy head of the national drug squad was caught smuggling heroin. The head of the People's Inspectorate, a body that is supposed to monitor government performance, was sacked for being involved in what a senior ministry official discretely called a 'business wrongdoing.' Health ministry officials stole donated contraceptives and sold them to Russia. Top officials in the foreign ministry enriched themselves by using the diplomatic bag to smuggle with impunity. The list of corrupt officials seems depressingly endless (Templer 1998: 133).

> Rob by night and you're a bandit, rob by day and you're a mandarin (Vietnamese saying).

Perceptions of Vietnamese corruption vary but the endemic nature of corruption is not in dispute. In February 2001 the official press released details of a report indicating that 69,000 (or 40 per cent) of the party members reviewed were guilty of some form of graft (Nhan Dan 14 February 2001). Between 1996 and 2000 Vietnam has seen two[1] cases of corruption resulting in the criminal trial of Supreme People's Court staff. [2] Although these cases are relatively small in dollar terms compared with the raft of recent major corruption scandals, they help to illuminate the state's attitude to corruption. They also assist to place in perspective the role the courts might play in trying and penalising corruption. This chapter therefore explores perceptions of courts and impropriety in contemporary Vietnam through analysis of the role of the Supreme People's Court, the corruption judgments and media commentary.

This chapter is structured in three parts. In the first part, Vietnamese legal culture is examined, with a particular focus on the traditional role of

1 The author contacted two Vietnamese lawyers (one state lawyer and one court official) to ascertain whether other cases of judicial corruption had been brought before the courts. Neither of them were able to locate statistics on this point (Lawyer V 2001 and Lawyer W 2000).

2 Compare this with the Australian experience where no superior court judge has been dismissed for accepting a bribe, although since the establishment of the Australian court system four judges have been sacked for incompetence and other misbehaviour (Waugh 1998: 223).

courts and dispute resolution in Vietnam. In the second part, the two cases are analysed and in the final part the role of courts and their treatment of corrupt judges and judicial officers is explored.

The Vietnamese courts

Several recent studies conclude that the Vietnamese have little, if any, trust in their courts.[3] Vietnamese also claim that it is too expensive to go to court (Author's interviews 1998). The explanation of this expense does not lie in high legal costs or court fees. Rather, users claim they have to pay court officials, including judges, to determine cases in their favour. Several lawyers have described how it is usual for those involved in litigation to approach the court to explain the details of their case before it is heard (Lawyer U, July 1997 and Lawyer V, June 2000). These perceptions indicate that a mix of costs and distrust result in a Vietnamese preference for avoiding courts.[4]

This preference is not new. A brief glance at the history of Vietnamese dispute resolution suggests the law and the courts traditionally have not received respect. By the mid-14th century Vietnam had a Confucian-inspired moral system that saw morals and not law as the guiding force in daily life. Confucianism essentially reflects a weighting of moral over legal systems. In short *le* (*li* in Chinese, meaning ritual or code of conduct) is valued over law (*fa* in Chinese or *luat* in Vietnamese). With the advent of the strong leadership of the Le dynasty (1428–1788), Sung Neo-Confucianism (Confucianism established during the period of the Sung Dynasty in China) became the predominant ideology in Vietnam, particularly among educated elites (Nguyen and Ta, 1986: 449; Young 1976: 7; Nguyen, 1985: 27–31). Over time, village life was increasingly guided by Confucian morals (Young 1976: 43).[5]

In addition to the importance of morality, Vietnamese rural life centred upon the life of the village (*xa*). The autochthonous nature of Vietnamese

3 Interview by the author with ten educated Hanoians in 1998 and analysis of Vietnamese court history (Nicholson 2000). Swedish lawyer Per Bergling interviewed 40 local Vietnamese businesses to ascertain their perception of commercial legal reform in Vietnam. The vast majority reported that courts could not be trusted to act according to law (Bergling 1999: 122-130). Macmillan and Woodruff interviewed 259 managers of privately-owned manufacturing firms in Hanoi and Ho Chi Minh City and found that only 9 per cent thought the courts could help them to resolve disputes. Explanations for not using the courts to enforce contracts or resolve commerce-related disputes included: "The court is weak and no entrepreneurs use it" and "They [the courts] usually just create more problems [...] in Vietnam no one believes we have a good legal system" (McMillan and Woodruff 1999: 5).

4 The Economic Court introduced in Vietnam in 1994 has increasing case numbers. Yet the numbers themselves remain very low (Nicholson and Nguyen 2000: 13).

5 An example of this is the 1663 moral code for village life, entitled "The Path for Religious Improvement", which contained 47 articles "loaded with Confucian morality". It was read to villagers on feast days and enforced by the chief of the village (Young 1976: 43).

village life is reflected in the age-old saying, "The laws of the emperor are less than the customs of the village" (*phep vua thua le lang*, Young 1976: 154).[6] Another Vietnamese saying is that "the village association is a small court" (*Huong dang, tieu trieu dinh*) (Woodside 1971: 154). These sayings reflect the fact that, in the first half of the 15th Century, the head of the *xa* was an official appointed by the central government, whereas after the 1460s it was quite common for the head of this community to be a local with some administrative experience (Woodside 1971: 154). Over time the leadership moved to a Council of Elders (*hoi dong hao muc*) with local responsibility for matters such as dispute resolution (Woodside 1971: 154-155).[7]

The Council of Elders' authority to resolve local disputes was technically held on behalf of the central imperial court, yet as a matter of practice it contributed to a sense in which local communities considered themselves independent of the central authority and its laws. Therefore, although there is a suggestion that the *Le* Code developed sophisticated doctrines of civil law (Ta, 1982: 523–553), it is unclear to what extent these permeated village life.[8] Certainly Le Thanh Ton in the mid-15th century crusaded against idiosyncratic and corrupt local dispute resolution by officials (Young 1976: 15). He commented that, "for some time officials have been settling cases according to their own whims (lit. their own stomachs), taking money illegally and sending up written reports late" (Young 1976: 15).

The French influenced the role of law and courts upon their arrival in Southern Vietnam in 1862 (Hooker 1975: 229).[9] This resulted in different court arrangements in each of the three parts of Vietnam: Tonkin, Annam and Cochinchina.[10] A hybrid system of Vietnamese mandarins and French

6 Another Vietnamese version of the same saying is *phep vua thua lang* (Nguyen Ngoc Huy and Ta Van Tai 1986: 493).

7 The Council of Elders was a hierarchical body with membership predicated upon age, scholarly pursuits and previous administrative experience. It was also responsible for collecting taxes on behalf of the state.

8 Ta Van Tai (who argues that the traditional Vietnamese legal system was sophisticated at this time) does not indicate whether the law was actually taken up. For example, he neither considers litigation nor enforcement issues in his analysis (Ta 1982; Ta 1998).

9 Hooker notes that in the 1860s the French passed several statutes dealing with the application of laws in the Eastern provinces of Cochinchina, which the French controlled from 1862.

10 Vietnam was divided into three parts under the French. From 1875 the French had sovereignty in the south, later gaining protectorates over the north and centre. Nguyen The Anh points out that the fragmentation of Vietnam resulted in a very effective erosion of the Vietnamese king's powers. In particular, Tonkin was increasingly under French control, although officially a protectorate. Nguyen The Anh refers to the appropriation of the king's power in 1897 by the *Residents Superieur* of Tonkin, enabling them to make all decisions and appoint or dismiss mandarins (Nguyen The Anh 1985, 148). The French position was strengthened when the Chinese were routed from Tonkin and the Yangtze River blocked, an act that ultimately ensured French-Chinese negotiations culminating in the total withdrawal of China from Tonkin (Ennis 1973: 49-51).

magistrates was used in the north and centre of the country. However in the south, where mandarins refused to work with the French, a French magistracy assumed control of the courts, gradually training local recruits as assistants. The French sought to apply Vietnamese law to Vietnamese citizens and French law to French citizens (Hooker 1975: 229–241).

There are two conflicting readings of this period of Vietnamese court history. The French tend to characterise their law reform initiatives in Vietnam as part of the *mission civilisatrice* (civilising mission),[11] while the revolutionary Vietnamese portray the French role in dispute resolution as oppressive and opportunistic. As Ho Chi Minh wrote:

> Justice is represented by a good lady holding scales in one hand and a sword in the other. As the greatness of the distance between Indochina and France was so great, so great that, on arrival there, the scales lost their balance and the pans melted and turned into opium pipes and official bottles of spirits, the poor lady had only the sword left with which to strike. She even struck innocent people and innocent people especially (Ho Chi Minh 1961: 96).

Not only was the critique presented in the damning rhetoric of leaders, but case studies were produced and used to argue for war against the French and the introduction of a more enlightened, socialist government.[12]

Into this complex history of "layers of law" (Mattei 2000: 36-39) and legal culture stepped the revolutionaries of 1945. They established their own system of courts, closely modelled on that of the Soviet Union (Nicholson 2000). By the early 1960s the Vietnamese in the North of the country had established a court hierarchy with the Supreme People's Court at its apex (Nicholson 2001). Today this court hears matters on appeal from lower courts, reviews decisions of lower courts and has some limited original jurisdiction (LOOPC 1992). It comprises a series of divisions (civil, economic, administrative, labour and military). The Supreme People's Court judges are appointed for five-year terms and are assisted by court secretaries and a range of court officers working, for example, in research, training and inspection of the work of lower courts.[13] The Provincial People's Courts and the Local People's Courts are below the Supreme People's Court in the court hierarchy.

It is important to observe the position of the court system in relation to the state and the Vietnamese Communist Party and the public perception of

11 Not all French commentators hold this view: see, for example, Ennis (1973), and Baugher (1980: 98). Baugher claims that, when drafting the revised civil code for Vietnam, the French "showed a determination to respect Vietnamese law".

12 Tran Tu Binh (1964: xi). Tran Tu Binh argued, on the basis of his experience of labour courts, that the French system of courts in Southern Vietnam was oppressive and a mockery of justice.

13 Law on the Organization of People's Courts (LOOPC), dated 6 October 1992, Arts 38 and 39. The National Assembly elects the Chief Justice of the Supreme People's Court, whereas the State President appoints other senior judges. For a discussion of judicial appointments and the manner in which people's assessors are elected to office see Nicholson (2001, 42–43).

these connections. Vietnam has no separation of powers and its courts are accountable to the National Assembly (Constitution 1992, Art 126 – 136). Judges and court officials are traditionally approved by the Party and therefore – as with all relatively senior bureaucrats – are required to implement the will of the Party according to the Communist Party Statute (SRVN CPV Statute, Art 2(1) and 23(1)). This is not to suggest that there is one Party view that can be ascertained and applied in contemporary Vietnam, but it does mean that the courts are required to uphold and implement Party policy as well as law and can be directed by the Party (Gillespie, this volume).

Historically there are several examples of Party-directed, quasi-judicial decision-making which have resulted in lasting Vietnamese perceptions of courts as arbitrary and brutal. The Vietnamese land reform of 1953 – 1956 (a campaign to redistribute land from landlords to peasants) was implemented via Special Courts (*toa an dac biet*). One professional judge and six to ten peasants judged land cases. Half of the peasants were appointed by the regional war committees (*uy ban khang chien hanh chinh*); the other half appointed by agricultural cooperatives.[14] Punishments for violations were severe, ranging from confiscation of land to the death penalty.[15] The use of beatings and torture during investigation and interviewing was prohibited,[16] although there were many allegations that these occurred.[17] Once the Mobile Land Court[18] had made a decision, this was supposed to be sent to the Inter-Zone War Committee for confirmation.[19]

The Vietnamese press, Asia-based press and eyewitness reports all describe the Land Courts as arbitrary and violent (*Nhan Dan* in Gittinger 1957: 118 and Burchett 1955: 168–169). The Vietnamese press itself reported as early as 1957 that up to thirty per cent of those condemned during the

14 Ordinance No 150 SL 12 April 1953 On Establishment of Special People's Court, Art 4.

15 Ordinance No 150 SL 12 April 1953 On Establishment of Special People's Court, Art 11 and Decree 264 – TTG 11 May 1953, Regulating in detail the Order 149, 150 and 151 12 April 1953, Arts 8 and 9.

16 Decree 264 – TTG 11 May 1953, Regulating in Detail the Order 149, 150 and 151 12 April 1953, Art 10.

17 Burchett (1955: 168-169). Wilfred Burchett, a Communist travelling in North Vietnam in the mid-1950s, provided an eyewitness account of the Land Courts operating and noted that the "forms and trappings of justice as known in the western world were absent". He noted that the accused was usually in a hole in the ground surrounded by an audience.

18 Ordinance No 150 SL 12 April 1953 On Establishment of Special People's Court, Art 4 and Decree 264 – TTG 11 May 1953, Regulating in Detail the Order 149, 150 and 151 12 April 1953, Art 13.

19 Decree 264 – TTG 11 May 1953, Regulating in Detail the Order 149, 150 and 151 12 April 1953, Art 16. Ordinance 151, 12 April 1953 guided decision makers and the War Administration Committees on appropriate penalties. For example, Art 6 set out one to ten years' imprisonment for "being in collusion with the enemy ... sabotaging the revolution, killing farmers, officials and government staff."

land reform should not have been (*Hoc Tap* in Gittinger 1957: 118).[20] Further, it noted that:

> [P]eople were arrested, jailed, interrogated and cruelly tortured; people were executed or shot out of hand and their property confiscated. Innocent children of parents wrongly classified as landlords were starved to death (*Nhan Dan* in Gittinger 1957: 118).

Such an experience of 'popular justice' has scarred the Vietnamese perception of revolutionary justice. For example, Duong Thu Huong's semi-autobiographical account of life in revolutionary Vietnam depicts Land Courts most unfavourably.

> At the entrance to the town was a huge village green, which doubled as a racecourse on festival days. At the time, it had been converted into a makeshift kangaroo Court (*truong cau, toa an cua nong dan*), where the landlords, the scapegoat 'model tyrants' from the surrounding villages and communes, were dragged before a jury of peasants to be denounced and judged. The glow of bonfires lit up the sky, eerie curls of smoke illuminating the night.
>
> The air echoed with the sound of fury: drums beat, bugles sounded the charge, mobs shrieked and guerrilla patrols crisscrossed the road, bayonets glinting at the tips of their rifles. The guerrillas kept their weapons cocked, threatening ready to do battle. Their bayonets reflected in the gleam of their eyes as they glared suspiciously at every passer-by. NO LANDLORD WILL SLIP THROUGH OUR NET. That was the new slogan, scrawled in lurid colours across the road (Duong 1994: 55).

The Military Courts, established immediately after the Declaration of Independence, existed to try and punish those convicted of committing a crime against the state.[21] Vietnamese court histories note that the court could order the death penalty. The name 'Military Court' referred to a court that could try civilians as well as members of the armed forces. These existed until at least 1960, when the courts were reorganised. As with the Special Courts, Military Courts were well known for their arbitrary adjudication. This phenomenon is usually ascribed to regionalism, poor coordination of courts and lack of legal training, which, in turn, are seen as a result of the war (Nicholson 2000: Chapter 3).

This history provides an explanation of why Vietnamese courts and judges are not held in high regard. Today judges are characterised as bureaucrats, without any particular status.[22] Historically judges and courts have not been relied upon to deliver justice. Instead they have been seen as

20 Estimates vary on the number killed during the land reform era. Recently Thayer (2000) suggested 15,000 people may have been killed.

21 See Order 33, Establishing a Military Court 13 September 1945.

22 Ho Chi Minh and his associates seemed aware that judges were not held in high regard in Vietnam in the early years after the revolution. They issued a circular which stipulated that "to maintain an imposing image of the judiciary, headquarters of courts must be in good condition" (Circular No 1000 NV/DL 20 March 1946).

instruments or tools of the state (be it imperial, French or socialist) that implement the will of rulers, rather than dispense impartial and reasoned decisions (Gillespie 2001).[23]

To balance this critique, it is important to recall that the Vietnamese system of courts, established by the new government after 1945, was constructed during wartime, with very few resources and little training (Nicholson 2000, Chapter 2). Judges often received no more than a few weeks of lectures on socialist principles and were then expected to administer 'justice' according to Party policy (Nicholson 2000, Chapters 3 and 6). Vietnamese court development therefore took place under very difficult circumstances.

Bui Van Tham: the 'scapegoat' judge[24]

In 1997 a Hanoi Supreme People's Court (Civil Court) judge allegedly received money from a female civil litigant, Tran Thi Chieu. Chieu took a land case, which had been heard at first instance and on appeal in Ho Chi Minh City, to the Hanoi Supreme People's Court. She approached the judge, Bui Van Tham, to influence the appeal and asked him to convey tea and cigarette money (*giao dich thuoc nuoc*) to those judges who might sit on her case. When Tham failed to produce the desired result, Chieu complained to the authorities, producing as evidence a tape of her conversation with Tham. Chieu and Tham did not agree on the amount Chieu had paid to Tham, although they both accepted that the amount paid had been refunded. The court accepted Tham's evidence that he had received US$ 500 and 7 taels (equivalent to US$ 3,500) of gold.

The judge was charged under the Penal Code, not with bribing other judges but with the offence of exerting undue influence on a person holding an official position.[25] No charges were levelled under the Vietnamese Anti-Corruption or Public Sector legislation. Article 228 of the Vietnamese Penal Code provides:

> (1) Any person who, directly or through an intermediary, accepts money or other material incentives in any form to use his influence and coerce a person in an official position to do or not to do something within his area of responsibility, or to do something he is not permitted to do, shall be subject to a term of imprisonment of between one and five years.

23 A State-employed lawyer also characterises contemporary courts as "tools of the State". This person points out that since the state reflects the will of the Vietnamese people, this is a fundamental improvement over the French-run courts (Lawyer Y, February 2001, correspondence).

24 The basis of this synopsis and ensuing discussion is the judgment of the Hanoi People's Court, in Judgment No 233/HSST 22 February 1997.

25 The Vietnamese Penal Code of 1985 has been amended four times: 28 December 1989; 12 August 1991; 22 December 1992 and 10 May 1997. The current Code was passed on 21 December 1999.

(2) If the offence is committed in serious circumstances, the offender shall be subject to a term of imprisonment of between three and ten years.

Tham received money on the basis that he would "use his influence and coerce a person in an official position to do something" (Art 228 (1)). He did not accept the money and gifts directly to affect his own conduct.[26] In other words, the nexus between the payment and the action sought was not direct. Tham was therefore convicted of 'exerting influence' under Art 228.[27] Since Tham was a Deputy President of the Civil Court within the Hanoi Supreme People's Court, it would have been clear to the court trying his case that he was in a position to exert influence (Lawyer Y 2001). Tham was not charged with fraudulent misappropriation of a citizen's money under Art 157(1) of the Code – presumably because all monies had been returned.

Tham received a two-year jail sentence from the Hanoi People's Court under Art 228 (2). Many jurists believe this was lenient treatment of a senior judge, given that there was concrete evidence of his corruption.[28] Further, although convicted under the article pertaining to more serious breaches of the Code, his sentence was reduced to fall within the range specified for less serious breaches. The judgment relied on Tham's previous good record, the fact that he repaid all monies to Chieu and his repentance of his bad conduct in mitigation of the offence. Bui Van Tham lodged an appeal to the Hanoi Supreme People's Court, however, this was subsequently abandoned (Lawyer W 2000).

Chieu was convicted of bribery and received a three-year suspended jail term. She was also placed on four years' probation.

Perhaps in keeping with the unusual nature of the case, the Hanoi People's Court judge and two people's assessors heard this case by candlelight, all electricity having failed on the day of the trial. The court chose to acquit Tham of bribery on the basis that he had not actually passed the tea and cigarette money onto the judges that heard Chieu's appeal.

26 Bribery, according to Art 226 of the Vietnamese Penal Code, requires the acceptance of money or other incentives to "perform or refrain from performing certain jobs as requested by the person offering the bribe." It is viewed by Vietnamese lawyers as a more serious offence than "exerting undue influence" (Art 228) as bribing carries with it a penalty of between one and seven years imprisonment (Art 226).

27 The summary of evidence in the Bui Van Tham judgment is scant and it is therefore not possible to determine how the court formed the view that no others were bribed.

28 The reporting of this case in the *Lao Dong* (Labour) newspaper on 28 February 1998 pointed out that the court had returned a verdict that was tougher than that sought by the procuracy. According to this report the procuracy had only sought re-education for the judge with a 30-36 month suspended sentence, while seeking six to eight years' imprisonment for the woman offering the bribe. Other Hanoi-based jurists point out that the judge could have been charged under other sections of the Penal Code, exposing the judge to substantially more serious sanctions.

Although Tham handed Chieu's petition to a court clerk and asked another court clerk to listen to Chieu's submissions, he did not enable her to meet with a judge of the court or pass her funds on to any court personnel. As a result, only the offence of 'exerting undue influence' was made out.

In addition to the conviction and two-year sentence - which is at the lower end of the sentencing options available to the court - Tham was dismissed from his office. No convicted person can serve as a judge and therefore Tham also lost a series of privileges such as medical benefits and housing which are attached to relatively senior positions on the public payroll.[29] Discussions with Vietnamese lawyers also suggest that Tham would have been expelled from the Communist Party of Vietnam. When I asked a lawyer based in Hanoi what work prospects Tham had, it was suggested that he might be able to work as a lawyer, providing one of the local Bar Associations would accept him (Lawyer V 2000).

Why did Tham withdraw his appeal? The main reason offered by one local lawyer for withdrawing the appeal is that Tham formed the view that an appeal was hopeless (Lawyer W 2001). Whether the court advised Tham informally of his poor prospects is a matter of speculation. Under the Vietnamese Criminal Procedure Code, if either the prosecution or the victim (in this case Chieu) lodges an appeal, the court may increase the penalty. In all other circumstances the penalty can only remain the same or decrease (Art 214). Therefore, although theoretically Tham's lodging an appeal did not risk an increase of the penalty, he nevertheless decided that to continue with the appeal was pointless.

In contrast, Chieu was convicted of bribery under Art 227(1) of the Penal Code and given a suspended sentence of 36 months.[30] In addition, she was placed on 48 months probation.[31] This penalty, the court stated, reflected her bribery of Tham, but also the fact that she was an elderly, uneducated woman of poor health who had exposed Tham to the officials. The court also ordered her to pay the amount of the refunded bribe to the state under Art 229 of the Penal Code.[32]

A significant aspect of this case is the apparently independent sentencing of the court. This may be more 'apparent' than real, as in the normal course of

29 See Ordinance on Judges and People's Assessors 1993, Art 22(2)(b) which provides that judges who break the law will be dismissed from office. Further, Inter-circular No 05/TTLN between the Ministry of Justice and Supreme People's Court 15 October 1993 provides that a person is assessed as having insufficient good ethics and virtue to hold office when they are convicted of a crime. Finally, Art 44 of the Ordinance on Public Servants makes dismissal mandatory where a public servant is convicted.

30 The court relied on Arts 38, in particular sub sections (a), (e), (g) and (h), of the Penal Code to suspend Chieu's sentence.

31 Art 44 of the Penal Code empowers the court to place people with suspended sentences on probation. In the event that Chieu breached her probation, she would face three years in jail.

32 It has been suggested to the author that it is very unlikely that this money would *actually* have to be paid back (Person X 2000).

events the procuracy and court would have determined the appropriate sentence in advance (Lawyer W 2001). However, the court 'apparently' rejected the procuracy's submission that Chieu be jailed for six to eight years. It also rejected the suggestion that Tham be given a suspended sentence of between 30 and 36 months. The audience condemned the procuracy's recommendations when they were announced in court, by 'booing' loudly (Yomiuri Shimbun 1997). The outcry presumably reflected a community perception that the person who reports the crime ought not be dealt with more severely than the official who committed it. As we have seen, the court chose to jail Tham and to release the frail Chieu on a suspended sentence and probation. If the court had accepted the procuracy's submission, it would have removed all incentives to report officials' corrupt behaviour.

It is not impossible to conceive that this sequence of events was orchestrated to present the court's treatment of the errant judge in the best possible light, namely as more harsh than the treatment sought by the procuracy. The manner in which the case unfolded and was reported in the press reduced the focus on whether the court's sentence was too light. Instead it portrayed the court as stricter with its personnel than was required by other agencies.

It is unknown to what extent any of the parties in this corruption case approached the court beforehand. Interviews with Hanoi-based lawyers suggest that no case proceeds to court without the parties' lawyers first appraising the court of the details of the case and the particular circumstances of their clients (Lawyer V 1997 and Lawyer V 2000). However, Vietnamese lawyers also note that the incidence of corruption is less frequent in the higher courts, particularly the Supreme People's Court (Lawyer W 2001, Lawyer Z 1997). We can only speculate how these two factors may have affected the outcome of this corruption case.

It has been suggested that whether the parties attended the court before trial or not, the court would have determined its decision in advance of the hearing (Lawyer W 2001). It appears common practice for the court to hold a meeting before trial in corruption cases, usually chaired by the Chief Justice, to settle the court's findings (Lawyer W 2001). This practice ostensibly avoids the judges sitting on these types of cases from wrongly applying the law or being subject to pressure to decide cases in particular ways (Lawyer W 2001). Presumably, it also ensures that a Party-endorsed judgment is reached.

The case demonstrates that while cases brought against judges are rare (even though their involvement in 'tea and cigarette' deals is said to be notorious), the state is not prepared to rubber stamp a release if a case proceeds to court. This suggests that while judges are not dealt with harshly, the court *will* jail its own – particularly if the case has come to public notice.

In many ways this hearing worked as a show trial. The hearing was reported in the local press and the story picked up and circulated in the Western media. This indicates that the Vietnamese authorities wished to teach the errant judge a lesson. Perhaps even more significantly, the government sought to be depicted as 'doing something' about judicial corruption.

In addition, it is suggested Tham's case was a show trial because Party officials are usually not tried for corruption in the courts, but instead face internal Party disciplinary procedures (Lawyer W 2000, Lawyer Y 2000). Depending on who commits the breach, it is usually either the local Party Standing Committee or its Discipline Committee that determines the case (Lawyer W 2000, Lawyer Y 2000). Various penalties can be invoked, including re-education, administrative detention in jails or house arrest.[33] These matters are mentioned in Chapter VIII of the 1996 Party Statute, entitled 'Reward and Party Discipline.' In particular, Art 36 of the Party Statute talks of "various forms of disciplinary action", although this phrase is not defined.

Finally, although Tham allegedly talked to several other court officials – including judges – none of them were charged. One the one hand, all monies were returned to Chieu, with the result that it may be the case that no other functionaries were bribed. Alternatively, if other court officials were paid, they returned all amounts to Tham, but he chose not to disclose this. It has been suggested that for a court officer or judge to inform on others would be the ultimate act of disloyalty to the court and would be viewed most unfavourably. It has been suggested that the personal security of 'inside' informants could be at risk (Lawyer W 2001).

Nguyen Dien Khoi: the fall of a court officer[34]

In January 1997 Nguyen Dien Khoi, an evaluator in the Civil Court of the Supreme People's Court,[35] met with Nguyen Thi Lien. The evaluator agreed to lobby for a suspended sentence for her, and light sentences for her two co-accused, Cong and Thuong (Lien's nephew).[36] All three had been charged and convicted of "resisting a person in the performance of their official duties"[37] in

33 Duong Thu Huong, author of *Paradise of the Blind* and other novels, experienced this treatment when she was expelled from the Vietnam Communist Party in 1989 and imprisoned for seven months in 1991. Ever since, she has periodically suffered house arrest (Duong Thu Huong 1993: 268–270; and Templar 1998: 184–185; see also Amnesty International 2000).

34 Analysis of this judgment relies on the decision of the Hanoi People's Court No 405/HSST 29 March 2000.

35 A civil court evaluator must check that the judgments of lower courts accord with the Supreme People's Court's view of the relevant law (Lawyer W 2000).

36 Only Thuong is mentioned as Lien's nephew. The relationship between Cong and Lien is unknown.

37 Art 205(1) of the applicable Penal Code sets out the offence of "obstructing (also translated as or resisting) a person in the performance of official duties". It provides "any person resorting to violence or threats of violence in order to obstruct a person in the performance of his official duties, or employing methods compelling him to commit unlawful acts, if not covered by the provisions set out in Arts 101(murder) and 109 (grievous bodily harm), shall be subject to a non-custodial reforms for a period of up to one year, or to a term of imprisonment of between six months and three years". In addition, more serious breaches of this provision can attract imprisonment for between two and ten years (Art 205 (2)).

the Hanoi People's Court on 27 December 1996. They approached Khoi to lobby judges at the Hanoi Supreme People's Court that would hear their appeal. They agreed that Khoi would receive four million *dong* (equivalent to approximately US $305) for his assistance. Chuc, Lien's brother, delivered the money to Khoi in February 1997. No charges appear to have been laid against Chuc. In April 1997 Uoc (Lien's husband) delivered a further two million *dong* (approximately US $125) to Khoi, who then arranged for Uoc to meet a Supreme People's Court judge, Mr Khoa. Uoc alleges Khoa received three million *dong* (approximately US $230). Khoa denies this. No charges were laid against Khoa.

The appeal was held on 12 June 1997 and dismissed. All sentences remained the same, despite two payments totalling six million *dong* (approximately US $457) to Khoi and allegedly three million *dong* (approximately US $228) to Khoa.

There were further attempts to obtain the assistance of Khoi. Thuong, still believing Khoi could assist, paid him an additional two million *dong* (US $125) in August 1997. In October Khoi took Uoc to see a prosecutor to see if the file could be reviewed. He advised it would be difficult. Khoi suggested Uoc pay the prosecutor. Uoc advised they were unable to pay and so Khoi refunded two million *dong* (US $125) and Uoc added 500,000 (US $38) to it and paid 2.5 million *dong* (US $191) to the prosecutor's wife. No prosecution arose out of this alleged interview and payment either.

In another incident, Uoc and Khoi's first wife, Ly Thi Duyen, approached Khoi (on behalf of Thanh, Duyen's adopted son)[38] and paid 2.5 million *dong* (US $191) seeking Khoi's assistance for a light sentence - six months to one year - for the offence of "resisting a person in the performance of their official duties". Khoi was unsuccessful in his lobbying and Thanh received a four-year sentence. From the judgment, Duyen does not appear to have been charged.[39]

As a result of complaint from the three defendants that Khoi had failed to assist, a total of three million *dong* (US $230) was refunded between October 1997 and March 1998. In total Uoc and his associates had paid 8.5 million *dong* (US $648) to Khoi, not including other payments allegedly made to the prosecutor and Khoa, of which five million (US $381) had been returned. In early 1998 Khoi and Uoc met again, Uoc taping their conversation. When Khoi did not refund the balance, Uoc denounced Khoi, producing the tape as evidence.

38 As information about the case was obtained only through the records of the trial, it has been impossible to establish the exact relationships of the defendants. Whilst Thanh is adult and the adopted son of Ly Thi Duyen, he does not appear to be the adopted son of Khoi. It is possible that Uoc (whose connection with Duyen is unstated) cultivated a connection with Duyen in order to gain access to Khoi.

39 It is entirely unclear why Duyen was not charged. The author hopes to establish shortly whether her matter was heard separately.

Khoi was found guilty of "appropriating civilian's property through swindling" and sentenced to ten months' jail under Art 157(1) and Art 38(1) and (2) of the Penal Code. No charges were levelled under the Vietnamese anti-corruption or public sector legislation.

Lien and Thuong were found guilty of handling bribes under Art 227(1) of the Penal Code. Pursuant to Art 227(1), Art 38(1)(h), 39(1)(i) and Art 42, Lien was sentenced to 15 months' jail for 'bribery' – cumulative upon her existing jail sentence of 42 months. Pursuant to Art 227(1), Art 38(1)(h) and 39(1)(i) Lien's nephew, Thuong, was sentenced to 12 months' jail.

Uoc was 'exempted' (*mien*) from the charge of handling bribes, the court relying on Art 38(2) in mitigation of his offence. This means he was charged and convicted, but received no penalty (Lawyer W 2000).[40]

The court legal officer, Nguyen Dien Khoi, was found guilty neither of bribery nor of exerting influence on an official, but rather of "fraudulently misappropriating civilian's property" (Penal Code 1985, Art 157(1)). The Penal Code suggests a penalty in the range of three months to five years for the first level of this offence. For serious offences of "fraudulently misappropriating civilian's property" the penalty is three years to twelve years. For extremely serious crimes, the penalty includes death. However, the court jailed Khoi for only ten months, relying on Art 38(2), which provides that, "[w]hen deciding the penalty, the court may consider other circumstances as extenuating but shall note them in the sentence." Like Judge Tham, Khoi lost his job and presumably any benefits that attached to it.

A reading of the judgment does not directly explain the lower sentence. It has been suggested that as Khoi was a court evaluator and not a judge he would not be able to exert undue influence (Lawyer Y 2001). This analysis goes on to suggest that lesser penalties apply because of Khoi's more junior position (Lawyer Y 2001). In addition, the lesser sentence may be a result of the smaller sums involved – 8.5 million *dong* is roughly equivalent to US $650. However, unlike Judge Tham, Khoi did not return all the funds and apparently tried to influence significantly more legal officers than Tham did. The lack of judicial reasoning makes it hard to reconcile the judgments.[41]

The procuracy charged all three complainants in this case with bribery under Art 227 of the Penal Code and they received wide-ranging penalties reflecting the varied characterisation of their roles in the bribery. Uoc received by far the lightest sentence. He was effectively acquitted. The bases of his 'exemption' were his confession, his assistance in the prosecution of the others, his age (68 years old), and his past war record. It would appear that the past war record counts for a great deal, as Chieu was only three years younger than Uoc and yet she received a three year suspended

40 Art 227(5) of the Penal Code provides that "[a]ny one offering bribes who, although not compelled to do so, on his own initiative makes a declaration before the offence is discovered, may be exempted from criminal liability".

41 Vietnam has a civil system of law and no court decision is formally binding in a later decision. Here the term "reconcile" is used to refer to consistency in sentencing rather than technical arguments about precedent.

sentence and four years' probation. Like Uoc, Chieu reportedly assisted the state with its investigations.

The remaining two defendants, Lien and Thuong, received fifteen months' and twelve months' jail respectively. Lien was jailed for a longer term reflecting her 'organisation' of the bribery. Both Lien and Thuong had their sentences reduced as a result of their admission of the crime, the relatively low amount involved and their demonstrated remorse.

The procuracy had suggested that Lien and Thuong be convicted and jailed for two to three years and that Uoc be convicted, but receive a suspended jail term and probation. Further, the procuracy suggested that the court official, Khoi, be jailed for three to four years. Although there is no system of common law-style precedent in Vietnam, these recommendations appear consistent with the first case decided in 1997, assuming that Uoc acted without the support of Lien and Thuong.[42] In particular, the procuracy recommended that the judge should be jailed for longer than the complainants, that those who informed the state of impropriety should not be jailed (Uoc and Chieu).

Both the procuracy and Khoi appealed the sentence in this case. The state was successful in extending his jail term to 15 months (although not quite as successful as they had hoped, having sought incarceration for between two and four years) (Lawyer V, 2000).

The 1997 Penal Code amendments to Art 227 are very significant. They provide that where members of the public are 'forced to offer bribes' but voluntarily report the act of bribery before it is discovered, they should be acquitted and all the property offered/payments made be returned" (Penal Code, Art 227 (5)). In the event that the person was not required to pay a bribe, but does, and subsequently voluntarily reports the offence before it is discovered, the person offering the bribe 'may' be acquitted and will get part of the property returned or payments made returned (Penal Code Art 227(6)). This amendment signals a shift in policy enabling those that report bribery – despite being participants in the offence – to be treated more mercifully by the court. This demonstrates a substantial official change in attitudes to bribery. Nevertheless, in the present case Lien and Thuong were found guilty of bribing Khoi and jailed, on the basis that they had not been 'required' to bribe Khoi.

Three years separate these two cases that deal with corruption of a judge and a judicial officer.[43] The Hanoi People's Court's attitude to

42 The judgement does not make it clear whether, when Uoc denounced Khoi, he acted with or without the support of Lien and Thuong. If this point had been explicit, it would be possible to work out whether the tougher penalties for these two sought by the procuracy and delivered by the court reflected their prior convictions. Alternatively these stiffer penalties may reflect the fact that only Uoc informed the authorities.

43 The Hanoi People's Court decided the case of Judge Bui Van Tham on 20 February 1997 and the case of judicial officer Nguyen Dien Khoi on 29 March 2000.

corruption cases involving judges or court officers would appear to have changed over that time. In particular, stiffer penalties for those offering the bribe in Khoi's case suggests a shift of emphasis – the court apparently being very tough on those bribing judicial officers. The amendments to Art 227, mentioned above, have not been considered in the judgment and it therefore must be assumed that the previous provisions applied. Alternatively, the case may reflect the fact that Tham was a judge whereas Khoi, although an employee of the court, was not nearly so senior and therefore could be treated more leniently. Finally, the fact that Lien and Thuong had prior convictions may have resulted in their longer jail terms. Whatever the motive, however, the judgment would certainly deter the community from complaining about the corrupt behaviour of court officials.

The judgment therefore does not appear to accommodate or even address the complex debates about corruption and its challenges for a public policy in favour of strengthening legal institutions. John Gillespie has written at some length on the recent Vietnamese public pronouncements in favour of rule of law (Gillespie 2001). However, he notes that 'rule of law' in the West is differently conceived and that Vietnamese legality continues to reflect a socialist legality (Gillespie 2001; Gillespie 1999, 124-125). This case confirms that the Vietnamese call for a rule of law (*phap luat*) is premised on socialist legal principles where morality and status are integral to law. In this particular case, socialist law has the person offering a bribe liable for any consequent wrongdoing. The case does not answer the call for strengthened legal institutions generally and the independence of courts in particular.

Lessons from two Vietnamese corruption cases

As the Vietnamese legal system is not based strictly on precedent, it is hard to compare the two cases. That being said, it is hard to imagine that the second hearing was not determined with the full knowledge of the case that had preceded it, especially as the courts have traditionally met to discuss cases before they are officially heard (Nicholson 2000: Chapter 6). The following general conclusions can be drawn from these two cases.

Findings on the facts

(1) Inappropriate conduct by court officials resulted in both cases in loss of employment.

(2) In each case the court official also received a jail term.

(3) In each case the court maintained that the offence was contained, in that it involved only one court official and no others.

(4) In the second case, those who bribed the state official received higher penalties than the court official.

Consequences for informed debates on the courts

(5) The second case sends very mixed messages to the community and risks further damaging perceptions of the state's integrity,[44] although it might be argued that the 1997 amendments to Art 227 are likely to reduce the penalties for those voluntarily reporting bribery in later cases.

(6) Neither case indicates that the taking of bribes by judicial officers is viewed very seriously, as it appears that 'contamination' by association of other court officials was not investigated.[45]

(7) There is a code of conduct that presumes that those accepting bribes will refund them in full if they fail to intervene successfully on behalf of a defendant/complainant.

In the context of a discussion about the transferability of notions of 'good governance', what do these cases tell us? Both indicate the importance of exploring local - in this case Vietnamese - treatments of impropriety to see how they are handled. Without the benefit of reading these judgments and comparing the cases, it is quite possible that a foreign commentator might anticipate 'Western-style' treatment by the Vietnamese courts of future improper conduct by judicial officers and judges.

It is also important to recall that the Communist Party of Vietnam metes out its own sanctions for improper conduct. To date it has not been possible to undertake any systematic analysis of how these are determined,[46] nor is it clear how such punishments effect the person punished. It is also hard to speculate about the impact of loss of privileges, Party membership and income, for example, on the family of the accused in these cases. Where disloyalty has been alleged, international organisations report the use of house-arrest.[47]

These cases also highlight the need to be cautious in expecting courts to take a leading role in Vietnamese legal reform. As stated at the outset, the Vietnamese people have little respect for courts, which are perceived as bureaucracies - with all attendant vulnerabilities, such as low wages and a culture of patronage. The background to these cases gives an insight into the

44 An alternative reading of the stiff penalties for those who bribe may be that the state must challenge endemic bribery by tough sentencing. This reading has the state attempting to quash the entrenched practice of bribing.

45 This is an assumption. The Party may have instigated an investigation or disciplinary proceedings against others involved (particularly in Khoi's case) but, if so, those interviewed knew nothing of it or feigned ignorance.

46 None of the lawyers consulted in the course of this research were able to advise of the Party's treatment of either of these judicial officers; or whether or not prior cases of bribery and exerting undue influence had been taken to the disciplinary organs of the Communist Party of Vietnam.

47 In addition, the various human rights organisations report on the use of house detention and isolation for political dissidents. See, for example, Amnesty International (2000).

accessibility of court staff to approaches by members of the public who expect that these staff will facilitate discussions to influence the outcome of cases.

The cases also reveal the determination of litigants to use pre-trial consultation with judges and their staff. In the case of the Khoi trial, a multitude of approaches to court staff emerges, suggesting the entrenched nature of pre-trial advocacy. This practice has also been confirmed by the author in discussions with Vietnamese lawyers over a ten-year period.

Finally, the handling of both these cases would not appear to have been calculated to increase respect for the judiciary or court officers in the short term. Local perceptions of judicial corruption continue. The case studies highlight the disjunction between, on the one hand, elite Party discussions, where the changing public face of law is debated; and, on the other, the realities of Vietnamese legal practice.

References

Amnesty International, (2000), Annual Report 2000, <http://www.web.amnesty.org/web/ar2000we…e70accab26802568f200552983?Open Document>

Baugher, Peter, (1980), *The Contradictions of Colonialism: The French Experience in Indochina 1860–1940*, Doctoral Thesis, University of Wisconsin, Madison.

Bergling, Per, (1999), *Legal Reform and Private Enterprise The Vietnamese Experience*, Umea Studies in Law No 1/99, Department of Law, Umea University, Umea.

Burchett, Wifred, (1955), *North of the 17th Parallel*, Foreign Languages Publishing House, Hanoi.

Duong Thu Huong, (1994), *Paradise of the Blind*, Translated by Phan Huy Duong and Nina McPherson, Penguin Books, New York.

Ennis, Thomas E, (1973), *French Policy and Developments in Indochina*, Russell & Russell, New York.

Gillespie, John, (2001), 'Self Interest and Ideology: Bureaucratic Corruption in Vietnam' 3 *Australian Journal of Asian Law*, No 1, 1-36.

Gittinger, J Price, (1957), 'Communist Land Policy', 29 *Far Eastern Survey*, No 8.

Hanoi People's Court, (1997), Judgment No 233/HSST, 22 February.

Hanoi People's Court, (2000), No 405/HSST, 29 March.

Ho Chi Minh, (1961), *Selected Works, Vol 2*, Chapter VIII 'Justice', Foreign Languages Publishing House, Hanoi.

Hooker, MB, (1975), *Legal Pluralism: An Introduction to Colonial and Neo-colonial Laws*, Clarendon Press, Oxford.

Internal Affairs Reporters, (1997), (Untitled article), Lao Dong (Labour), 28 February.

Mattei, Ugo, (2000), 'Legal Pluralism, Legal Change and Economic Development' Paper presented to the World Bank Summer Research Workshop, 'Institutions for Markets', July.

McMillan, John and Woodruff, Christopher, (1999), 'Dispute Prevention without Courts in Vietnam', unpublished paper, 11 February.

Nguyen Ngoc Huy, (1985), 'Limits on State Power in Traditional China and Vietnam', The Vietnam Forum, Summer/Fall, Yale Center for International and Area Studies, New Haven.

Nguyen Ngoc Huy and Ta Van Tai, (1986), 'The Vietnamese Texts', in MB Hooker (ed), *Laws of South-East Asia*, Vol 1, Butterworths, Singapore.

Nguyen The Anh, (1985), 'The Vietnamese Monarchy under French Colonial Rule 1884 – 1945', 19 *Modern Asian Studies* 148.

Nhan Dan, (2001), 'Vietnam Corruption Reported' 14 February [circ. Vnnews - 1].

Nicholson, Penelope (Pip), 2001, 'Judicial Independence and the Rule of Law: the Vietnam Court Experience', 3 *Australian Journal of Asian Law*, No 1, 37-58.

Nicholson, Penelope (Pip), 2000, *Borrowing Court Systems: the Experience of the Democratic Republic of Vietnam, 1945–1976*, Doctoral Thesis, University of Melbourne.

Nicholson, Pip and Nguyen Ngoc Minh, (2000), 'Commercial Disputes and Arbitration in Vietnam', *Journal of International Arbitration*, October, 1-18.

Ta Van Tai, (1982), 'Vietnam's Code of the Le Dynasty', 30 *The American Journal of Comparative Law*, 523-553.

Templar, Robert, (1998), *Shadows and Wind: A View of Modern Vietnam*, Penguin Books, New York.

Thayer, Carlyle A, (2000), 'Pham Van Dong: Vietnam says Farewell to a Member of the Communist Old-Guard', *Vietnam Business Journal*, May [circulated on vnnews].

Tran Tu Binh, (1964), *The Red Earth: A Vietnamese Memoir of Life on a Colonial Rubber Plantation*, translated by John Spragens, Jr, David Marr (ed), *Monographs in International Studies, Southeast Asia Series*, No 66, Ohio University, Athens.

Waugh, John, (1998), 'A Question of Capacity: the Case of Justice Bruce', *Public Law Review*, 223.

Woodside, Alexander, (1971), *Vietnam and the Chinese Model*, Harvard University Press, Cambridge, Massachusetts.

Yomiuri Shimbun (The Daily Yomiuri), (1997), 'Corruption: Name of the Game in Vietnam', 9 April, Retrieved by Westlaw.

Young, Stephen B, (1976), 'The Law of Property and Elite Prerogatives During Vietnam's Lệ Dynasty, 1428–1788', 10(1) *Journal of Asian History* 1-48.

Interviews

All interviews were granted with the author on the basis of anonymity:

Lawyer U (a Socialist Republic of Vietnam or SRVN lawyer), 1997, Hanoi, July

Ten educated members of the public, living in Hanoi, were interviewed in 1998.

Lawyer V (SRVN lawyer), 2000, Melbourne, June

Lawyer V (SRVN Lawyer), 2000, October (correspondence)

Lawyer V (SRVN lawyer), 2001, February (correspondence).

Lawyer W (SRVN lawyer), 2000, Melbourne, October.

Lawyer W (SRVN Lawyer), 2001, February (correspondence)

Lawyer W (SRVN Lawyer), 2001, Melbourne, May

SRVN Person X, 2000, Melbourne, October

Lawyer Y (SRVN State-employed lawyer), 2000, December.

Lawyer Y (SRVN State-employed lawyer), 2001, February (correspondence).

Lawyer Y (SRVN State-employed lawyer), 2001, February (correspondence).

Lawyer Z (Foreign lawyer based in Hanoi), 1997, June

Index